MAN OF THE OVAL

THE INTERNATIONAL LEGACY OF JOHN CHAPLIN AND WSU TRACK & FIELD

BRUCE BLIZARD

Design and Interior formatting services provided by:

SWEETSPIRE LITERATURE
—— MANAGEMENT ——

DEDICATION FROM JOHN CHAPLIN

This book is dedicated to the love of my life Linda Beth Klebaum, the rock that our family of James, Matt and Megan and Sheree, along with granddaughter Hailey Michelle and the three boys Tyshawn, Dewayne, and Prescott was built on.

TABLE OF CONTENTS

AUTHOR'S NOTE AND ACKNOWLEDGMENTS

FROM BRUCE BLIZARD

One of the most interesting and rewarding aspects of this project is the that I have had the opportunity to speak with people who I had admired from afar for most of my life in track and field, which began in the spring of 1966 when I was a ninth grader at Granite Falls High School in the foothills of the Cascade Mountains.

Athletes and coaches and personalities like Charlie Green, Brooks Johnson, Mel Pender, Stephanie Hightower, and Vin Lananna were all people I have admired from afar and who at one time or another were at the forefront of my thinking about this sport. So, when I began to organize this project, I was grateful that all of these individuals (and many others) were so willing to be so generous with their time and their recollections when it came to talking about John Chaplin. I owe an enormous debt of gratitude everyone who contributed their thoughts and recollections to this book.

Of course, I was aware of some of Coach Chaplin's supposed controversies and so was curious about the unwavering level of loyalty that he seemed to garner from his athletes, despite those supposed controversies.

And like everyone close to the sport in the State of Washington, I was also aware of John Chaplin's success at Washington State University. My wife, Tina, and I had witnessed the first of Henry Rono's major cross-country races and the second of his world records.

I was familiar with and/or acquainted many of the athletes mentioned in these pages. I know Robert Price well and have coached with and against Phil English. I was around Kiona-Benton High School when Chris McBride began his unlikely rise to becoming one of the best 800-meter runners in the Pac-10 conference. Tina knew Josh Kimeto, and I had listened with incredulity the time he insisted that WSU had a new runner on the cross-country team who was much better than he and the other two Kenyan internationalists on the WSU roster at the time. Much better? That runner was, of course, Henry Rono. And the rest, as they say, was history.

There are too many people who contributed to this project to name them all. The cover was designed by Brett Grimes of *Brett Grimes Designs* from a painting by Brian Friel, the grandson of the man WSU's Friel Court is named after. Porsche Steele and her international crew at MystiqueRose Publishing are among the best in the business. They handled the editing and interior design and will also manage the marketing of the book.

But most of all, for the faith and trust he has placed in me, I owe debt of gratitude that cannot ever be adequately repaid to Coach John Chaplin.

For more on this book and to find my three novels (*God's Instant, A Better Place, and Always a Runner*) go to http://bruceblizard.com/

FORWARD

BY VIN LANANNA

Many illustrious individuals have impacted our storied sport of athletics over the years. But true aficionados and experts of the inner workings of what happens in and out of the oval recognize one name that has influenced track and field at a deeply profound level: John Chaplin.

Those who invest the time to delve into the many complexities of John's persona will quickly learn that he is an incredibly intelligent, articulate, and deep-thinking person. It is not easy for anyone to listen to John's words because he is always speaking, and always at a rapid pace. However, if one truly hears his message, one will learn what I have about this remarkable leader. He is always passionate and usually correct when he speaks. As John often said, "Your greatest asset is your greatest liability." By this, he means if one is a *AAA* personality, people say, 'why can't he or she lighten up?' If he is a *B* personality, 'why can't he or she be more outspoken?'

Few have dedicated as much time, energy, and expertise to the sport of track and field, while at the same time being willing to roll up their sleeves and get their 'hands dirty' when needed. Even today, after decades in the sport, John continues to be an ever-present guiding light, never shy about advising the next wave of leaders and administrators. John Chaplin has been an influencer in the sport for decades as an athlete, a coach, an administrator, and a parent. Coach Chaplin has been a successful leader nationally and globally. He has contributed to track and field as a high school coach, a college coach, and an Olympic coach. He has been a voice of reason on both the field and the track oval.

John is bright, innovative, and creative. He never minces his words and is always willing to share his perspectives. He is often misunderstood because his style can be perceived as caustic or offensive. Despite this perception, those who have worked with John have grown to appreciate his commitment to fairness and perfection. His care and concern for 'doing the right thing at all times' define his deeply rooted principles.

Some might say that John is a study in contradictions. His deep appreciation for art, music, and fine dining stands in contrast to his sincere desire 'to tell it like it is.' He rarely sugarcoats the message he is trying to convey. He believes that everyone is entitled to know exactly where he stands, regardless of his popularity. He says what he means, and he means what he says.

One of my early recollections of John's commitment to follow his convictions was when I attended my first Pac-10 meeting in 1993. It was my first coaches' meeting as the head track coach at Stanford University. John was the rules chairperson for the conference coaches' group. At the meeting, he was debating whether a Cal triple jumper should be permitted to compete in his event at the conference meet. Most of the coaches favored disqualifying the student-athlete from the event because he was entered in an event on the first day but did not compete.

The athlete's excuse for not competing on the first day was that he chose to attend his college graduation. *(The honest-effort rule stipulates that if an athlete fails to compete when entered in an event, then he or she cannot compete in any remaining events in that meet unless there is a medical exception).* A lively debate ensued at the meeting, and it appeared that the student-athlete would be disqualified. John launched into a long tirade, citing the importance and significance of the student's attendance at his college graduation ceremony, a once-in-a-lifetime event for the student. As a result of the tirade, John was successful in reversing the decision, and the student-athlete was permitted to compete. During this encounter, I gained a true appreciation of Chaplin's commitment to doing the right thing for the right reason, regardless of self-interest.

Make no mistake about John's competitive spirit. He is a ferocious competitor, but at the same time, he has always been steadfast in his commitment to fairness, regardless of how it might impact his personal situation.

Beneath John's telling-it-like-it-is façade is a man of great compassion and kindness. Two years ago, John and I were having dinner in Eugene in advance of the 2021 Olympic Trials. We decided to visit a beloved friend, former University of Oregon track coach Bill Dellinger. Bill suffered a severe stroke twenty years ago that severely impacted his speech. Chaplin and Dellinger were archrival coaches in the Pac-10 Conference for many years. As Bill was sharing some of his impressive memorabilia, he was unable to complete his sentences. John did not flinch. John quipped that even before Bill suffered the stroke, John had often completed his sentences. We all chuckled and agreed. As Bill pointed to the photos depicting the 'old days," I observed the two 85-plus-year-old archrivals sharing memories hand-in-hand. It was an impactful image. That image represents the John Chaplin that most don't know.

Our sport has evolved and continues to remain relevant globally in the field and on the oval. At the core of this evolution, the positive influence of John Chaplin on the sport cannot be overstated. I am honored to call him a confidant and friend, and I am looking forward to following his story.

(Vin Lananna is the President of USA Track and Field and the Director of Track and Field at the University of Virginia. He was previously the director of track and field at the University of Oregon and Stanford, the head men's coach at Dartmouth University, and the head men's coach of the 2016 U.S. Olympic Team.)

INTRODUCTION

J ohn Prescott Chaplin, a member of the US Track & Field and Cross-Country Coaches Association (USTFCCCA) Coaches Hall of Fame, suggested the title for this book—*Man of the Oval*—very early in the writing process. When I asked why that title in particular, he explained that the oval shape of the track, combined with the 440-yard or 400-meter distance of a single lap, plus the demands of racing that one lap, seemed to characterize his career as an athlete, a coach, the chair of the International Competition Committee and chairman of the Men's Track & Field Committee for USA Track & Field (USATF), and finally, an international technical official with the International Amateur Athletic Federation (IAAF, now called World Athletics).

"The year I was born [1937]," he said, "Washington State College set a world record of 3:12.3 in the mile relay at the Pacific Coast Conference Championships, the forerunner of today's Pac-12 championships in Los Angeles."

Later, Chaplin himself would go on to set school records for the 440-yard dash at Wilson High School in Los Angeles (49.2) and Pasadena City College (47.2), tie the outdoor record at WSU (46.9), and set the WSU indoor record of 47.9 on a 220-yard dirt track. Then he became the head men's coach for the US team at the 2000 Olympics in Sydney, Australia, where the US won the 4x400-meter relay. For the record, though, after the 2000 Olympic Games, one member of the US team in the 4x400 final tested positive for a banned substance, and Nigeria was awarded the gold medal. Coaching the 2000 Sydney US Olympic team would be Chaplin's last official coaching position.

As the head coach at Washington State University (WSU), Chaplin would produce the best 400-meter runners in the school's storied history. In 1981, Chris Whitlock ran 45.84 seconds to become the first WSU athlete under 46.00, and then in 1983, he became the first Cougar to run under 45.00 when he ran 44.80. The following year, WSU sprinter and Cote d'Ivoire native Gabriel Tiacoh would win a silver medal in 44.54 at the Los Angeles Olympic Games. Two years after that, in 1984, he would lead the world with a 44.32, and then again at 44.30, in 1986.

So...

John Chaplin views his life in the sport not as a straight line but as an oval, encircling one lap of the quarter mile (440 yards or 400 meters) oval over and over, again and again. The one-lap race is long, it's hard, and it requires an unwavering commitment. The 400-meter athlete does not get to relax, coast, ease up, or slow down. After spending many hours with John Chaplin during the last twenty months, I'd agree that one hard lap of the oval is the perfect metaphor for John Chaplin's career in track & field—an all-out sprint, tenacious and unrelenting.

Track & Field News, the self-described and universally accepted "Bible of the Sport," once ran a cover photograph of the great Kenyan distance runner Henry Rono cresting the top of a hill. Behind and below Rono stretched an endless vista of rolling countryside, empty and devoid of any sign of nearby civilization. Casual readers at the time assumed the photo was taken in some remote corner of Rono's home country. But the picture was snapped just as he reached the end of a steep climb to the rim of the Snake River Canyon. The canyon was south of Pullman, Washington, where Rono and the other great Kenyan athletes, along with the rest of WSU's distance runners, had worked out twice a week in the mornings before their afternoon session on the track.

Lower Granite Dam sits at the bottom of the canyon, more than 1,800 feet below Pullman. Driving from the canyon floor to the rim is enough to make your ears pop. So, you can imagine what running up the approximately two-mile grade in the company of several other world- and national-class distance runners might be like. It was hard, it was fast, and it tested the strength, stamina, and will of several generations of WSU athletes. The Snake River Canyon run has for years served as an accurate barometer of what may be possible for a particular athlete. But according to Coach Chaplin, no one at that time had run the two-mile grade out of the canyon quite like Henry Rono.

During the last third of the twentieth century (from 1965 to 1999), beginning with Gerry Lindgren, continuing with Chaplin's long line of great Kenyan distance runners, and ending with Bernard Lagat, Cougar athletes put WSU at the epicenter of the international track & field world.

Chaplin also noted, "In 1978, the Australian National Team trained at WSU before going up to the Commonwealth Games in Edmond, Alberta, Canada. A major newspaper in Australia printed a map showing San Francisco, Pullman, and Edmonton so their readers would know where their team was going. So, we can say accurately, and with tongue in cheek, "WSU track & field did put

Pullman on the map." Chaplin and his wife, Linda, also hosted three USATF international junior meets in Pullman and three more in Vancouver, British Columbia, in the 1980s, featuring national teams from the US, Australia, Mexico, Canada, Japan, China, and Cuba, as well as individual athletes from Jamaica.

When the US State Department would not allow Cuban athletes to enter the country to compete, Washington congressman Tom Foley (then the speaker of the US House of Representatives), who represented Washington's Fifth Congressional District (which included Pullman), intervened, and the Cuban kids were allowed to compete. Chaplin said, "All these junior meets would not have happened if it had not been for Jack Pelo Sr., the local Coca-Cola distributor, who helped with expenses and who secured funding to get and keep a new scoreboard for the relocated WSU track."

Anyway, back to Rono...

Rono and WSU teammate Samson Kimombwa spent the summer of 1977 racing in Europe under the auspices of the Cougar Track Club. Kimombwa was the star of that summer tour. He broke British great David Bedford's record for 10,000 meters when he ran 27:30.47 in Helsinki, Finland, on June 30. Rono didn't have a bad summer himself. By lowering his personal record in the 3,000-meter steeplechase to 8:29.0, posting a world-ranked time of 13:21.9 in the 5,000-meter, and running an eye-popping 27:37.1 in the 10,000-meter, Rono established himself firmly as a member of that tiny fraternity of runners who can legitimately be identified as *world-class*. Then, when Kimombwa and Rono came home and ran the steep grade out of the Snake River Canyon with their WSU teammates, John Prescott Chaplin had a revelation.

After watching him demolish Samson on the Snake River Canyon run, Chaplin remembered, "I brought Henry into my office and said,

'Henry, I think that you could be the first man in history to hold the world record in all three Olympic distance races.'"

Chaplin's prediction came at a time when the world of international distance running had recently been elevated in the public mind by the likes of New Zealand's John Walker and Finland's Lasse Viren and by the exploits of American athletes like Gerry Lindgren, Billy Mills, Frank Shorter, and Steve Prefontaine. Needless to say, Chaplin's belief in Rono's potential must have come as something of a shock to the soft-spoken young Kenyan.

"But," Chaplin remembered, "Henry replied, 'Do you really think I can do this?'" Chaplin, in his inimitable style, didn't hesitate because he'd already had a vision, and he had formed a plan.

"I suck myself up, like any coach would, to answer that question and said, 'Yes. But we will have to first look at the schedule, then work out a program where you run a race to prepare, and, in the second race at that distance, correct any problems, and then you'll run for the record.' And that's what he did!"

More specifics on that preparation later.

So...

Chaplin had recently worked to convince administrators at the school to allow a statue honoring Rono (who has been selected as the track & field Athlete of the Century by the Pac-12 Conference) to be erected on the WSU campus. Initially, according to Chaplin, his appeals were met with a distinct and frustrating lack of enthusiasm by the athletic director and by the WSU Foundation Development office. But anyone familiar with John Chaplin's tenure as one of the most successful collegiate track & field coaches in the country and *the* most successful coach of any men's program at WSU knew administrative indifference would not deter or distract him, even at age 85.

"Finally," he said, "with the help of WSU President Dr. Kirk Schulz and local businessman Duane Brelsford and fruitful discussions with all parties, a plan was developed, and the problem was solved." A statue honoring Rono is in the works. Rono is not the only WSU athlete honored by the Pac-12. John Olerud, who starred in the major leagues for the Toronto Blue Jays and the Seattle Mariners, was the Pac-12 Conference Athlete of the Century for baseball. WSU baseball alumni, under the direction of a local WSU baseball alum (Phil Hinrichs), are raising a statue of Olerud at the Bailey-Brayton Baseball Complex on campus.

Chaplin does have a reputation for being a controversial figure. He remains brash, forthright, often profane, and, to anyone more interested in acquiescence than candor, a bit difficult.

But…

"If you don't understand me, the rest is irrelevant," Chaplin said. "I am not complicated. If I say I will do something, I will do it. If I say I won't, I won't. But I'm not closed to reevaluating anything. If you say you *can't* do something, I will listen, but if you say I *won't* do something, it's game over. I am a lot of things, but insecure is not one of them."

Once, during an annual visit with his doctor, Chaplin asked, "How is my blood pressure?" The doctor laughed and answered, "Hell, John, you don't have high blood pressure. You give it."

"My public persona is nothing like I am. But I made it, so if other coaches and/or track & field governing bodies wanted to play hardball, I could play hardball too. Messing with the track & field program is not the best thing for you to do in life."

What is sometimes lost when considering Chaplin's legacy, not only at WSU but also as a major figure on the national and international stage, is that his recruitment of international athletes was not unusual. But what seemed to rankle some people is that so many of Chaplin's successful imports were from African nations. To Chaplin, the objections were disingenuous at best, and, at worst, were…Well, his good friend and coaching colleague, Brooks Johnson, the former coach at Stanford University, will have something to say about that later.

"An example is Jim Bush, a great track & field coach at UCLA, who, in my opinion, should have been a head coach for the US at the Olympics," Chaplin said. "From 1965 to 1984, Bush had several foreign athletes on his teams, and those athletes helped him beat archrival USC in 1966 in their annual dual meet for the first time in school history. But he was all over *me* for recruiting foreign athletes."

Notice how Chaplin managed to simultaneously praise Bush and take issue with the UCLA coach's attitude about WSU's recruitment of African athletes. This ability to hold two seemingly contradictory ideas at the same time is a consistent feature of John Chaplin's view of the world and one that will repeat itself again and again.

"So, in 1977, when the Pac-8 Conference Championships were hosted by UCLA, I decided that enough was enough."

To make his point, Chaplin showed up at the meet in a safari suit and pith helmet and then wore his exotic getup onto the infield when the coaches were introduced. "Bush almost lost his marbles, but after that, the rhetoric on foreign athletes [from Africa] was toned down."

Was this highly visible nod to his willingness to search far and wide for great athletes over the top? Sure. Was the gesture controversial? Probably. Did Chaplin care if the gesture may have caused certain of his colleagues a measure of well-earned discomfort? Not at all. He had made what he believed was a serious point in a manner no one was likely to forget.

"*They* say I'm controversial, but you can hardly find anything I ever *said* that was controversial, other than that stupid statement about…"

Chaplin paused, not sure just how far he wanted to go. Yes, he can be blunt, even abrupt, but he measures his words when they need measuring. He was speaking of an incident following a meet in Eugene, Oregon, on April 15, 1978. Henry Rono was in the early days of that remarkable 81-day stretch in 1978 (from April 8 to June 27), in which he would set world records at 5,000 meters, the 3,000-meter steeplechase, 10,000 meters, and the flat 3,000 meters.

See Rono's 1978 81-day racing schedule in the appendix.

The story goes that Chaplin had Rono back off in the final 600 meters of the 3,000-meter steeplechase in a dual meet against the University of Oregon at venerable Hayward Field in Eugene. Chaplin has since been accused of wanting to deny the knowledgeable and enthusiastic fans in Eugene the satisfaction of seeing the world record set in their stadium. But the truth is either more complicated or more interesting, depending on your point of view. With a lap and a half left in the race, Rono was running close to the steeplechase world record of 8:08.02, held at the time by Anders Garderud of Sweden, but Chaplin believed the water jump pit at Hayward Field was too shallow.

"I didn't want Rono to set the record there and then have it disallowed later," he explained, "so, I yelled at Henry to slow down." Rono did as he was instructed. He still finished in 8:14.75, a new collegiate record, and the fastest time ever on American soil at the time.

"I knew that if the IAAF [International Amateur Athletics Federation, the worldwide governing body for track & field in charge of ratifying world records] measured the Oregon steeplechase pit and it was found to be not deep enough, the headline in the Eugene paper would be 'Chaplin Embarrasses Oregon.' Hell, as an old newspaperman myself, I would have written the same headline."

Then the *fun* began.

"After the race, Carl Cluff, a reporter for the Portland *Oregonian*, asked me in front of Rono and other members of the media, 'But can the kid read or write?'"

Remember, Henry Rono was a black man from Africa, setting records in track events that, up until then and from the limited perspective of some American observers, had been the exclusive province of white athletes. "First, I said 'next question.' Then I said the stupidest thing I ever said in track & field. 'You have crazy fans…'"

At this point, he paused again, this time to clarify what he meant—that Oregon track & field fans tend to be more like college football or basketball fans in their enthusiasm for the sport and their devotion to University of Oregon athletes in dual meets. He was also quick to add that when it came to championship events held in Eugene, fans were (and are) uncommonly generous to all athletes, regardless of affiliation. But then he added, "…and you have a shitty press." Significantly, he did not pause here to clarify. "And their press doesn't deserve a world record."

Then Chaplin threw gasoline on the inevitable media fire by announcing Rono would break the steeplechase record at the University of Washington five weeks later, on May 13. Anyone familiar with the rivalry that exists between Washington and Oregon's two largest universities also knows Chaplin's announcement had to sting.

"Yeah. I really put my foot in it. But Henry would bail me out." At this point, Chaplin said he made a mental note *to never again predict a world record.*

"Another example was Blaine Newnham," Chaplin went on, referring to the sports editor of Eugene's *Register-Guard* at the time. "Even Kenny Moore called him out as a *homer* in an article for *Sports Illustrated* in 1978."

Moore, who died on May 4, 2022, was a Eugene native, Oregon alum, and world-class marathon runner. He wrote eloquently about the sport in several national publications and authored the definitive book on Oregon track & field, *Bowerman and the Men of Oregon.* WSU has had a similar description for its distance runners: the Long Crimson Line, made up of nearly 50 conference champions and more than 50 NCAA All-Americans.

"Finally, it got so bad that I had to change my policy about the kids talking to the press. When the University of Oregon came to Pullman, everyone was allowed to talk to the press. But in Oregon for dual meets, the athletes were instructed that when we crossed the Columbia River, all they were to say to the press was 'no comment.'"

Chaplin applied this same rule to his own relationship with the Oregon press. "I made sure if I was quoted in the *Oregonian,* everyone knew it was a damn lie."

Five weeks later, on May 13, 1978, the Northwest Relays (a low-key meet in an all but empty 58,000-seat Husky Stadium in Seattle) took place. Present were about one hundred and fifty damp and shivering fans and a couple hundred sodden ex-WSU track & field athletes, along with a handful of reporters ready to jump on Chaplin when Rono failed to fulfill his coach's world record prediction. Instead, they witnessed what is certainly one of the least observed world records in track & field history. Rono cruised seven and a half laps around the cavernous and nearly empty stadium, negotiating twenty-eight hurdles and seven water jumps in 8:05.4, a new world record, just as his coach had predicted back in Eugene.

Chaplin has never fit the mold of the laid-back, easy-going distance runners' coach—a stereotype that doesn't really hold up anyway, not when you consider the top college coaches in the US.

Most burn with the same emotion and intensity Chaplin wears on his sleeve, even if their intensity is less visible or their emotion more cautiously held in check. And Chaplin lacks the distance runner's self-conscious introspection. To this day, he insists long, slow, leisurely runs have very little to do with racing with the best in the world. He also believes fervently that track & field, coupled with cross country, is a major sport, and for more than fifty years, he has battled conventional wisdom, media neglect, and institutional stubbornness to have the sport treated as such.

In an August 23, 1987, article in the *Moscow-Pullman Daily News*, after citing WSU's sixty straight dual meet victories, numerous top-ten finishes (including finishing second three times) at the NCAA meet, world record holders, and an Olympic champion, reporter Peter Harriman quoted former WSU athletic director Dick Young as follows: "I'd say [Chaplin's] a borderline genius who isn't very challenged by his position as a track coach."

I don't know what Chaplin's reaction to Young's assessment was at the time, but in the same article, the coach explains his success at WSU by crediting the Long Crimson Line of extraordinary athletes. "I never made a great athlete," Chaplin said in Harriman's article. "Great athletes made me."

After Harriman's article was published, former WSU football player Keith Lincoln, who was the director of the WSU alumni office, repeated to Chaplin a comment by WSU Vice President Stan Schmidt. "It's not that he is not challenged by his job as a track and field coach," Lincoln said, quoting Schmidt, "it's just that he's the only intellectual in the building."

This book will touch lightly on John Chaplin's controversies because those issues were dealt with, often in a biased and inaccurate manner, in real-time and as they happened. This book is not about the people he made uncomfortable or the feathers he ruffled. This book is about the vital contribution he's made to the sport in the Pacific Northwest, across the United States and internationally, and to the personal and athletic development of the young people who came through the WSU program during his tenure. This is not an exposé or a tell-all. This is a book about John Chaplin and the elite athletes he attracted to a tiny town in the rolling hills of southeastern Washington's wheat country and how, together, they raised WSU to the very pinnacle of international track & field.

John Chaplin left WSU in 1994, frustrated by new institutional restrictions on how he would be allowed to grant scholarships. Athletic director Jim Livengood downsized both track & field and baseball by insisting half of all scholarships go to in-state athletes. Baseball coach Bobo Brayton left WSU at the same time and for the same reason.

"If I had one regret about how the program was treated during my tenure of twenty-seven years at WSU," Chaplin said, "it was that in all that time, not one athletic director ever came into the track office and asked, 'How can WSU and I help your program?' In fact, I don't remember more than a few times that a WSU AD was ever at a dual meet at Mooberry [Track & Field Complex].

"The NCAA places a limit on scholarships for all sports," he explained, "which meant track & field went from no limit on scholarships to 24.5, then down to the current limit of 12.6 on the men's side. However, WSU never offered more than 17 full scholarships."

Despite all that, Chaplin's dual meet record was an astounding 202-15. He had a run of sixty straight dual meets victories and a winning record against every team on his schedule. Chaplin was dismayed by what he saw as the coming diminishment of collegiate track & field, so he stepped away to take on a more active role in the administrative, technical, and officiating side of the sport at the national and international levels. On his way out, Chaplin warned of the possibility that collegiate track & field programs could be cut over tenuous, *even* disingenuous, budget considerations.

He believes that *when you try to legislate equality, you only get mediocrity.*

"In the last several years, there has been an uptick in coaching salaries and interest in track & field at some of the major powers," he said. "But for the most part, track & field is simply a way for schools to count three sports toward NCAA Division I participation requirements on the men's side. Since I only coached men at WSU, I will leave comments about the women's side to others."

Chaplin was driven to place collegiate (particularly, WSU) track & field and cross country where he believes they belong—alongside and equal to the other major sports that have come to dominate the college and university landscape. In 2001, Chaplin was awarded an IAAF Veteran Pin Award, an international award few Americans (and almost no coaches) have ever received.

John Chaplin was a pioneer of a trend that, in the years since he left WSU, has become standard practice in collegiate track & field. At the 2022 NCAA Division I championships, international athletes from ten different countries won eleven individual titles—six for women and five for men—in the thirty-four individual events contested. Whether or not this is a good thing is still debated, albeit quietly, because the practice of recruiting athletes from other countries has become so common. In fact, it's now common practice for American colleges and universities to recruit foreign-born athletes in nearly every NCAA sport.

I think there are two reasons for this:

First, the depth of talent coming out of American high schools has improved dramatically in the last several years. For example, sixteen high school boys have run under four minutes in the mile since Jim Ryun became the first in 1965, but eleven of the athletes who have broken four minutes have done so since 2015, four in 2022 alone. Eight of the top ten times ever recorded for high school girls for two miles, or 3,200 meters, its closest metric equivalent, have been accomplished since 2013, and all are under 9:55. The counterintuitive point is that because more elite American high school athletes have become available, the competitive incentive to recruit from elsewhere is increased to match the influx of domestic talent.

There is a school of thought among some coaches and outside observers that international athletes come to American college campuses with fewer years of hard training and fewer races on their legs. So, even if their times may not be as impressive as the top American kids, their potential upside is greater over the long haul.

Of the American high school boys who have run the mile under 4:00 since 2015 and prior to 2022, only Grant Fisher, running for Stanford University, has won an NCAA title, at 5,000 meters in 2017. Fisher has since broken American records for the 5,000 (both indoors and outdoors) and the 10,000 outdoors. *Note: Fisher's indoor 5,000-meter record was beaten by former University of Portland athlete Woody Kincaid in February of 2023.*

None of the rest improved markedly, if at all. This not a criticism of collegiate coaching or a condemnation of the American high school system, which often requires elite athletes to run anywhere from twenty to thirty races during a single season, but rather to point out that success, even phenomenal success, at the high school level is no guarantee of elite-level success at the college level. Couple that with the increasing availability of professional opportunities for elite high school runners and it is easy to understand why contemporary college coaches might take the same road traveled by John Chaplin as far back as the early 1970s in pursuit of high-end talent.

Not to get all high-handed and philosophical here, but it is a truism that lasting innovation is nearly always initiated by individuals with a unique vision and who are criticized, scorned, or condemned for that vision, especially if it challenges conventional wisdom.

That is, until the innovation becomes conventional wisdom.

The late great ABC sportscaster Keith Jackson, a WSU graduate, once complained on air or in print, I don't remember which, that Chaplin was perpetuating a disservice by granting scholarships to international athletes at the expense of American high school kids. During the early days of preparing this book, I interviewed more than a dozen former WSU track & field athletes, but only four (Joseph Taiwo, George Ogbeide, Patrick Muturi, and Georges Kablan), were born outside the US. The rest went to high school in Washington State, most in either Seattle or Tacoma, which is certainly not "Cougar Country" in the way people in the Pacific Northwest think about the kind of kids who would, under normal circumstances, attend WSU.

Not a single former athlete would find fault, criticize, or second guess John Chaplin's philosophy: to recruit the very best athletes from the state of Washington and then fill out his team with the very best athletes from wherever he could find them, anywhere in the world. As Chaplin pointed out, *"The cost of out-of-state tuition is the same whether a kid is from Arizona or from France."*

In 1985, a WSU 4x400-meter relay team consisting of Lee Gordon (from Mercer Island, Washington), Dennis Livingston (from Seattle's Ingraham High School), Calvin Harris (from Lakes High School near Tacoma), and Gabriel Tiacoh ran 3:05.58 (an average of 46.45) to win the Pac-10 title. That time remains WSU's school record. A year later, as Tim Manson, the Pac-10 800-meter champion who grew up in Tacoma and attended Lincoln High School (and from whom we'll hear more later), pointed out, another WSU 4x400-meter relay team ran 3:06.4 (an average of 46.6). That team consisted of Manson, Kris Durr (from Rogers High School in Puyallup, just outside Tacoma, Washington), Harris, and Tiacoh. In these admittedly limited but by no means unique samples, the Greater Seattle/Tacoma area might have been as fertile a recruiting ground for Chaplin as the Rift Valley in Kenya.

Yes, WSU's all-time lists contain a generous sprinkling of international athletes, and some events, particularly the longer races, are dominated by athletes from other countries. But the assumption some people made at the time and the impression that lingers to this day that Chaplin's success at WSU was due solely to ready-made international athletes is simply wrong, as nearly every single American-born athlete who competed for WSU during Chaplin's tenure will attest without question or reservation. In fact, at the time of publication, all but one of WSU's top-ten lists contains both American and foreign athletes.

WSU's all-time top-ten list for the 400-meter hurdles consists entirely of American kids. Seven of the ten were All-Americans: Jim Allen was the Athletic Association of Western Universities (AAWU) champion ranked second in the world at 50.1 in 1962; Boyd Gittins set the world record at 49.5 and later, in 1968, ran 49.27 (49.1 hand-timed); Eric Dudley was the Pac-10 champion in 2005; Jeshua Anderson ran 47.93, won four conference titles, three NCAA championship championships (in 2008, 2009, and 2011), the USATF title in 2011, and was the world junior champion in 2008; and C.J. Allen won two Pac-12 titles and then ran 47.96 in 2022 after his WSU career. *Note:*

Loren Benke (1937 NCAA 440-yard dash champion at 46.9) was an NCAA All-American in the 440-yard intermediate hurdles in 1936. He tied the American and colligate records in the prelims at the 1936 AAU Championships with a time of 51.8 for a one-turn race. He hit the sixth hurdle in the finals and place third to Glen Hardin, who set a new American and collegiate record at 51.6.

CHAPTER 1

THE LITTLE HEATHEN

John Prescott Chaplin's 70-plus years in track & field began when he was a star on the Los Angeles Wilson High School C team as a precocious, if under-sized, ninth grader in the spring of 1952. This was at a time when sprinters still had to use a trowel to dig holes in the track for their feet at the start. Chaplin had his first experience with distance running in the fall of 1952, his sophomore year in high school.

"Coach Paul Barthel, the track & field coach at Wilson High, recruited me for the newly established cross-country team. I think it was because I ran the 660-yard race on the C team in ninth grade. Barthel says, 'You're going to run cross country.' I say, '*What?*' But it's only 1.8 miles, and I became a varsity letterman in tenth, eleventh, and twelfth grade in cross country and captain of the team my senior year in 1954."

Despite that early exposure to distance running, Chaplin recognized his future would lie on the track and at much shorter distances. "My best time as a high school student for 440 yards was 49.2," he pointed out, adding that he lowered that to 48.9 at a summer AAU meet after he graduated from Wilson.

Those times would be considered very good even today, and at the time, Chaplin had been identified as one of the better-than-average high school quarter milers in the country. His involvement with elite-level track & field did not end when, more than four decades later, he resigned as the head coach at WSU. After leaving WSU, he served as the head track & field referee at the 1996 Atlanta Olympics, as the head coach for the US men's team at the 2000 Olympics in Sydney, and later as an IAAF technical official. During his 24-year tenure as chairman of the International Competition Committee for USATF, he chaired the committee in charge of the Olympic Trials and other US foreign competitions. Also, in his role as the head of USATF's Men's Track & Field Committee, he has adjudicated the sometimes-contentious interpretations of the often-arcane track and field rulebook as the referee at major meets all over the world. He also chaired the USATF committee that selected the coaches and managers for international competitions. He continues to be in demand for speaking engagements at coaching clinics across the globe, and he remains the head of the jury of appeals for the USATF junior and senior national championships. The USATF Men's Executive Committee has named him *emeritus* for all those years of strict, fair, and conscientious enforcement of the rules. No one in the world is more familiar with the legalities that govern track & field than John Chaplin. Interestingly, he invests some time as the chair of the cemetery committee for the city of Pullman.

Despite all that, Chaplin is best known and most visible as the head track & field coach (from 1974 to 1994) and head cross-country coach (from 1968 to 1993) at WSU. During those twenty-seven years,

Chaplin, following in the shoes of three WSU Hall of Fame coaches, elevated the track & field program at a small, land-grant university in a tiny farming community, in a remote corner of a remote state, to a position of national and international prominence.

Washington State University is considered by some in the state of Washington and around the country as the poor, albeit personable, little brother of the University of Washington (the Evergreen State's flagship university). With enrollment in excess of 40,000 students, the U-Dub is located on the shores of Lake Washington in the cosmopolitan and urban metropolis of Seattle. The damp view through the open eastern end of the (recently renovated and expanded) 75,000-seat Husky Stadium is of the lake and the picturesque Lake Washington floating bridge disappearing into the misty distance toward the trendy suburbs of Bellevue, Redmond, and Medina. On a rare clear and still fall day with the sun shimmering off the calm surface of the lake and with the Cascade Mountains and Mount Rainier looming beyond, it's not difficult to understand why Husky Stadium has been called the best venue in all of college sports. On game days, some fans travel to the stadium by boat and celebrate their own aquatic version of the time-honored tradition of tailgating.

WSU, on the other hand, has around 23,000 students. The school sits atop a series of steep hills in the heart of the Palouse region, hard against the Idaho border and on the southeastern verge of Whitman County, which proudly boasts of its status as the number one wheat- and lentil-growing county in the entire country. The view from atop the 34,000-seat Martin Stadium (less than half the size of Husky Stadium) bears this out. The campus ends, and the wheat fields begin. No picturesque lakeshore. No suburban transition zone. No quaint hobby farms. No crowded freeways. Just wheat, barley, lentils, chickpeas, and other field crops rolling off into the distance as far as the eye can see. Highway 27 winds through these fields (and little else) and links Pullman to the next closest towns in Whitman County. Fifteen miles to the north is Palouse (population fewer than 1,000), and fourteen miles to the south on Highway 195 is Colton and its 418 industrious souls. The only other significant population center in Whitman County is Colfax, the county seat fifteen miles northwest of Pullman on Highway 195, with a population of 2,911. The agricultural character of Whitman County and the multi-varied, cosmopolitan culture of Seattle, and by extension, the respective cultures and world views of the two universities, are so different that comparisons are sort of pointless.

Seattle is the financial and political center of a region that stretches from Sacramento to Fairbanks and from Honolulu to Boise. It is the region's heartbeat and hub. Seattle and its suburbs are home to most of the region's (and a significant number of the nation's and the world's) movers and shakers. Bill Gates and Jeff Bezos live just across Lake Washington. Boeing is there. So are Amazon, Nordstrom, Microsoft, and Starbucks. More people live within twenty miles of the University of Washington campus than in the entire 46,620 square-mile expanse of Eastern Washington.

People in Washington who live east of the Cascade Mountains often look west at Seattle's power and wealth and influence and shake their heads in wonder because that same power, wealth, and influence so often seem to look east and see a culture and a people easy to look down on. Some people on the lush, drizzly west side of the mountains seem to think their neighbors on the arid east side of the state are not all that smart, not at all well-educated, and not worth considering all that much—an attitude John Chaplin has fought against tirelessly in his 60-odd years in Pullman. He notes that Paul Allen, co-founder of Microsoft, is a WSU graduate. And that Pullman is also the home of

Sweitzer Engineering Laboratories, a worldwide supplier of electrical switching equipment. Chaplin's point is that Eastern Washington, although mostly rural and sparsely populated, is not as backward as some might wish to assume.

This point was made pointedly and ironically by a columnist for the *Seattle Times*, who made the following observation when a nascent movement to tear down the dams on the Columbia and Snake rivers—dams that provide the entire region with the nation's cheapest electricity and the farms and ranches in Eastern Washington with abundant irrigation water—was gaining political traction: At times, it seemed as if people in the urban enclaves on the west side of the mountains must not know where their food comes from. He then went on to imply that, at best, they were ignorant or indifferent to the role Eastern Washington plays in the region's prosperity, and at worst, they probably *didn't* know where their food comes from.

So, it should not be surprising that WSU alumni and Cougar supporters, who are often fanatically devoted to the school's athletic teams regardless of their success, or lack of, are also among the country's longest-suffering fans when it comes to comparisons to rival teams from the University of Washington. This is largely due to the material and geographical advantages the much-despised *Dawgs* from Seattle have over their much-loved Cougs from the Palouse. With that in mind, it is to be expected that successful WSU coaches have been elevated to near-mythical status. Conversely, coaches who are otherwise uncommonly successful are looked at somewhat askance, even disdainfully, if they fail to beat the University of Washington, at least occasionally.

The late Mike Leach is the best recent example. His WSU football teams were consistent winners and ranked, at one time, in the top ten in the nation. By most measures, it was an eight-year record of accomplishment nearly unparalleled in the history of WSU football. Still, Leach's teams had only one win against the University of Washington in those eight years.

"At an event in Coeur d'Alene [Idaho], an alumni gathering," Chaplin recalled, "I said, 'We need to take a page out of Washington's book. Let's give him four or five years before we start throwing darts at him.'" I got the impression that in Mike Leach, Chaplin recognized a kindred spirit, someone who could take a school like WSU to the very top of the collegiate football world, given adequate time and resources. "He was a character," Chaplin went on, "and I liked him."

So, despite whatever success WSU achieved on the track or in cross country, the Cougars are still considered the University of Washington's *little brother*—tolerated, occasionally annoying, but not really of much consequence, especially when it comes to intercollegiate sports. "First of all," Chaplin explained, "I never bought into that. And second, I never discussed it."

Chaplin's record in dual meets against the University of Washington was either 22-1 or 21-1. There was some confusion over the scoring of a meet at Corvallis, Oregon, involving Washington, WSU, and Oregon State. After twenty-five years in the record book, Washington now considers the meet a three-way. But Chaplin insists Oregon State scored the meet as three separate dual meets, so Chaplin counts it as a dual-meet win over the Huskies.

Unfortunately, from Chaplin's point of view, As of February 2023, the annual Washington-Washington State dual meet does not appear on the schedule of either school. Chaplin indicated that apparently, "beginning in 2023, WSU and the University of Washington will not have a co-ed dual meet, and if this continues in the future, WSU track & field will have limited competition opportunities to develop young talent, and as a result, there will be fewer chances to shine in the *Big Meets.*"

The impression you get from talking to John Chaplin is that he accepted and was challenged by the notion he would have to do things differently to succeed at a place like WSU. "But we never broke the recruiting rules," he said. This seems important to Chaplin, now 85 and as cantankerous and plain-spoken as ever. And he underscores his point by noting he was at one time the assistant athletic director in charge of eligibility and an assistant admissions officer—appointments that were thrust on him by WSU administrators, positions he did not seek or want. The assumption at the time, I think, was that the only way Chaplin could have possibly attracted the kind of athletes who were consistently showing up in Pullman would have been to stretch the rules. That is to say...cheat. This assumption was reinforced and provided fodder for his critics when, in 1994, Chaplin left his coaching position at WSU to take a job in the provost's office. He also taught a geography class, which some students in the College of Education needed for their secondary teacher's certification in social studies.

The WSU interim athletic director at the time, Marcia Saneholtz, claimed that both Chaplin and iconic baseball coach Bobo Brayton were forced to resign as part of satisfying sanctions demanded by the NCAA against the WSU track & field and baseball programs. "To say the relationship that Brayton and I had with Saneholtz was not without conflict was to push the envelope a bit," Chaplin said. "At one time, she was our direct boss, and that did not go well."

Saneholtz further claimed that Chaplin's job in the provost's office was a position he was forced into as a result of the NCAA sanctions. The problem with Saneholtz's claim that the sanctions against the two most successful coaches at WSU resulted from something "more than bookkeeping errors" is that they are not true.

The best, or at least the most accurate, account of what happened when Chaplin and Brayton resigned is an article by reporter Tim Sullivan that appeared in the *Moscow-Pullman Daily News* on March 9, 1994. In the article, Sullivan cites high-ranking WSU and NCAA officials who contradict Saneholtz.

For example, Sullivan notes that David Swanks, at the time the chairman of the NCAA infractions committee and an assistant professor at the University of Oklahoma Law School, stated flatly that the problems within the track & field and baseball programs were the results of a "bookkeeping error."

In its official statement on the matter, the NCAA did not include any requirement that Chaplin or Brayton resign. "The NCAA did not take away our four NCAA outdoor runner-up trophies [from 1983 to 1985 and 1991]," Chaplin pointed out, "or the runner-up [trophies] in 1984 and third place in 1991 [that] we won indoors. The conference took the 1983 and 1991 conference titles away, but they let us keep the trophies. Was Saneholtz in a position to influence the process? Who knows?"

In Sullivan's article, Chaplin is quoted as saying, "I was never asked to resign my [coaching] job. She [Saneholtz] knew I wasn't asked to resign. That's character assassination. The consent agreement never said I had to resign. We were given an additional year of probation and were not allowed to participate in the conference championships in 1993." That year, the baseball team was also not allowed to participate in the postseason.

"I agree it was a violation in the eyes of the Pac-10, and I took the punishment, which was the loss of a few partial scholarships that were taken back in the 1994 season," Chaplin went on. "But the interpretation of the question that was asked was given to our faculty representative, Dr. Ed Bennett, by the conference." Chaplin noted here that Bennett had an impeccable reputation and was well regarded in the academic community beyond WSU.

Under the rules at the time, only an institution's faculty representative and president could communicate directly to the conference office or the NCAA national office. And individuals in each institution who were responsible for eligibility were not allowed to attend the NCAA National Convention, where the rules for eligibility were established every year in January. And they could not call the NCAA office if they had questions. Now, that has been rectified. In addition to university presidents and faculty reps, eligibility officers and the primary woman's administrators all have access to both the conference and the NCAA.

"I told the press that no matter how it happened," Chaplin concluded, "as the head coach, I was responsible for anything that happened in or to the program."

Chaplin was offered a job in the provost's office in the summer of 1994, "And I took it," he said. "I stayed with the provost's office and taught classes off and on from the summer of 1994 to the spring of 2002, when I turned 65 and retired from WSU. It's one of those unfortunate screwups where all hands weren't on board together. Somebody dropped the ball, but not deliberately."

Sullivan also quotes Sallie Giffin, WSU's then vice president for business affairs, who oversaw the athletic department: "Chaplin and Brayton were not forced to resign." And, according to Sullivan's article, Sally Savage, the executive assistant and counsel to then WSU President Sam Smith characterized claims that the two coaches were forced out as "inaccurate."

For more on Chaplin's relationship with the Pac-10 Conference and the NCAA, see the appendix.

And finally, Sullivan quoted WSU's vice provost for academic affairs, Geoff Gamble, on why Chaplin was asked to return to the provost's office. "We're trying to capitalize on John's strengths and his international reputation and involvement with international students....He had an ongoing relationship with the provost's office, and we agreed to bring him back."

Now, getting back Chaplin's coaching story:

"But my problem as a track coach," he explained, "was the same as every other program at WSU—no depth."

Recruiting athletes to WSU can be a challenge, at least recruiting the type of track & field athletes it takes to be competitive with the likes of UCLA, USC, and Oregon. Chaplin was emphatic when he pointed out that even though Pullman, with one public high school, is the largest city (population 34,000) in the 2,178 square miles of Whitman County, the population of Los Angeles County is 9.86 million, greater than the entire state of Washington by more than two million. The city of Los Angeles, where Chaplin went to high school, had 60 public high schools in the 1950s, but today there are more than 180 high schools with a total enrollment of 469,633, plus an additional 281 private high schools, with a total enrollment of 79,6125, as of the beginning of the 2022-2023 school year. Clearly, recruiting at WSU presents challenges that California universities and, to a certain extent, the University of Washington need not contend with. Chaplin's solution to overcoming WSU's geographical and demographic disadvantage was to give in-state and other US kids a red-shirt year so they had more time to develop and then go as far afield as necessary to find athletes who could compete at both the elite level of the NCAA and at the highest level of international track and field. As Chaplin pointed out, whether you were from a different state or a different country, out-of-state tuition was the same.

WSU already had a national reputation in track & field, with Hall of Fame coaches like Doc Bohler, Karl Schlademan, and Jack Mooberry. After a short stint as an assistant coach and ticket manager at Oregon State University, Mooberry hired Chaplin in 1968 to be his first-ever full-time assistant. He also made Chaplin the head cross country coach, responsible for the distance runners during track season. In addition, Chaplin would coach the throws and the 400-meter hurdles. Both coaches worked with the relays.

By the time Chaplin arrived in 1968, Mooberry had been WSU's coach since 1946 and had already established the school as a favored destination for great middle- and long-distance runners. Athletes like Lindgren and Rick Riley, who was the eighth-ranked 10,000-meter runner in the US as a high school senior in 1966, had established WSU's reputation for distance-running excellence. Lindgren had been an Olympian and set the world record for six miles. The versatile Riley became the first WSU athlete to break four minutes in the mile when he won that event at the 1970 Pac-8 championships, and he was an all-American at 10,000 meters in both 1969 and 1970.

Chaplin wants it known that WSU's tradition of great middle- and long-distance runners did not begin with him and even predates Mooberry. As far back as 1925, Cougar athletes were setting records and winning titles. John Divine won the NCAA two-mile title that year, and in 1939, Dixie Garner defeated world two-mile record holder Miklos Szabo of Hungary. Garner also set an indoor world record of 9:11.1 at the Cow Palace in San Francisco, CA, and then set the collegiate two-mile record outdoors at 9:07.9. Clem Eischen made the 1948 Olympic team at 1,500 meters and was All-American at 880 yards.

Canadians were a big part of the WSU middle- and long-distance legacy. Bill Dale was third at 800 meters in the 1938 Empire Games and a member of the gold medal 4x400-meter relay team. Another Canadian, Bill Parnell, made his country's Olympic team at both 800 and 1,500 meters in 1948 and 1952 and won a gold medal at the mile run at the 1950 Empire Games with a record of 4:11.0. Don Bertoia won the 800 meters at the 1963 Pan American Games in 1:48.46 and placed third in the 1,500 meters to American greats Jim Grelle and Jim Beatty. John Valient placed fourth in the NCAA meet in 1964 and set WSU records in both the steeplechase (8:57.1) and at 10,000 meters (29:57.2). Valient also placed eighth in the 5,000 that year in 14:20.9, setting a WSU record in all three events. Remarkably, it was the first time he'd ever run the steeplechase or the 10,000 meters.

And then there were American athletes like Noel Williams, Richard Paeth, Al Fisher, George Stimac, Chris Westman, Dean Clark, Art Sandison, Calvin Harris, James Brewster, Dale Scott, and Eric Anderson, and more recent athletes Paul Ryan, Zach Stallings, Colton Johnson, Jesse Jorgensen, and Joe Abbott. All have excelled at distances ranging from 800 yards to 10,000 meters. Sandison, from Port Angeles, Washington, was the 880-yard NCAA runner-up at the 1969 NCAA meet and the silver medalist at the 1971 Pan-American Games. Sandison still holds the WSU 800-meter record at 1:45.6. Larry Almberg was from Evergreen High School in Seattle and would go on to run 4:04.0 in the mile and set a world age-group of 3:50.43 for 1,500 meters—all after turning 40.

For ambitious young athletes today, a glance at WSU's school records and the level of performance it takes to make it on the all-time top-five list in the middle- and long-distance races might serve either as inspiration, motivation, or intimidation: 1:45.5 to 1:46.84 in the 800; 3:30.56 to 3:38.77 in the 1,500; 3:55.65 to 3:57.84 in the mile; 7:32.1 to 7:45.84 in the 3,000; 13:06.2 to 13:21.6 in the 5,000; 27:22.47 to 28:00.6 in the 10,000; and 8:05.4 to 8:20.67 in the steeplechase.

As Mooberry's assistant at WSU, Chaplin was exposed to world record holders Lindgren, John van Reenen, and Gittins. It is hard to imagine any two athletes less alike than Lindgren, the sparrow-like distance runner from just up the road in Spokane, and van Reenen, the larger-than-life shot and discus thrower who came to WSU from South Africa, halfway across the world. Gittins was a hurdler, a junior college transfer from a Seattle suburb. These three athletes set the stage, or at least suggested a paradigm, for how Chaplin would develop the WSU program after he succeeded Mooberry as the head coach in 1973. And all three were on the 1968 NCAA team that lost the NCAA Division I team title to USC by a single point: 58-57. After that NCAA meet, Mooberry was named the first national collegiate track & field coach of the year.

Lindgren was already a distance running legend from Spokane's Rogers High School when he arrived in Pullman in the fall of 1964. The diminutive phenom had run 8:40 for two miles and 13:44 for 5,000 meters while still in high school and nearly became the first high school athlete to break four minutes in the mile when he ran 4:01.6 his senior year. In the 57 years since Lindgren graduated from Rogers High, those times remain unmatched by any high school runner from the state of Washington. In 2019, the popular and influential YouTube channel *Total Running Productions* named Lindgren the second-best high school runner ever, behind world record holder and Olympic silver medalist Jim Ryun. Significantly, both Ryun and Lindgren qualified for the US team and competed in the 1964 Tokyo Olympic Games as high schoolers.

Lindgren and Ryan, along with Henry Rono, have all been inducted into the inaugural 30-member class of the United States Track & Field and Cross-Country Coaches Association (USTFCCCA) Athletes Hall of Fame. The event was held in Eugene, Oregon, on June

5 and 6, 2022 in conjunction with the centennial anniversary of the first NCAA national championship in track & field, which was also the first NCAA championship in any sport.

Lindgren caught the nation's attention when, in 1964, at the height of the Cold War, he defeated the best distance runners from the Soviet Union in the US vs. USSR dual meet as a high schooler. He went on to win three NCAA cross-country titles for WSU and set a world record for six miles when he and 1964 Olympic gold medalist Billy Mills both ran 27:11.6 at the 1965 AAU championships. At the time, six miles was the preferred distance in both the US and countries of the British Commonwealth. Later, he broke the American record for three miles, 5,000 meters, and six miles five times and broke collegiate records over the same distances plus the 10,000 meters seven times. His best times at WSU were the aforementioned 27:11.6 for six miles, with American records at 12:53.0 for three miles, 13:33.8 for 5,000 meters, and 28:40.2 for 10,000 meters, all performances that hold up remarkably well today even though they were attained more than half a century ago. At the time of Lindgren's first year at WSU, freshmen were not allowed to compete at the varsity level.

van Reenen was Lindgren's opposite in every respect except for his competitive success and assault on the record book. For one thing, he came to WSU from about as far away as it is possible to come. His native country, South Africa, was banned from international competition until 1992 because of the government's apartheid policies, so van Reenen sought education and the opportunity to compete at an American university. He settled on WSU after getting offers from four other schools. In 1970, he set WSU records in the shot put (65-0) and discus (208-10). Three years later, he broke the world record in the discus with a throw of 224-8. van Reenen was an NCAA individual champion in both events and the first man to throw over 200 feet at the NCAA championships. He was so impressive athletically that even though he only played one season of American football, he was selected by the San Diego Chargers in the fourteenth round of the 1972 NFL draft. The Chargers hoped he might find success as a running back based mostly on a single play. WSU head football coach Jim Sweeney sent van Reenen into a game against UCLA, and the massive fullback carried five or six UCLA players into the end zone from the eleven-yard line with seeming ease.

But it is not simply the difference in Lindgren and van Reenen's stature—Lindgren was about 5'3" and 110 pounds, and van Reenen was at least 6'7" and nearly 270 pounds—or the differences in their background that made them, along with a junior college transfer like Gittins. As Chaplin pointed out earlier, these three athletes provide an early example of the paradigm for success WSU would experience in the years after Mooberry retired and Chaplin became the Cougars' head coach.

van Reenen and Lindgren were established stars when Chaplin arrived at WSU. By 1968, each had an international reputation and had claimed an undisputed place among the very best in the world in their respective disciplines. But Gittins came from the other end of the spectrum. He was a junior college transfer with unimpressive junior college credentials and was typical of a number of in-state athletes who would develop into national or world-class performers while at WSU.

Chaplin paused to explain how a misjudgment on his part cost John van Reenen, a three-time NCAA discus champion, a world record. "One of the craziest things I have ever done as a coach," he said. "It was in 1970. John van Reenen had been throwing the discus well over 215 feet in practice, and since the discus throwing ring was opposite the finish line, his throws were bouncing near where the officials were located. So, I put up a set of barriers at 225 feet. The world record was 224-4 [68.40] by Jay Silvester, set in Reno, Nevada, in 1968, and what do you know? John hit the damn thing eighteen inches above the ground, costing him a world record. Lucky for me, he broke the world record at 224'8" [8.48] in 1975 in South Africa." Later, Jay Silvester would become Chaplin's weight coach at the Sydney Olympics.

Chaplin's unique upbringing and his own history in the sport had taught him that talent takes time to develop and that it comes in all shapes and sizes, and, significantly, from all over the world.

John Prescott Chaplin was born in Los Angeles on April 9, 1937. He grew up there in the years during and immediately after World War II. His father, James Prescott Chaplin, who went by Prescott Chaplin in his role as a writer and artist, was an intellectual and an adherent of radical politics. But his mother, Ruth Mariam (Heishman) Chaplin, was traditionally minded enough to see that her precocious son was educated in LA's Catholic school system from the sixth grade through eighth grade. Chaplin had three siblings: Michael Christian Chaplin (1938–2018) was a financial editor and a credit union banker for the *Los Angeles Times*; sister Colleen Ann (Cody) Chaplin (born in 1943) worked for the city of San Juan Capistrano, and brother Kent Lowell Chaplin (born in 1953) was a full colonel and an intelligence officer in the US Air Force.

We talked about his upbringing, his early education, and the influence of his parents during the first of many long conversations at his home—a spacious dwelling that sits on a gravel road a mile from the nearest paved highway, smack in the middle of Palouse's endless fields of wheat, barley, and other crops, and shaded by the only trees visible for miles. "I tell people I live in the middle of a park," Chaplin said, indicating with a wave of his arm the endless green of early spring wheat rolling away in every direction. "But the farmers take care of the park." He met Linda, his wife of nearly sixty years, at a hamburger stand in Wapato, Washington, the tiny Yakima Valley hamlet where his coaching career began.

When you enter the Chaplin home, you might expect to see trophies and mementos of Chaplin's seven decades in track & field. But except for a couple of plaques in the well-stocked library/bar and a single photograph of Henry Rono hanging in a corner, what is remarkable is the absence of the typical coaching memorabilia, photographs, or paraphernalia. If a visitor did not know how John Chaplin had spent the last sixty years, a reasonable assumption would be that he was an art collector (which he is), an historian, or a philosopher (also true) rather than a track & field coach. I have known a lot of track & field coaches, and most lean hard in a philosophical direction. Such are the vagaries of the sport.

The walls are covered with original works of art, and in every corner, a statue or bust in bronze, marble, or ceramic is displayed. Chaplin delighted in explaining the history of each piece and how he obtained it. The library shelves contain no books on coaching, no athletic histories or sporting-life biographies, no arcane technical journals or airy guides to the psychological or emotional benefits of running. Instead, Chaplin's extensive library includes authors from Shakespeare to Umberto Eco and Sydney Lanier and includes books on world religion, politics, history, geography, biography, and philosophy. And (I think Chaplin would consider this significant) most of the books are hardbacks, solid and permanent. There are few paperbacks, which, by contrast, seem transitory.

"You ask any athlete I ever had," Chaplin said, leaning far forward in a narrow chair in a corner of his library and jabbing a finger to make his point, "they'll all tell you the same thing. 'The first thing

Coach [Chaplin] cared about was our education.' Everyone will say that. *Every* one of 'em." Of course, this is the mantra repeated by every high school or college coach from the beginning of time, so often that it's become a cliché, whether true or not. But Chaplin insists he has evidence to back up his claim.

"Because I proved it when it really counted." Then he offered an example. "We had a meet against [the University of California]. And whoever wins gets the *Track & Field News* ranking as the number one dual-meet team in the country."

So, the meet with Cal is a big deal. Imagine Alabama-Georgia in college football. "And well, Josephat Kapkory is a chemical engineering major," Chaplin explained. "And he has to take a test as part of the process to gain certification as a chemical engineer."

The only time the test would be offered was on the day of the dual meet. "If he doesn't take the test on that day, the test doesn't come around again until the next year." Kapkory was the two-time NCAA indoor 3,000-meter champion and meet record holder with a best of 7:50.90. He had personal bests of 13:27.00 for 5,000 meters, 28:20.64 for 10,000 meters, and 8:20.67 for the steeplechase. He was the Pac-10 champion at 1,500 meters, the 3,000-meter steeplechase, 5,000 meters, 10,000 meters, and cross country. And he also won an NCAA cross-country title. He is also the only athlete to win the steeplechase, 5,000 meters, and 10,000 meters in the same Pac-12 championships. In other words, if WSU was going to defeat Cal for the national dual-meet title, the Cougars would need Josephat Kapkory.

But…

"I told the team that Kapkory would not be running, and we lost the meet by one point," Chaplin said. "And not a kid on that team cared about the one point." He raised his voice then, insisting his point not be missed. "They all knew we did the right thing."

"In addition," he continued, offering further evidence of the emphasis he placed on academics, "you can check with Rueben Mayes, Garry Hill, and Dominique Arnold about when I got after them to complete their degree." At one time, Mayes held the NCAA single-game rushing record. Hill is the editor in chief of *Track & Field News*. And Arnold was an NCAA hurdle champion who would eventually set the American record in the 110-meter-high hurdles.

Chaplin's insistence on the primacy of education can be traced directly to the early days of his own schooling and a complicated relationship with a father who was not only a thinker but also on the fringe of radical politics and political activism.

"My father was 40 years older than me and twenty years older than my mother," Chaplin said. "He fought in World War I, and he was a Wobblies [International Workers of the World] organizer. He wrote movies and TV sitcoms and was an internationally known woodcut artist. He was blackballed in the fifties for his socialist/leftist views. But he wasn't a communist. He was a socialist. *"He was so far left, he'd put a communist on the right."*

Then, Chaplin recites much of his father's resume and accomplishments in the arts as if he is aware that the coach and educator he would become was inextricably linked to the unorthodox (maybe even counterculture) legacy left to him by Prescott Chaplin.

"He was the screen writer for movies with W.C. Fields and John Wayne," Chaplin said. "He wrote TV scripts, sometimes under someone else's name while he was blacklisted. *The Ann Southern Show*, for example. He was a staff writer on *Perry Mason*. And later he was president of Manson's Paisano Productions. He studied art with George Wesley Bellows, William Merritt Chase, Max Bori, and John Davidson Butler. He studied writing with George Sterling, Jack London, and Arthur Herbert Forder. He was the writer eight movies. *The Island of Lost Women* in 1959, *Woman of the North Country* in 1952, *Flame of the Barbary Coast* in 1945, *My Buddy* in 1943, *Sleepy Lagoon* in 1941, *Never Give a Sucker an Even Break* in 1933, *Laughing at Life* in 1933, and *Private Jones* also in 1933. And he was a collaborator on the musical revue *Step This Way* along with Merritt Maloney, Tedwyl Chapman, and John Hobble.

With his immediate ancestry in mind, the artistic contents of Chaplin's home and the nature of the books in his library are not nearly as surprising as the fact that he ended up in a profession so far removed from the influences of his formative years.

Or maybe not.

"This room [the library] is like the fourteenth century," he explained. "Because that's where I belong. My father was an intellectual, a liberal. Homeschooled. Studied at the Art Institute of Chicago. Got a degree in metaphysics."

The Chaplin family crest is on the black marble fireplace in the library. Chaplin explained, "My ancestors on my mother's side [the Chilton's] were on the Mayflower.... I am a direct descendant of James Chilton. I guess I'm a typical WASP [White Anglo-Saxon Protestant] without the religious 'protestant' part. My mother's ancestors also go back to the families of the earls of Derby and barons of Groby de Ferrers...from 1066, direct descendants of William the Conqueror, some fifty generations removed from the present, who intermarried with all the great houses of England and Europe. In addition, there were several generations of de Ferrers Earls and Barons, Templar Knights who fought in Crusades between 1095 to 1291, and two of my direct ancestors died at Acre serving Richard the Lion Hearted. I am also a direct descendent of Empress Victoria I, whose Grandson George IV was the founder of the current reigning Royal House of Windsor in Great Britain and N.I. My father's ancestors came to English America in 1638 on the ship *John,* which was bringing a printing press to Harvard. They were upper middle class and/or feudal gentry, *men of substance,* exclusively English, and they *'came to America primarily to establish religious freedom but were just as intolerant as the Church of England they had fled.'"* Built in 1641, you can still see the old Chaplin home in New England in Rowley, Massachusetts.

Here is where some of the assumptions and misconceptions about John Chaplin, the track coach, begin to diverge, and a more accurate conception about John Chaplin, the humanist educator, begins to come together: coaching, like teaching, is at heart a future-oriented humanist enterprise.

"From the age of fifteen to eighteen, every Wednesday night, I had to walk down the hill with my father—he did not drive—to catch the Red Car, and then meet with these old German socialists in downtown LA," he remembered. "I had a reading list. Kant, Nietzsche, Spinoza, and others.

"So, these are the things I think [about]. I'm explaining this so you get an idea of where I'm coming from."

More specifically...

"My father never worried about tomorrow."

Now the logic of the content of the library and the collection of high-end art begins to coalesce. But still, how does all this reconcile with Chaplin's eventual decision to become first an athlete and then a track & field coach?

"My dad had lung cancer," he said. "I don't think I ever saw him without a cigarette hanging out of his mouth. My wife and I went down to visit my parents, and Linda had a good time talking to my dad." Chaplin paused here, searching for the significance in a memory nearly sixty years old.

He went on to explain that his father had three wives (one every ten years) and children with all three. "With his first wife [Paula Doris Schultz]," Chaplin said, "he was callous. With his second wife [Lucy Llewellyn Miller], he was deceptive, and with his third wife, my mother, he was caviler." Still, while working on a family history years later, he discovered marriage certificates for all three marriages in which his father had listed himself as "single."

"Without passing judgment on his behavior in the matter," he said, "I will say my father was not a responsible parent with the children from his first two wives. But he was loving and caring with me and all my siblings." He paused again, thinking back. "But it's a long story." A story he prefers to be told by the way he's conducted his life in the six-plus decades since.

When Chaplin discusses a topic or comments on an issue that engages his well-honed passion, he speaks in a rapid-fire staccato, as if what he needs to say had long before been formulated and organized in his mind but could not be contained once he had an attentive audience. "My father told me, 'I have done some things in my life that I am not particularly proud of.... It's your turn to right the ship.' That was the second time we ever sat and had a whiskey."

Then he makes an ironic connection between his father and the athletes who would come through the WSU program during his time as the head coach. "Most kids don't think about the future. Like my father. He was [metaphorically] stark naked.... The world ended each day. He gave no thought to what happened beyond that. He died, and he didn't make any arrangements. So, my answer was, *if anything happens, I'm going to make sure that I'm ready for tomorrow and my family will be taken care of.* That's the [counterintuitive] lesson I learned. You have to live for tomorrow and for the future because the sun is gonna come up. Come hell or high water."

To make his point, he explained that when his athletes finished their careers at WSU, he gave each his crimson WSU jersey with these words of advice: "You owe me nothing, you owe WSU nothing, but if you want to impress me and my wife, you will tell us what you are doing to help others. You can't just dance through the world free after you have been given this opportunity to get a college education." As they left college to get on with the rest of their lives, he added one of his favorite aphorisms: *"Remember, you can't eat the medals."*

Despite the obvious influence of his father's radical notions of everything from politics to the nature of the passage of time, it was boredom that set Chaplin on the road that would lead him to coach at WSU and, eventually, the US Olympic team. Chaplin did not inherit or absorb his father's attitude on the *un*importance of planning for the future, but he did inherit and absorb his father's attitude about religion. "I don't believe in God in the traditional sense. I am agnostic at best." And yet… "I was absolutely bored to death [in public school], so my mother put me in Catholic school with the Dominican nuns."

Chaplin remains frank about his religious beliefs, or if you prefer, his uncertainty about religion. "I was once asked in a philosophy graduate seminar in college about my idea of the 'Creator.' My answer was simple. All religions that believe in a single god—for example, Zoroastrianism, Judaism, Christianity, Islam, and their various offshoots—come down to two things, assuming you believe in order, because there is order in the universe regardless of whether or not there is a Creator. First, if there is a 'Creator,' which I doubt, does the Creator know it exists? And second, does this entity care about you as an individual? Which does not seem provable. Simple questions, but with hard answers. Remember, *God,* if there is a god, is in the heart and soul of the believer. Ha! And that begs another question… What about the soul?"

Chaplin explained that while he was okay with the parochial school education, he was about to receive from the nuns at All Saints Catholic School in Los Angeles, not everyone at the school was equally enthusiastic about the possibility of having the un-churched son of a far-left activist potentially corrupting the student body.

"There's the head nun, Sister Luchetta…she should be in Heaven, if there is a heaven." Chaplin smiled at the memory. "The parish priest says to her while my mother and me are standing there, 'Young John has never been baptized,' and the sister says, 'Father, are you telling me that I have to take this little heathen?' The priest did not miss a beat. 'Sister, we all have our crosses to bear.'

"My Father did not have us baptized. With Michael and Cody [Chaplin's brother and sister], and myself, he let us decide. Michael and Cody did choose a church, and later Kent was baptized in the Anglian Church, but I chose not to be baptized."

Catholic school may not have awakened in the young John Chaplin a nascent spirituality (at least not in orthodox terms), but it did provide him with his first taste of athletic success, a fact that proved to be, if not distressing to Sister Luchetta, at least inexplicable.

"In eighth grade, they have this All-Little Catholic thing, a competition among many of LA's numerous Catholic grammar schools," Chaplin said, again smiling at the memory of the role racing was about to play in his ironic, formative education. "And I won the 180-yard dash, and so I'm All-Little Catholic. But I was a heathen, remember, because I wasn't baptized. I mean, at one time, the Dominicans would have put you on the rack for that. They were the [Spanish] Inquisition. The priest tried, but he could not explain to Sister Luchetta how I could be All-Little Catholic without being a Catholic.

"When I started at All Saints, they had just opened and only had grades one through six. Then the next year, they added a seventh grade and then an eighth grade. "But what Sister Luchetta, who had me for all three, understood [was] that I was bored, so she gave me advanced work above grade level. I still managed to graduate with a straight-A average."

It is interesting, and I think significant, that when Chaplin and I first met to talk about his life in the sport, this is the point at which he began to tell his story. Not with his 22-1 dual-meet record against the archrival Washington Huskies. Not with countless conference and national champions, not with the 200-plus All-Americans. Not even with the Olympic team or his role as chief referee at the 1996 Olympic Games in Atlanta. He began with his father's determined view of the world, his mother's insistence on a traditional Catholic education for the "little heathen," and winning a sprint championship of 180 yards.

CHAPTER 2

HOLES IN THE TRACK

O ne of the principle issues in track & field these days seems to be whether the recent plethora of records being set at every level is the result of superior talent and improved training or a consequence of recent advancements in the design and construction of particular shoes worn by certain athletes. When considering John Chaplin's career, those questions and the resultant controversy seem apt because Chaplin has been present for every technological innovation in the sport, from starting blocks to rubberized tracks to "super shoes."

Ever since he entered Wilson High School in Los Angeles in the fall of 1951, Chaplin has seen just about every technological and scientific development in the sport up close. When he began his track & field career in earnest, sprinters were still digging holes in the track to gain traction at the start and wearing shoes with long spikes that could not be removed, so the shoe controversy must seem at least a little bit ironic to the 85-year-old Chaplin.

"That's right," he recalled. "I went out for track at Wilson High School in 1952, and that was the last year we dug a hole in the track with a trowel at the starting line. The next year, a guy named Arnett made an adjustable starting block." Arnett's starting blocks were revolutionary in that they had footpads that could be adjusted and moved back and forth. "So, you didn't need to dig a hole. But you did have to pound two huge spikes into the ground [to hold the starting blocks in place]. There were no all-weather tracks, only dirt or cinder or crushed brick tracks."

The composition of running tracks makes the marks achieved by athletes from that era all the more remarkable. "In fact," Chaplin continued, "I never ran on an all-weather track during my career."

I came along later than Chaplin [and in the interest of full disclosure, quite a bit slower], but I did not run on an artificial surface track until the state meet at the end of my senior year in high school in 1969. My first "championship" meet experience in 1966 was run on a 460-yard grass track in Monroe, Washington. I can even remember at least one meet in which runners had to share a large rock to pound in the spikes securing the starting blocks because no one had a mallet. And, of course, my exposure to athletes like Henry Rono and John van Reenen is mostly from a distance and as a fan or semiprofessional observer. I wonder how different the sport might be today if races were still contested on dirt tracks and without the aid of composition vaulting poles or in rigid leather shoes not yet enhanced by sophisticated engineering. Not to mention pharmaceuticals. Less spectacular, for sure, but perhaps more interesting.

The closest I ever came to engaging competitively (a real stretch, in this instance) with world-class athletes happened in a college cross-country race in 1969 or 1970. To say I was a mediocre cross-country runner would be generous. I was terrible, a quarter-miler from a tiny high school who had not seen a cross-country race before I got to Everett Junior College in the fall of 1969. But in a six-mile race on the Thorp Golf Course outside Ellensburg, Washington, I was passed on a bridge by Gerry Lindgren and Rick Riley. They were approaching the finishing line, and I still had more than a mile left to run. But as they raced by me in a flash in one direction while I stumbled along in the other, I could see or sense, or otherwise recognize, that they possessed something different, something significant that I would come to appreciate but never possess.

I have since noted that the very best coaches in the sport also have something that the hardworking, day-to-day coaches at every level and in every sport can recognize but don't usually possess—a set of personal characteristics, difficult or even impossible to define or identify. Today in collegiate track & field, success depends as much on institutional amenities that attract the very best athletes, like travel budgets and facilities, as it does on coaching acumen. It's hard to imagine a very good high school kid with knowledge of, say, the University of Oregon's track & field history as they tour that school's new state-of-the-art stadium (perhaps the best in the world, with its out-of-the-weather training areas, barber shop, and nail salon) and then saying no when the scholarship offer comes.

But there must be more to recruiting than just that. Right? Once a kid agrees to compete for a particular university, he or she needs to get better, usually a lot better. Very few kids step directly out of high school and into the upper echelons of collegiate track & field, and as we've seen, many kids from even the most elite level of high school track & field do not always succeed at the highest collegiate level. It happens, but it is rare. It takes time for a talented and motivated high school kid to develop into an adult athlete relevant in the NCAA or beyond.

The NCAA Track & Field Championships is the third- or fourth-best track meet in the world, surpassed only by the World Athletic Championships, the Olympics, and the US Olympic Trials. The difference is that the NCAA championship meet is an annual event, rather than being held every two years in the case of the world championships or every four years like with the Olympics. In each instance in which a kid succeeds at the NCAA level, there is a coach who has been skillful at more than simply recruiting top-end talent.

These coaches understand what a talented kid needs most are time and care.

If the assumptions about John Chaplin were accurate, it would be easy to conclude that those qualities—a willingness to spend time and take care of one's athletes—did not apply to the WSU program. A misunderstanding of Chaplin's persona suggests he was willing to take shortcuts, disregard academics, and put winning track meets ahead of the well-being of the young people he brought into the program. Once again, Chaplin's former athletes are unanimous in their disagreement with that point of view, but Chaplin's own words are what matter most on this point. "My persona is nothing like what I'm really like."

Chaplin explained to me that "in college, a program that is successful is 50 percent recruiting, 25 percent taking care of the children, 10 percent putting them in the right event, 10 percent teaching them skills, running mechanics, and/or tactics. For the last 5 percent, you can pat yourself on the back for your *great* coaching!"

Back to Chaplin's athletic endeavors...

High school track & field in the Los Angeles public schools in the 1950s was different enough from the way high school track is contested today—almost unrecognizable. For example, Chaplin, who would eventually make a name for himself as one of the best high school and collegiate quarter-milers in the country, was not even allowed to run the 440-yard dash until the twelfth grade. In LA in the 1950s, even the mile relay, still the most popular and often the most exciting event on the schedule of any good high school, college, or international track meet, did not involve a single 440-yard leg. The mile relay in LA was 8x220 yards.

In LA, high school competition was broken into A, B, and C divisions based on age, height, and weight. Chaplin was very fast, but "I was also small for my age," he explained. "So, my first two years, I was a C. And since there was no 440-yard dash for C's, I ran the 70-yard dash, the 660, and the 4x110 relay."

At this point, Chaplin made sure to note that LA public schools did just about everything differently than the rest of the country and even the rest of the state of California. "For instance, kids could not play both football and basketball because both were considered contact sports," he explained. "And no parents could see the basketball games until the city championships. No one from the general public." Chaplin pointed to National Football League Hall of Famer Ben Davidson as an example. Davidson was a basketball player at Wilson High who went to East Los Angeles Junior College for a year and played football well enough that he ended up on the football team at the University of Washington, which led to a long NFL career with the Oakland Raiders. But he never played high school football.

I spent nearly 20 years as a writer for various small- and medium-sized newspapers around the state of Washington, and I cannot imagine high school football and basketball without a significant adult presence in the stands. However, I can imagine certain situations when an event might have been enhanced by the absence of particular adults in the crowd, and by the time my younger daughter was playing high school basketball and soccer, I may have at times been one of those *particular* adults.

Chaplin moved steadily through the LA school system's age-height-weight caste system.

Then, of course, as time passed and Chaplin got older, he got bigger, as a natural result of growing and maturing physically. "In my junior year, I became a *B*," he said. "And since I'd been running the 660-yard run, the new coach, Joe Berry, who came from Jefferson High, where he and Estel Johnson had won several state titles, to be the head coach at Wilson, says to me, 'You're going to be running the 1,320 [three-quarters of a mile], anchor the 220 in the 660-yard medley relay [2x110, 2x220] and run either 100- or the 180-yard dash.'"

Remember, the mile relay in LA in those days was 8x220 yards. There was still no quarter mile if you were a *B*. Chaplin believes that if Berry had not left Wilson for Washington High, "he would have turned me into a 400/800 runner. *In fact, if I was coaching myself now, that is what I would have also done with me.*"

Finally, by the twelfth grade, with Paul Bartell back as the head coach, Chaplin was old enough and large enough to be considered an *A* in the LA school's peculiar athletic hierarchy and was at last allowed to run the quarter mile. "My senior year, I ran the 100 [yards] and the 220 [yards], but mostly the 220 and the 440. But I never ran a 440, ever, in a relay." Los Angeles was locked into the 8x220, but, unlike the rest of the country, the California state meet contested the 4x220 rather than the 4x440—the point being that opportunities to run the 440-yard dash were limited.

Chaplin was the team captain for the track & field team his senior year in 1955, as he had been for cross country. "I finished my high school career at five-foot-three or five-foot-four inches and about 110 pounds and did not shave until I was twenty-one."

"They ran the LA City Championships, along with a B 660 and medley relay [2x110, 2x220, respectively] and a C [4x110 relay], at the Los Angeles Coliseum," Chaplin said, relishing the memory. "The meet was held in conjunction with the Coliseum Relays in front of a crowd of about 60,000."

Here, we get an early glimpse of Chaplin's prodigious memory and penchant for detail.

"At the city championships, the varsity teams came out of the tunnel," he said, describing the start of the 8x220-yard relay and the resultant high-speed anarchy, "running a straightaway in lanes for the first 220 yards. Then they broke for the pole with the next seven athletes running without lanes or stagger. In those days, the LA Coliseum was configured so that a 440 or 660-yard race would begin with a 220-yard straightway. In a dual meet or at league finals without a 220-yard straightaway, they just broke for the pole after the first turn, the way 800-meter runners do today, or ran it from scratch like the mile race."

Sounds like fun. Chaotic, but fun.

"In 1957, Manuel Arts [High School]," Chaplin said, "had eight guys who averaged 21.8 seconds for eight 220-yard legs, for a time of 2:54.6 [2:53.8 in meters]."

I was incredulous because 2:53.8 is faster than the current world record for the 4x400-meter relay, which is 2:54.29, and because only eight sprinters in the entire state of Washington ran 200 meters under 22 seconds during the 2021 track season, and 200 meters is slightly less than 220 yards. *Track & Field News* subtracts .1 from your 220-yard time to get an equivalent 200-meter time. Is it even reasonable? I wondered if eight kids from one high school could have run that fast on the Coliseum's cinder track sixty-five years ago. But then, when I suggested in an email that just maybe Manuel Arts High School's performance had been enhanced by the passage of time...

"Oh, ye of little faith," Chaplin said. Then he provided the names of each of the eight kids on that remarkable relay team. "It was a team of Ken Harris, Ralph Waddy, James Bates, Ken Hayes, Harold Willard, Ernest Taylor, Cecil Green, and Alvin Williams." Somewhere in his labyrinthine archive of track & field statistics or cataloged in his encyclopedic memory, he had dredged up the results of a high school relay race from 1957. Later, in junior college in 1959, Chaplin would compete against and defeat a member of that relay team, James Bates (who ran 9.4 and 21.2 in high school) in the 100-yard and 220-yard dashes.

The point of all this is how John Chaplin's formative years in track & field influenced the next 70-plus years of his life. How many people can claim to have survived in the sport long enough to go from digging holes in the track to gain traction at the start of a sprint race, to developing one of the top collegiate programs in the country, to coaching one of the best distance runners in history, to officiating in the high-tech world of the highest levels of contemporary international track & field?

In the fall of 1953, during Chaplin's junior year in high school, Chaplin participated in a program sponsored by the *Los Angeles Examiner* called SSA (Scholastic Sports Association). "I and a bunch of high school reporters from around the city wrote stories on the Friday track meets for the *Examiner*," he said. "We were at the *Examiner*'s downtown office and the majority of the writers were at the meets and then called in the results to us, and we wrote the copy to be published."

Then as a senior, he was the editor of that group, but like most kids at that age, he was not at all sure what he should do when his high school days ended. Apparently, the dilemmas faced by twenty-first-century kids are not so different from those faced by a kid in the middle of the last century. Chaplin was also the sports editor for his high school newspaper, *The Hitching Post*.

"I got a scholarship offer from Pepperdine through the *Examiner's* SSA program," he said. But the religious nature of Pepperdine, while still evident today, was strict, even rigid, at the time, so… "That was a problem. I had still not been baptized, and I do not believe in God. Everyone knows it. So, Pepperdine would not have been a smart choice."

With no clear plans for his future, he went back to work for the *Examiner*, this time as an entry-level cub reporter. The newspaper business was as much in his blood as the 440-yard dash was. He was the sports editor for the WSU student newspaper during his undergraduate years, and he would later cover the 1984 Olympic Games in LA with a series of columns for the *Salt Lake City Tribune* and its subsidiaries. Chaplin indicated that at "one point, me and a woman coach from Idaho along with a judge from both states had a local TV program called the High Court, we all wore black robes, and each week we talked about local sports." He also wrote a weekly sports opinion column for the *Moscow-Pullman Daily News*. He was also a card-carrying member of the Track & Field Writers of America for many years. Considering Chaplin's later, uh, tense relationship with certain members of the Fourth Estate, the fact he came close to becoming one of them strikes me as…ironic.

"Then I start thinking about what I'm going to do with my life," he said. Apparently, as a young man, he was not convinced the newspaper business was an attractive option. "And my parents were not in a position to help me with college. I know they're going to draft my ass anyway, so I went down and enlisted in the regular army for three years."

Chaplin does not speak about his decision to join the army in terms of duty or patriotism, but he does concede there is a history in his family that suggests a certain level of obligation. Considering the totality of my impression of John Chaplin by this time, I'd begun to realize that despite the bombast and the harsh exterior he often displayed to the public and the media, there is a hard ethical center at the core of his worldview and an ingrained sense of responsibility that directs his conduct.

"In my family, there have been soldiers since the colonels William and James Prescott in the American Revolution. I was *not* going to be drafted. Even my radical father enlisted in the army in WWI. He was *not* drafted."

At this point, all discussion of his time in the military ends. As we'll see later when he talks about his competitive career at WSU, Chaplin refuses to engage in useless or self-serving recollections or "war stories," and he does not make specific his duties or his rank. It's not that the years between 1955, when he enlisted, and 1958, when he was discharged, are blank. They are simply, for whatever reason, not spoken of. But they did leave an impression on the still-young Chaplin, and his army years did make it possible to return to two important areas of his pre-service life—track & field and school.

"I get out of the army in the fall of 1958," he said. "By then, I was 5'11" and 178 pounds. It's too late to go to college [that semester], so I come out and go back to the *Examiner*. I'm a low man on the totem pole, so I get all the county jail crap and the fights and the bookies, that kind of stuff. I also tended bar to make more money for my college fund." Not exactly the kind of glamorous assignments a young reporter working in LA might envision for himself, but fortunately for the future of track & field, he had an option.

"My grandmother lived in Pasadena," he explained. "She was a geriatric nurse, and she says, 'Come and live with me.'"

So, he moved in with his grandmother and, for a year, attended Pasadena City College and ran on the track team. "The reason I was able to go to PCC was that under the Soldiers' and Sailors' [Civil Relief] Act, I was exempt from having to go to an intercity JC in Los Angeles," he said. "Then, after my spring track season, I ran a couple of meets with the LA Striders in the summer of 1959. All these kids who had gone off to run other places around the country came back to run for the Striders."

During this time, Chaplin made his first of many essential connections to athletes competing at the highest levels of track & field. Among his teammates on the LA Striders was Mike Larrabee. Larrabee would overcome the disappointment of untimely injuries in the lead-up to the Olympics in both 1956 and 1960 to finally win the gold medal at 400 meters and in the 4x400-meter relay in the 1964 Tokyo Olympics. Along the way, he would become just the fourth man in history to run 400 meters in less than 45 seconds.

"Mike Larrabee and his sidekick John Bragg [both worked for Adidas] were good friends of mine." As we'll see, Chaplin is proud of his connection with many of the legends of the sport and would rather talk about their exploits and accomplishments than he would his own.

During that single season with the Pasadena City College track team, Chaplin ran a personal best of 9.6 for 100-yards, tied Mack Robinson's [Jackie Robinson's brother] PCC 220-yard record of 20.8, and ran 47.2 for 440 yards. Then, "later that summer, running unattached, I ran 46.8 in a meet at Fresno."

Also, during that single season at PCC, a seed was planted that would grow into an important branch of his future coaching philosophy. "I was running three or four races in every meet in junior college," he said. "I ran the 4x110-yard relay and the 4x440-yard relay as the anchor leg, and I ran the 100 and either the 220 or the 440. I was always the anchor leg on any relay in high school, in junior college, and at WSU." A crowded competitive schedule, but one that produced a revelation.

About halfway through that 1959 season, Chaplin and his coaches at PCC, Mickey Anderson and Otto Anderson, all arrived at the same realization. Anderson had been the 1936 California State 100-yard champion for John Muir Tech in Pasadena, played quarterback and fullback for the 1938 USC national championship football team that beat undefeated and unscored Duke in the 1939 Rose Bowl, was a member of three (1938, 1939, and 1940) NCAA track & field championships teams at USC under Dean Cromwell, and ran the second leg on the school's 1938 world record (40.5) 4x110-yard relay team at the West Coast Relays in Fresno, CA. Otto Anderson played football at USC, competed in the triple jump in the 1920 Antwerp Olympics and in the decathlon at the 1924 Paris Games, equaled the world record for the 220-yard low hurdles in 1923, and was the captain of the USC track & field team in 1925. That is a lot of experience at the highest competitive level available in the early years of the twentieth century.

The revelation? "It wasn't that I was better," Chaplin said. "The difference was that I was twenty-one or twenty-two years old that season, and these other kids were seventeen or eighteen."

The three years he'd spent in the army meant Chaplin had the advantage of being three to four years older than the typical community college athlete. Then as now, age and physical maturity were distinct and unqualified advantages at that early point in an athlete's career. "Especially," he said, "when track season was only from January to June with no year-round training."

"I was naturally stronger. I could recover quicker," he said. "It was the same thing when I got to the Washington State track team. They [the younger athletes] could not run three to four races in every meet, so Mooberry didn't have them do it." Instead, Coach Mooberry (just like he did with Joe Nebelon, also from California, just out of the army, and an NCAA All-American at 440 yards) had the older and more mature Chaplin run three or four races in every meet. And his success, or more specifically, his survival, provided a lesson that would pay off when he began to develop his own philosophy of coaching college-aged athletes.

Chaplin survived that strenuous year at Pasadena, but he did not necessarily enjoy it or intend to make track & field his life's work. Not by a long shot. Despite his success and his durability, John Chaplin was not enamored of running. "*You have only so many heartbeats in life,*" he said. "And I am not going to use mine all up with physical exercise.

"I went to college to get a classical education," he said. "Anybody can get a job. I marked off the days [until he was finished]. Just like the army." With a flourish, he crossed off an imaginary item from an imaginary list with an imaginary pencil. "Every goddamned day."

His lack of enthusiasm at that time and the conventional wisdom that track & field, especially at the highest levels, was a younger man's sport, had Chaplin convinced it was time to go another direction. In fact, no less an authority than the legendary University of Southern California and US Olympic team coach Dean Cromwell—the coaching genius who had by then produced a dozen Olympic gold medalists and fourteen world records holders—told Chaplin so, and in just so many words.

"So, I'm 22, and Larrabee takes me to USC to see Cromwell, and Dean Cromwell says, 'I hate to tell you this, but the world has passed you by. You're too old.'" Even after all this time, the memory makes

Chaplin laugh. But even at 22, and unlike his father, Chaplin was nothing if not future-oriented. So, neither conventional wisdom nor the judgment of the best-known coach in the US at the time was going to dent his well-honed practicality.

"Remember, there was no pro track at that time. Everyone graduated at around 21, and then you were done," Chaplin explained. "But I'm thinking if this running thing works out, I may have some different choices [for getting an education] on this deal."

He began looking around to see if his success and record for durability might land him an opportunity to complete his college education. "I got offered [scholarships] from Pittsburgh, and I had a girlfriend who was at Mary Washington just down the road in Virginia from Pitt.

"And I got an offer from Stanford and, I don't remember how, to Holy Cross," he explained. "Coach Payton Jordan was at Occidental when I was a senior at Wilson, and he did talk to me about going there. Then when I got out of the army, I talked to Payton, now at Stanford, again, and he told me that he was having trouble with the administration and might not be there the following year. Coach Jordon was my mentor. Somehow, he just took a liking to me and schooled me during my early years as a young college head coach."

"Then, when it came to Holy Cross, I had to think twice about it. Holy Cross might not be a smart move." Remember the little heathen, the agnosticism, and the lack of baptism? "So, I'm sitting with my grandmother at her kitchen table in the fall of 1959, and she says, 'Why don't you go to Washington State?' And I say, 'Go *where?*'

"She says, 'Your uncle Jack [Heishman] majored in engineering and went to WSC [WSU was formerly known as Washington State College] prior to WWII.' He was in a fraternity called the SigEps and was in naval ROTC over at the University of Idaho. My uncle

Jack was a captain in the navy and a naval pilot and fought battles in the Pacific, like Midway. Later, he was the naval liaison officer to Congress and then commanded the aircraft carrier *USS Lexington* [the Blue Ghost]."

It is interesting and a little ironic that Chaplin's reaction to the possibility of attending WSU was the same response *Coach* Chaplin would get years later when recruiting athletes from other parts of the US and especially from other parts of the world.

But he was curious, so Chaplin returned to the offices of the *Los Angeles Examiner* to research a school he had never heard of and had never considered as an option for continuing his education or restarting a running career he was still ambivalent about. The first thing that impressed him when he looked up WSU was the football team's record. "This was the fall of 1959," he said. "They were 6-1 in football, and they ended up 6-3."

Chaplin was impressed with WSU's football team, but not excited. His excitement came from something else: "They had a 6-11 high jumper, Hank Wyborney. A 235-11 javelin thrower, Dick Rubenser, who won a PCC title. A hurdler, Spike Arlt, who ran 13.8 and 51.0 and who later coached at Central Washington University. And a 1:48.46 half-miler, Don Bertoia, a skier who turned out for track after the ski team was dropped. He later won the 800 meters at the Pan Am Games for Canada. "And I'm thinking *it's in the Pacific Coast Conference* [the precursor to the AAWU and the Pac 8, 10, and 12]. So, I take my clippings and my times of 9.6, 20.8, and 46.8, and in October, I send them to 'Track Coach Washington State College, Pullman, Washington.'"

He waited, but not for long.

"About ten days later, my grandmother says there's a coach on the phone. I said *hello,* and he said, 'This is Coach Mooberry from

Washington State.' What I did not know is that Coach Mooberry never recruited a kid from out of state unless that kid called or wrote him first."

The irony, of course, is in the fact that despite the enormous effect Jack Mooberry would have on his future, Chaplin would become best known for recruiting from *way* out of state. According to Chaplin, "Mooberry thought it was unethical to recruit out-of-state or foreign athletes unless they contacted him first, and [that] coaches from other states should do the same. He recruited mainly from the annual high school state meet, which was held in Pullman for more than 60 years, and some in-state junior college athletes." Mooberry had a tremendous effect on Chaplin's coaching philosophy, but not apparently in his attitude about out-of-state recruiting.

In any case, Mooberry offered Chaplin all he was allowed to offer by way of financial aid. (Interestingly, football and basketball players were allowed to get more than athletes in other sports in those days....They got books and laundry money. Are we circling back to that situation?) Chaplin sent the transcript from his first semester at Pasadena City College, with a promise to bring his second-semester transcript with him to WSU. He connected with another LA kid who was also traveling to Pullman and started driving north.

I don't want to beat the irony horse to death here, but athletes I spoke with who would compete for Chaplin after he became WSU's head coach all mentioned the "culture shock" of moving from wherever they were to a place like Pullman, Washington. The irony comes from the fact that the remote, small-town character of Pullman suited the African athletes, who, almost without exception, came from small farming communities, and, despite the climate and the language barrier, often felt more at home than many of the in-state kids who often came from urban enclaves like Seattle, Tacoma, and Spokane.

So, you can imagine the empathy Chaplin must have felt for those kids, given that he was driving the 1,100 miles from Los Angeles to Pullman in the days before the interstate highway system had been completed and the fact that the farther north he drove, the more primitive travel became.

"So, I drive up to Pullman in my car," he recalled. "And I come through Lewiston." And up the notorious Lewiston grade, then a seven-plus-mile tangle of sixty-four treacherous twists and turns that rise 2,000 feet from the floor of the Snake River Canyon. "And I drive right out of this little town, and I go, *'I'll be damned, I missed it.'* So, I turned it around, and right where the city library is now was a Chevron station. I pulled in there, and I said, 'Can you tell me where Pullman is?' And the guy says, 'You are in it.'" Pullman was about half the size it is today, and WSC had only about 6,000 students. It did not become a university until January 1960, just as Chaplin arrived.

Pullman is still by far the smallest city in the Pac-12 conference today. In fact, the entire population of Pullman in 2021—including all 23,000 students at WSU—was 34,000 and would fit into every other football stadium in the conference with room to spare. Chaplin was coming from the largest metropolitan area on the West Coast, so it is not hard to imagine the culture shock he must have experienced at that moment. But that experience would also make it easy to empathize with kids who came to Pullman from Seattle or Tacoma once he became WSU's head coach. The difference was that Chaplin had been in the army, and he was older, so he took it all in stride.

Chaplin and his traveling companion spent a night in the Hilltop Motel in Pullman, no doubt well-named because the city of Pullman and the WSU campus occupy five notoriously steep hills. To travel on foot from one side of town to the other or from one end of the campus to the other can be as taxing as a steep hike in the nearby

Moscow Mountains. The local joke is that WSU students have the best calves in the NCAA.

The next day, Chaplin made his first visit to the campus and found Mooberry in the unheated field house, supervising a workout on the 220-yard dirt track. It was snowing outside, and WSU was no longer in the Pacific Coast Conference; the school was an independent. He introduced himself; Mooberry walked him over to the admissions office, got him enrolled, and just like that, John Prescott Chaplin was a Cougar.

He said, "I joined my uncle's fraternity SigEp, which, by the way, was Jack Mooberry's and Bobo Brayton's fraternity. Then in the fall of 1962, WSU rejoined the old PCC members, making it a six-team league called the Athletic Association of Western Universities (AAWU)."

At this point, most former athletes would want to regale the listener with their exploits on the track, tales of great performances, and titles won. But not Chaplin. He was as reticent and direct about his competitive career as he was about his time in the army. "I ran indoors and got hurt," he said. "So, I had three seasons of eligibility for both [indoors and outdoors]: '61, '62, and '63. Then I graduated."

When questioned about how he performed at WSU, he said simply, "You can look up all the marks." He was not going to talk about it, so I did look up all the marks. During his time at WSU, Chaplin set a then indoor world best for 330 yards at 33.4. He ran 9.5 for 100 yards, 10.2 for 100 meters, and 46.9 for 440 yards. Bear in mind that 220 and 440 yards are slightly longer than the 200 and 400 meters commonly run today. He also set a WSU indoor record of 47.9 for 440 yards.

When he says, "If you don't understand me, the rest is irrelevant," I think he is making sure we know that his life before he arrived at

WSU had more to do with the way his adult life would unfold than the time he spent becoming one of the best sprinters in the northern division of the old Pacific Coast Conference, which consisted of WSU, Washington, Oregon, Oregon State, and Idaho.

I asked Chaplin to summarize his three-year colligate career at WSU, and he said, "I had three full seasons, and then I graduated." From his point of view, that was the end of it, but he failed to mention that he was elected captain of the team for his senior year. It is interesting and revealing that Chaplin was elected captain of his high school cross country and track & field teams and his junior college and university track & field teams.

CHAPTER 3

THE SUPERINTENDENT WALKS INTO A BAR...

"**T**hen I graduated."

So, now what? John Chaplin had a degree in geography with a minor in history, and along the way, he had taken non-credit courses in philosophy with graduate students. Even by today's touchy-feely standards, not the most practical course of study for someone about to enter the job market.

But...

"Any idiot can get a job," he said. "I went to college to get educated. To see another point of view." Another point of view? This notion would come up again and again when we considered the value his athletes placed on the education each received at WSU. "In my whole life, I never worried about getting a job."

Like a lot of bright young people, then as now, law school was the first thing Chaplin thought of when he received his newly minted WSU diploma. "But I knew I had to wait eighteen months [to start law school] until I could get my GI Bill financing, so I called an administrator I knew in the placement bureau. He was one of our track officials."

I think we can all look back at moments when a decision that seemed insignificant at the time, but which had been made as a result of getting good advice, had a profound effect on the direction our lives ended up going. "And he said, you've got a teaching degree. Why don't you go and teach for a year or so [while you wait to get into law school]?" So, the administrator in the placement bureau set him up with three interviews for teaching jobs. "The first is [in] some dinky little town between Olympia and Oregon on the coast. Can't remember it now, but if I had taken that job, I'd still be there. It was a cool place to live."

Next was a job opportunity in Vancouver, Washington. "But they wanted me to teach eight periods of *dumbbell* English. I said no." His final opportunity was in the tiny Yakima Valley hamlet of Wapato, Washington. "He [the guy in the placement bureau] says they're looking for a track coach, assistant football coach, someone to teach world problems, and to be the senior class advisor." And that seemed like a good fit.

Chaplin's administrator friend arranged an interview with Dr. Urdahl, the superintendent of the Wapato School District. At the time, Chaplin was cooling his heels living with fraternity brother Corky Hicks, whose family owned an oyster farm on Mud Bay near Olympia, and working in the Weyerhaeuser paper mill, a job secured by Corky's mother, Marjorie. Today, Corky Hicks is a retired Superior Court judge and still lives in Mud Bay.

"I get in my car, and I drive over there," he said. "I have a 10:30 appointment to meet with the guy in a hotel, but 45 minutes later, he's not there." So, Chaplin does what any self-respecting recent college graduate would have done. "I'm twenty-six years old, so I go in the bar and order myself a gin and tonic and figure I'll just drive myself back to Olympia."

But, just as Chaplin is about to enjoy his drink, "A guy [Dr. Urdahl] comes into the bar and says, 'Is there a Mr. Chaplin here?'"

So, the superintendent of the conservative rural school district walks into the bar looking for a track coach and social studies teacher. "I told the bartender to hold my drink, but Dr. Urdahl has seen me at the bar, so I figure this is not going to take very long." The attitude people had about the relationship between teachers and alcohol in those days was considerably less tolerant than it is in most places these days.

He explained there was one other candidate for the job waiting to be interviewed by Dr. Urdahl. "There's this guy sitting in the corner. And he's about five-foot-two with big glasses about this thick." He held his thumb and forefinger about an inch apart. Chaplin did not say whether what happened next had an impact on whether he got the job or not, but his reaction was something of a harbinger of what was to come once he began his coaching career in earnest. "I figure I've already blown it with Dr. Urdahl, so I say, 'Just between you and me, I'm sure the gentleman over there can teach world problems, but if you really believe he can coach the track team, you might be biting off more than you can chew."

And that was that. Chaplin made sure Dr. Urdahl had his address and phone number, drove home to LA, and waited. "I'm home almost a month when I get a call from this Urdahl." And just like that, he's the new track & field coach and world problems teacher at Wapato High School.

Wapato had a typical small-town attitude toward its high school teams. That means football was king, basketball was the crown prince, and the other so-called minor sports (like track & field) were often treated as an afterthought, even though in 1930, Wapato had won a state title. Weirdly, in those days, there was no team scoring at the state meet. The state championship was awarded to the team with the highest score in the district meet.

But then John Chaplin showed up.

The Wapato Wolves now had a track coach who had come up through the hypercompetitive LA public school system, trained with Olympic medalists like Mike Larrabee, competed at the highest levels of collegiate track, and even set an indoor world best. With all that in his recent background and with everything the track world was about to discover about John Chaplin, it should come as no surprise that Wapato High track was not going to remain an afterthought for long.

But first, he had to get to Wapato and set up housekeeping in a community that was even more unlike the streets of LA than Pullman had been. Wapato was and is all about farming. Today, Wapato, located on the northern edge of the Yakama Indian Reservation, is home to a large and vibrant Hispanic community whose roots were put down by migrant farm workers, mostly from Mexico, in the 1950s and 1960s. There were also several Japanese row crop farmers and a Buddhist Church in Wapato, plus farmers and ranchers who grew fruit and hops. The town was not unlike a dozen or so similar communities, nestled along the Yakima River in the 75 miles between Yakima and the river's confluence with the Columbia River in Richland and the Tri-Cities in the south-central section of Washington State. These communities remain insular and conservative, and while they can be welcoming, they often tend to keep newcomers at bay.

Chaplin put that welcoming attitude to the test and his inclusion in the community in jeopardy on his first day in town. A common practice in those days was for small school districts to maintain housing for teachers because new teachers usually came from somewhere else and usually did not stay in town for long.

When Chaplin arrived in Wapato, the first thing Dr. Urdahl did was introduce him to a row of cheap houses owned by the school district where he could live during the school year. Teachers in those days were paid very little and only for nine months. In recalling what happened next, Chaplin clearly appreciated the gesture.

But…

"I was with this girl," he recalled. "I'd gone out with her a couple of times, so I said, 'I got to go to Wapato. I got this job.' And she said, 'Can I go along?' Not thinking, and like an idiot, I said, 'Sure.'"

Chaplin does not remember much about the young woman, "I don't even remember her name." And he does not mention where she was from. Whoever she was, though, and wherever she was from, she clearly did not realize that a certain level of decorum was expected in a small town like Wapato.

"So, we drive there, and I need to get some utensils and stuff." Chaplin left the young woman at the house, and when he returned, she was lying out in the sun in the backyard. The young woman had been noticed by the neighbors. "Three days later, I come back to town, and at the first teachers' meeting, Dr. Urdahl says, 'Oh, by the way, is your wife here?' I haven't even started school yet, and the whole town thinks I've got a wife. I say, 'I don't have a wife.' The girl was real, but how people came to believe she was my wife, I do not know."

There was no more mention of the girl, which is just as well because Wapato is where Chaplin will eventually meet Linda, to whom, at the time of this writing, he has been married for fifty-seven years. John and Linda were married on June 19, 1965, in the Lutheran church in Wapato. Keith Lincoln, the WSU football player who would become an all-pro in the NFL, was the best man. Lincoln and his wife, Bonnie Jo, would also be godparents to the Chaplins' two sons and an adopted daughter.

Chaplin indicated it is necessary to note here that "I did have my children baptized in the Anglian church, the same church that my father was baptized in, because this is a mostly a Christian country, and I did not want to have them be conflicted over why they were not baptized."

But before Linda came into the picture, he'd settled into the typical life of a small-town teacher and coach. The demands on an educator's time and energy are one of many things that never seem to change in a small town. School staffs are so small that teachers are called to fulfill a multitude of roles along with their classroom duties. So, it is a good thing Chaplin had an ample supply of both time and energy. "I was also the assistant football coach my first year," he explained. Wapato was *the* prep football power in the Yakima Valley in those days. Just prior to Chaplin's tenure as an assistant coach, Wapato's football team had reeled off 29 wins in a row.

"I did the scouting," he explained. "I'd write it all down and then put it all together"—with typical attention to detail. Chaplin does more than simply pay attention to detail; he is obsessed with getting the details right, figuring out what works, and then doing the work on the little things to make sure the big things work according to plan. "I coached the JV team at home and away," he explained. "And I assisted the head coach with the varsity."

If I'd learned anything about John Chaplin by this time, it was that he was not going to be interested in leading a track team that was not competitive, regardless of whatever perceived disadvantages or challenges a small school like Wapato High would present. High school track & field is really a numbers game. Meets are not usually won or lost by a team's best athletes. It is the average kids, those struggling in third, fourth, or fifth place, that mean the difference between winning and losing. Wapato had won just a handful of dual meets in the five years prior to Chaplin's arrival, so the first detail Chaplin had to take care of was to make sure he had enough kids on the team to be able to pick up those crucial points below first place.

"So, I go before the whole student body," he explained, "especially the ninth graders. And I tell them anybody who turns out will get to compete in at least three meets." Since varsity-level track & field meets usually limit the number of competitors in each event, that meant Chaplin had to invent competitive opportunities for kids who were not yet or who never would be varsity athletes. "I had to run nineteen scoring track meets a year," he said. "Sometimes on Tuesday or a Thursday but most on Friday or Saturday. I had all kinds of kids on the track team, but we went 17-2-0." There was no limit on the number of meets on a school's schedule in those days. "But many of the meets were double dual meets that made up the larger part of the schedule."

In those days, high school sports like track & field were not divided up with the larger schools in one division and smaller schools in lower divisions. A small school like Wapato had to compete against local big-school powers like Davis and Eisenhower in Yakima and Richland and Pasco from down the valley, in the Tri-Cities. And again, we get just a hint of what is to come at WSU: A small school in a small town competing successfully against major powers like Washington, Stanford, Oregon, USC, and UCLA. "I went 50-4-1 in three years," Chaplin said, just as pleased today with the success of Wapato High School as he would be of WSU's success in the upcoming years.

He points to three of his team's most significant accomplishments. "We gave Eisenhower its first loss in the history of the school," he said. "We split our team and won the West Valley and Toppenish invitationals on the same day. And in 1966, we won the district meet in Pasco." Here, Chaplin emphasized the fact there were no enrollment classifications in Washington in those days. Just as in the regular season, Wapato had to compete for the district championship and a high place at the state meet against the larger schools.

During this time, we also get our first hint of Chaplin's propensity for innovation. High school sports at the time were somewhat hide-bound and resistant to change, but after just one year as the track & field coach, Chaplin convinced the athletic director at Wapato and the coaches and ADs at several other small schools in the Yakima Valley to add cross country to the schedule.

And because he had seen young girls compete overseas while in the army, Chaplin was an early advocate for the inclusion of girls in high school track. Girls were virtually excluded from high school sports at the time, more than ten years before Title IX changed the gender landscape of high school and college sports. When Chaplin was the head coach at WSU, there was a title IX lawsuit against the school that was tried in the Whitman County Courthouse in Colfax. "I was the only one from the men's side to speak for the women," he said. "And the Judge, Wally Friel, gave me a great deal of latitude. In my mind, there was one basic issue. If women are not allowed to have [competitive] sports, they will be at a disadvantage economically in the 'good old boy network' when it comes to advancing up the corporate ladder."

Chaplin's point was a straightforward way of saying that high schools, colleges, and universities (at the time) justified sports programs because of their educational value. Then why were those programs denied to more than half of each school's student population? The suit by WSU female athletes was a pivotal moment in the explosive growth of women's and girls' sports that continued for the next 50 years.

At Wapato High School, Chaplin was approached by a girl in one of his classes. She had a sister, and they wanted to run track. "They wanted to know why they couldn't run track," Chaplin said. "And I told them, 'Because you don't have any meets.' And they say, 'Well, can't we get some?'" Chaplin sent the sisters away with instructions to talk to some of the other girls at school. "And we ended up with between twelve and fifteen girls on the track team."

The following year, he sent the Wapato girls' team with their parents to Spokane for an age group AAU meet at Whitworth College. "We win the team title," he said. "And the story is in the Yakima paper. On Monday, the principal called me in and said… 'the superintendent wants to see you.' So, I go over to Dr. Urdahl's office, and he is almost busting at the seams, and he says, 'When did we allow girls to have sports teams at Wapato?' I say that we started one this spring and ask if there's a problem with that. Then I explained that I paid for all their uniforms and equipment from my Pepsi truck. He then says, 'We can't have this.' I say, 'Are you telling me that girls at Wapato can't have sports? What will their parents say about this?' And by the way, one or two of the girls' parents were tight with members of the school board. Then I suggest he should take the credit and tell the school board that Wapato is a pioneer in girls' sports. He thinks it over and says, 'I will get back to you.' Then we had a girls' track & field team."

He then established the Wapato Relays, one of the first high school track & field meets in the state of Washington to include competition for girls and the first to include the triple jump.

High school track in Washington was experiencing something of a golden age in the 1960s. Charlie Greene from O'Dea High School in Seattle was rewriting the state's sprint records and would go on to star at the University of Nebraska before winning two medals (bronze in the 100 and gold in the 4x100) at the 1968 Olympics. Gerry Lindgren, up at Rogers High in Spokane, was setting state records that still stand, and he qualified for the 1964 Olympic team just a month after graduating from high school. Casey Carrigan, from tiny Orting, Washington, a town with a school even smaller than Wapato, was just an eleventh grader when he made the 1968 Olympic team in the pole vault.

The point is that with all that star power around the state and with his major college experience behind him, there is no reason Chaplin should not have considered Wapato High School track & field a "major" sport. With John Chaplin in charge, track & field was going to matter. Under him, Wapato produced Don Fate, a 229-foot javelin thrower who later threw at the University of Washington; Dave Fox, the state 880-yard champion, who ran 1:48.5 for the half-mile and went on to run for WSU; and Roger O'Dell, who ran 9.6 for 100 yards and 49.5 for the quarter mile. O'Dell went to Whitworth College and would later become the head track & field coach at Wapato High.

It's also about this time that we get a glimpse of the blunt nature that will characterize much of his public persona in the years to come. During Chaplin's very first meet in his very first year, Wapato was hosting Sunnyside and Ellensburg high schools for a double dual meet, and "Ellensburg shows up for the double dual meet," he said. "But the [Ellensburg] coach does not want to run a double dual. So, I say, 'Fine, Coach. Get your ass back on the bus, and Sunnyside and Wapato will have a meet.'"

I can only imagine what the veteran Ellensburg coach must have been thinking as the upstart from tiny Wapato turned and walked away. I suspect he thought Chaplin was just going to say something like *Fine, Coach, whatever you want.* Chaplin's terse response and aggressive insistence that the meet be conducted as planned must have come as a surprise, at the very least, if not a complete shock. "Then I told the Sunnyside coach, and he says the Ellensburg coach is sometimes an ass." It *is* important to note here that the Ellensburg team ended up competing in the meet under the rules sent out ahead of time and agreed upon by all three schools. With John Chaplin in charge of the meet, the Ellensburg coach really had no other option.

Chaplin's interest in the triple jump (at the time called hop-step-and-jump in the US) began when, as an athlete at WSU, he was sitting in the Cub (the student union building at WSU). Another student approached him and asked, "What is that Big 'W' on your sweater for?" "I told him it's for being a first-year varsity letterman in track," Chaplin recalled. "We get to talking, and I find out that he's Elf Fredrickson, an exchange student from Norway who competed in the triple jump. I ask him his marks, and he tells me in meters, which I figure is around forty-eight feet. I go to Coach Mooberry... WSU did have a triple jumper named Clint Richardson, who was an NCAA All-American in 1952. The triple jump was only held at the NCAA meet in Olympic years... and I say, 'Coach, there's a guy here on campus that jumps forty-eight feet in the hop-step-and-jump.'"

Long story short: Frederickson joins the track team, ties the school record in the long jump, sets a school record in the triple jump, and wins the AAWU and several other collegiate titles. And he places second and third in the 1962 and 1963 NCAA national meets. "That was my first recruiting experience.

"My second was after the 1963 Pac-8 championships held at Berkeley," Chaplin continued. "I talked Coach Mooberry into going down to the Modesto Relays. I convinced Dick Hickman, a junior college transfer, to agree to go to WSU. He ended up winning the Pac-8 100-yard title in 1965."

Of course, Chaplin's natural inclination to innovate, to think outside the box, to promote the sport, and to advance his team's chances to succeed began back at Wapato.

"…When I get to Wapato, I add the triple jump to the program, and the WIAA [Washington Interscholastic Athletic Association] asks me to give a clinic on the triple jump at the annual coaches convention in 1965."

Chaplin's most remarkable trait might be his ability to keep so many varied balls in the air at the same time. Every time we talked, he came back to his insistence that despite his coaching successes, track & field was just a means to an end. He was never far from his foundational belief in the primacy of education. Track & field mattered, but school mattered more.

"The first year, I had four or five classes of world problems, which all students were required to take, and a prep period as senior-class advisor," he said. "And the second year, I said to the principal, 'This is insanity. We got a big room over there by the lunchroom. Why don't we have two classes of world problems in the morning and one in the afternoon, and I will teach a class in sociology with its economic consequences for interested students as an elective." He pointed out to the principal his belief that it was essential that students in a small town like Wapato understand the one-sided economics of local agriculture, especially the economic discrepancies between wealthy farmers and business leaders and the laborers in the field.

"I must admit that after the first semester, my world problems classes had parents who came to watch me teach topics and have guest speakers that were not necessary on their top ten list," he added. "I made the students buy *Time Magazine* for the world problems class, and you would have thought it was illicit material based on the reaction of some of the school district's right-leaning parents."

This is a perfect early example of Chaplin's tendency to adjust some small detail to make it possible to get more done with more efficient use of time and energy. It is also a perfect early example of how Chaplin's straight-ahead, get-it-done approach to problem-solving could rustle the feathers of those used to a more cautious and measured approach.

"The principal thought that was wonderful," he said. But, not surprisingly, "the teachers didn't like it at all. You don't volunteer to teach anything, right?" In today's school climate—micromanaged as it is by school district policy, union rules, and class size and workload restrictions—Chaplin would not be allowed to simply volunteer to take on an additional class.

Chaplin had not intended to coach more than one year at Wapato. After one year, he intended to resume his pursuit of a law degree. But, as he says, "all men are little boys at heart, and I was having fun, so I decided to stay another year and see if I could get cross country in our new league, the Mid-Valley League.

"The second year, I met my wife in the hamburger booth at the Wapato Harvest Festival," he said. "We went out every day for four days, and two days later, she goes to California for her new job. I call her and ask her if she wants to get married. She had already talked to her friend and says, 'I met this guy who's going to ask me to marry him, and I'm going to say yes.'"

Linda returned to Wapato, and "there's several months before the wedding," Chaplin recalled. "That's so she has time to get out of it." He laughed and added, "You know what I mean?" The Chaplin marriage has thrived for more than fifty-seven years. "That's because I'm on the road a lot," Chaplin added with a note of affection. Several of Chaplin's former athletes credit Linda Chaplin for being the gentle counterbalance to John's gruff demeanor.

"Maybe I just fell into it [the role of moderator]," she said, discounting her role. "I didn't view myself as a moderating influence. I did at one time work in athletic eligibility, so John and I were in the same office when he was doing eligibility for a while."

Linda Chaplin worked for the university in several capacities over than 30 years, but it was through her job in athletic eligibility, in the same office where track athletes came to see the coach, that the athletes would first encounter Linda.

"My desk was right where kids would come into John's office," she explained. "And the track kids would be in and out every day. I got to know a lot of them pretty well. Some of the kids just needed someone to talk to. And as you know, John *is* volatile, so…" She let that last statement hang before going on to explain that during this time, Coach Chaplin was frustrated over WSU's decision to change the way he would have to allocate scholarships.

"I remember talking to John at one point," she said. "He was really grouchy and grumpy and yelling at people. And I told him, 'You know what? Enough. You are being unkind.'"

The problem from Linda Chaplin's point of view was that the coach was beginning to feel like his goal of winning an NCAA outdoor title was being thwarted by what he viewed as unnecessary and unwarranted university policy. "He felt like he was not getting the support from the athletic department to be competitive. He wanted that NCAA championship, and there was a lot of stuff going on in the teams he competed against he didn't think was fair. And then they start cutting scholarships, and he felt like he was being pinched."

Chaplin himself credits Linda with providing the final word when it came time for him to decide, finally, what direction his professional life was going to go. And her explanation for the change in his career trajectory was typically insightful, simple, and direct. "I think he had a lot of fun as the track coach [at Wapato]. And that's what attracted him."

After three years at Wapato High School—years that even today he refers to as the most fun he ever had in track & field—Chaplin had a decision to make. He had stayed at Wapato longer than he'd intended, and he still harbored a desire to go to law school and become an attorney specializing in civil and maritime law. It's not clear whether this desire was sincere or whether he'd not yet come to grips with the notion that coaching track & field was a suitable career path. Interestingly, his good friend Brooks Johnson had similar ambitions. He graduated from the prestigious University of Chicago Law School and, for a time, worked in Washington, DC, for the Government Affairs Institute in the State Department.

"I knew after three years at Wapato I'd have to decide one way or the other [about law school]," Chaplin explained. "Because you had to get a fifth year or do a master's degree [to continue teaching]. I had already taken the LSAT in the summer of 1963 and was getting ready to begin the process of applying to various law schools. I was considering Boalt at UC Berkeley, the University of Virginia, and Tulane.

"Then I get a call from Mooberry, and he said, 'John, I got a call from *the* Sam Bell.'" Bell was the long-time track & field coach at Oregon State University, who was just about to take the head coaching job at the University of California. "They just hired a guy named Bernie Wagner, and he is going be the coach." Wagner was in the market for a grad-student assistant coach and had called Mooberry for a recommendation.

"He says, 'I gave him your name. I hope you don't mind.'"

Wagner asked Chaplin to come down to visit Oregon State. He was worried Chaplin might find the small-town atmosphere in Corvallis, Oregon, unsatisfying. Chaplin laughed at the notion. He had, after all, spent the last six years in Pullman and Wapato.

"So, I go down there, and sonofabitch, he offers me the job," Chaplin said. "I tell Linda I'll go to Oregon State for one year and work on my master's degree, which I am going to need anyway if I am going to stay in teaching, and if I'm going to law school, it's not going to do me any harm."

In the fall of 1966, Chaplin jumped into his new job at Oregon State with the same enthusiasm and the same determination to raise the profile of track & field that he'd employed at Wapato. He designed and produced the school's first-ever press book for cross country and helped organize the Far West Basketball Tournament in Portland. Wagner and the athletic director Jim Barrett, who Chaplin calls "one of the best ADs in the conference at the time," were so impressed with the young coach's initiative, enthusiasm, and attention to detail that Barrett offered Chaplin a job as the athletic department's ticket manager.

"But I said 'no, no, no. I'm going to law school,'" Chaplin said. Barrett asked Chaplin what it would take to keep him at Oregon State. "And I casually said, 'If I could be the assistant track coach in the spring and the ticket manager in the fall...'"

Barrett was convinced. "I'll do better than that. I'll give you a country club membership and seven thousand dollars." Chaplin was only making $3,500 a year teaching and coaching at Wapato High School, so the deal was done, and Chaplin became a Division I track & field coach.

Collegiate track & field was growing rapidly in the 1960s. Dirt and cinder tracks were being replaced by composition surfaces that allowed athletes to run faster in all weather. Pole vaulters were soaring over previously unimagined heights due to the introduction of poles made first from fiberglass and later, other composite materials. The longest distance race was extended, from two miles to three miles and then to six miles (eventually to be replaced by the 5,000 and 10,000 meters). The steeplechase became a regular feature of major meets (even if most universities did not yet have the necessary facilities to contest the event regularly). New field events were added: the triple jump (which Chaplin had introduced to Washington high school athletes during his time at Wapato) and the arcane, complex, and potentially dangerous hammer throw.

Of course, Chaplin realized immediately these new events provided schools like Oregon State with an opportunity to get in on the ground floor competitively and score big points at both the NCAA championships and later in the Pac-8 conference meets. He recalled a conversation he had with Wagner. "I said to Bernie, 'We got this walk-on 50-foot shot putter from Eugene, Steve DeAutremont, but he's no shot putter at all.'"

Imagine Bernie Wagner's reaction when his brand-new sprint coach approached him with the opinion that one of his shot putters was *no shot putter at all*. Incredulity comes to mind, but Wagner must have been open to the idea because...

"I say, 'Why don't I teach him the hammer throw?' And Bernie thought about it and said, 'That's a pretty good idea. We could get some points there.'"

So, Oregon State built a hammer cage and prepared a landing area in a remote location on campus.

Chaplin said, "I call Irv Black, a friend of mine in Connecticut and one of the few coaches in the country who understands the complexity of the hammer throw. So, I take Super 8 movies of the kid and send them to Coach Black, and he tells me what he is doing wrong, and I teach him the hammer."

By the fall of 1967, DeAutremont was throwing over 200 feet in practice, and "in those days, two hundred feet could win the NCAA." Chaplin said. "And Bernie was excited. We did get *some points*. Steve won two NCAA titles, in 1969 and 1970." In 1970, after Chaplin had left OSU for WSU, the Cougars' Tony Tenisci placed third in the hammer at the national meet in 1969. "Steve was a good friend," Chaplin said. "He died on November 13, 2021. He will be missed."

So, like the coming explosion of great international distance running talent waiting just over the track & field horizon, Chaplin was ahead of the curve when he recognized the scoring opportunity in the hammer. "Even though the hammer was a scoring event on the NCAA program, almost no schools outside the Ivy League and Rhode Island threw the hammer. Chaplin and Oregon State changed that. "No one saw that coming," he said. "But when it finally arrived, a lot of coaches looked the other way and failed to take advantage of the opportunity. As long as it was just the Ivy League and a few lesser track powers throwing the hammer...so what? But if teams in the Pac-8 [or one or more of the other *major* conferences] start throwing the hammer [and scoring points in the national meet], that was a horse of a different color. They were not going to let track powers like the Pac-8 conference pick up easy points. In 1967 in Provo, I told the coaches that if the Pac-8 takes up the hammer, in a decade or so, we would have most of the hammer throwers, and it would take 220 feet to make the final, and not just 200 feet to win the national title."

Between 1967 and 1997, Pac-8 and Pac-10 athletes won fifteen hammer titles. Included among those national champions was Balázs Kiss of USC and Hungary, who was the 1996 Olympic champion and 1998 European champion.

There finally came a point after three years at Wapato and an 18-month stint at OSU when Chaplin had to choose between a lucrative career in the law or a tenuous future in the uncertain world of Division I college sports. Then, during the fall 1967 indoor season, Chaplin got another phone call. "So, I'm sitting in my office, and I get another call from Mooberry. He wants to meet me in a local restaurant in Corvallis. He tells me Stan Bates [the WSU athletic director] finally gave him an assistant." Apparently, things were done a little differently in those days. Bates had budgeted for a track & field assistant for the entire year, but Mooberry did not find out about it until the indoor season was underway, and then only because one of his friends mentioned it in passing during a poker game. "And I [again] think Mooberry wants me to give him some names for assistant coaching candidates," Chaplin said. "But Jack Mooberry had told Stan Bates there was only one person he wanted."

John Chaplin.

When WSU coach Jack Mooberry offered him the opportunity to become his first paid assistant, Chaplin was uncertain and, therefore, reluctant. "I said I got to talk to my wife." John still wanted to go to law school, but he was clearly intrigued by Mooberry's offer. "So, I talked to Linda," he said. "And she throws up her hands and says, 'Why don't you just give it [law school] up? You're going to be a track coach.'" And so, John Chaplin's future was sealed, and track & field in the Pacific Northwest would never be quite the same.

The new job at WSU was to begin in January, but he still had indoor track obligations to fulfill before he left Oregon State. "So, I accept the job, but first [before his new job at WSU began], there's an indoor meet in Portland." Chaplin, amused by the situation, chuckled even before he was done telling the story. "I'm wearing Oregon State colors [orange and black], and I'm there with Willie Turner, a kid I'd recruited, and some other guys." It's interesting, I think, that Turner had been a standout sprinter from Yakima, Washington, and grew up virtually next door to Wapato. "Larry Scheurer is at Washington State." Scheurer was from Newport, Washington, a Seattle suburb. "Willie beats Scheurer."

Just a week later, Chaplin is at the Seattle indoor meet in his new capacity as the WSU assistant coach. "I am wearing crimson and gray, WSU's colors. And this time, Larry beats Willie, and the two kids come up to me and say, 'Now we know there's something to this coaching deal.' Willie said, 'When you are at Oregon State, I win, but when you're at Washington State, Larry wins.'" Chaplin paused at this point, which is remarkable, because when Chaplin is talking about track & field, pauses are rare. "It's wonderful, you know. Kids are funny and insightful at times."

Mooberry took a creative approach when assigning coaching duties to his new assistant. Chaplin was to coach cross country in the fall and the throwers, the 400-meter hurdles, and the distance runners in the spring. "He wanted to give me events I had the least amount of knowledge in, so I'd learn, because Jack is grooming me to follow him as the head coach. So, I have John van Reenen, Gerry Lindgren, and Boyd Gittens. A great way to start a career."

Plus…

"Mooberry said he told Stan I was to be the new head cross country coach and his assistant track coach."

When Mooberry turned over WSU's nascent cross-country program to Chaplin, there was a National Division I Cross Country Championship, but the position of a head cross-country coach was not fully recognized by most schools that had cross country. And the Pac-8 conference had no schools with cross-country programs that existed separate from their track & field programs. The cross-country team was simply an extension of the track & field program. Similar arrangements continue to exist today, at least in a de facto manner, but administratively, track and cross country are viewed as distinct programs separate from each other to make adherence to various federal Title IX regulations easier to manage. Today, scholarships allotted for cross country are included in the total allowed for track & field. The only exception to that rule is for schools that have only cross country. They are allowed six scholarships.

So, in 1971, after WSU had won both the northern division and Pac-8 team titles in cross country, the conference named Mooberry Coach of the Year. When Bates received the coach-of-the-year plaque from the conference office, Mooberry had to inform his AD that it was John Chaplin who had coached the conference championship team. Until 1973, the collegiate cross-country championships had always been held in the eastern half of the country. In 1972, Chaplin, still an assistant to Mooberry but the head cross-country coach at WSU, convinced the NCAA to hold the 1973 and 1977 Division I meets at the Hangman Valley Golf Course in Spokane.

Even though cross-country had until then been the province of eastern universities, Chaplin pointed out that the origin of the sport at the collegiate level was directly connected to WSU. "Karl Schlademan was head track & field coach at Kansas from 1919 to 1925," Chaplin explained. "He helped start the Kansas Relays." Then, from 1927 until 1940, Schlademan was the head track & field coach at WSC. His WSC teams placed fourth at the NCAA track & field meet in 1937 and 1939 and won seven northern division track & field titles. He was Jack Mooberry's coach at WSC. He continued his career at Michigan State from 1940 to 1959, winning eleven (ICAAAA) and seven NCAA cross-country championships. MSU hosted the first NCAA cross-country championship race in 1938 and continued as the host school every year until 1964, and under Schlademan's direction from 1940 until 1959.

"Once cross country became established in the Pac-8 and elsewhere out west," Chaplin explained, "it did not take long for those programs to succeed." The conference has won 24 individual cross-country titles over the years: Oregon with eight, WSU with seven, Arizona and Colorado with three, and USC, UCLA, and Oregon State with one each. Additionally, Oregon has six team titles, and Stanford and Colorado have four each.

As noted earlier, the three athletes who had the greatest impact on Chaplin's philosophy once he became the head coach were all in the program when he arrived in the January of 1968. "I had John van Reenen, so I wasn't too worried about the shot and the discus. I had [Gerry] Lindgren because I was going to have him in cross country in the fall. And I had a kid named Boyd Gittins."

Van Reenen and Lindgren are obvious examples of the type of athlete WSU was to become known for in the years after Chaplin became the school's head coach, when Mooberry retired after the 1973 season.

But it is with a certain level of satisfaction that he describes Boyd Gittins' journey. He was the two-time NWAACC champion in both the high hurdles and the intermediate hurdles, with a best time of around and 53.9 in the one-lap intermediate hurdles but still attracted little more than indifference from other Division I coaches. Despite all that, he still blossomed into a world-class 400-meter hurdler. As Chaplin pointed out, "He placed second in the NCAA meet and later tied the world record with 49.5 and made the 1968 Olympic team." Athletes like Lindgren, van Reenen, and Gittins would form the foundation for WSU's success in track & field during the last third of the 20th Century.

"Gittins was a junior college transfer," Chaplin explained. "He ran 53.9 in junior college. But one day, I said to him, 'Why don't we try running 13 steps [between hurdles] after the first hurdle and for the next five hurdles, and then go to fifteen steps for the last four hurdles…as a start.'"

At the time, most 400-meter hurdlers would take 15 steps between hurdles for the entire race, and only a few had toyed with the idea of taking 13 for the first half of the race. But back in 1962, Chaplin had a teammate, Jim Allen, with similar credentials to Gittins. Allen was a 14.9 high hurdler who worked his way up to running 13 steps for seven or eight hurdles and posted the second-best time in the world that year at 50.1 for the 400m intermediate hurdles. So, Chaplin knew Gittins could do the same. Gittins wasn't convinced at first, but when he asked why the coach wanted to make this radical change to his normal stride pattern, Chaplin came up with a typically straightforward and practical response.

"I said, 'Listen. That means you'll be taking two steps less than the other guys for as long as you can. Your present best time is, what, 49.2? Your best projected quarter mile is 47.1 or 47.2, and some of these guys can run 45.0.'" The implication was that if Gittins was going to compete with the best in the country and then the best in the world, he would have to make up for his lack of flat quarter-mile speed with a superior and heretofore untested, tactical approach. Gittins worked on the innovative stride pattern and qualified for the NCAA championships in his junior year, 1968.

"We finally get up to [taking 13 steps] for eight hurdles. Anyway, he goes to the NCAAs, and he has a 52.2 going in. He places second and beats the good USC kid, Geoff Vanderstock." Gittens ran 50.7 in the finals, just behind eventual Olympic champion David Hemery from Boston College and Great Britain, who ran 50.6. The eight points Gittins picked in that race were critical to WSU's second-place finish in the 1968 NCAA meet, just a single point behind the University of Southern California.

"He comes back [to Pullman]," Chaplin continued. "We do some more training, and he goes up to altitude and runs 49.5 in the [preliminary] rounds...but the record was never ratified." At the time, the record was a world record. The existing world record, Chaplin pointed out, had been run on an unusual 500-meter track. Vanderstock of USC, who was third at the NCAA, beat Gittins in the final at the trials, setting a new world record of 48.8. Gittins was second, at 49.1. After 1968, outdoor world records could only be set on tracks that were no more than 400 meters long.

Of course, 1968 was an Olympic year, with the Games to be held at the 7,349-foot elevation and in the thin air of Mexico City. In order to simulate the brutal demands of racing at high altitudes, the US Olympic Trials were held on a unique track carved out of the forest at South Lake Tahoe, California. The running surface was state-of-the-art for the time, but the organizers had simply decided to leave the forest in place in what would have normally been the infield.

Obviously, Gittin's performance also earned him a place on the US Olympic team for the Mexico City Games. Unfortunately, an ironically prescient turn of events—an adverse reaction to a mandatory vaccine—forced him to withdraw two days before the race.

"But he was, for a short time, the world record holder," Chaplin said with no effort to hide his satisfaction with Gittins's accomplishment.

He added that Gerry Lindgren had set a world record at six miles in 1965, and van Reenen would go on to set a world record in the discus after college. Of course, Chaplin was not yet WSU's head coach in 1968, but the ball had begun to roll, and Chaplin and WSU were on the verge of emerging as a consistent national and international force in the world of track & field. In 1968, all three (Lindgren, van Reenen, and Gittins), plus Carl O'Donnell, an NCAA champion in the javelin, were coached by Chaplin.

CHAPTER 4

RONO'S RACES

I've mentioned this earlier, but at this point, it bears repeating: Very few track & field athletes have had a record-breaking streak like Henry Rono in 1978. Britain's Sebastian Coe broke the world records for 800 meters, 1,500 meters, and the mile in a span of just 41 days in 1979. Between August 14 and October 7, 2020, Ugandan Joshua Cheptegei obliterated the world records for both the 5,000 and 10,000 meters after breaking the world best for 5,000 meters earlier that year. But Coe's assault on the record books was accomplished in the relatively friendly environs of Europe, and Cheptegei's records were accomplished in the progressive contemporary days of professional track & field with financial and material support and incentives from sponsors and meet organizers. In 1978, Henry Rono faced a much different and, in almost every way, more difficult competitive environment.

After Chaplin sat Rono down in his office and convinced him he could break all four records, the singular Kenyan "looked at me and said, 'If you think so, then okay.'" What I think is implicit in Rono's reply is that regardless of what his ambitions or aspirations might have been at that moment, on some level, he trusted Chaplin's judgment, or at least he had faith in the training system and tactical philosophy that Chaplin had devised.

"But I told him first, we would have to look at the schedule," Chaplin explained, "and then work out a program where he'd run a race in preparation, and in the next race, we correct any problems. And then, 'You run for the record.'" And that's what he did.

"Coming out of the 1977 cross-country season," Chaplin continued, "Henry wanted to see how fit he was on the track. So, on January 28, in Auckland, New Zealand, he won a 10,000-meter race in 27:48.6." Following that performance, Rono had a shortened indoor season with little speed work. His short indoor season consisted of just a few meets: On January 21, Rono ran two miles in 8:18.3, a new collegiate record; on February 10, he ran 13:24.6 for three miles; and on February 17, he ran 8:20.0 for two miles, going through 3,000 meters in 7:49.1 on the way, another collegiate record.

"But I felt obligated to send Henry and Ian Campbell, the defending triple jump champion, and few others to the national meet," Chaplin explained, "because WSU was the defending NCAA team champion. Henry was not ready for a tough indoor two-mile and finished second, but we were both focused on the primary goal of breaking those three world records outdoors."

He concluded the indoor season on March 18 in Pullman, after the NCAA indoor championships, by running 8:34.8 for 3,200 meters, despite the tight turns on WSU's indoor track. "Henry accelerated through the middle 600 meters with 200-meter segments of 27, 26, and 25 seconds. That's 600 meters in 78 seconds," Chaplin said. "He was getting ready for the outdoor season, in which we would attempt to break the world record in the three Olympic distance events [the steeplechase, the 5,000, and the 10,000]."

Rono took the next step on March 25 at the Bruce Jenner Invitational at San Jose State. "I told Henry his weak spot was his second mile," Chaplin explained. "So, I say, 'Henry, you need to run between 4:03 and 4:05 in the second mile of the 5,000, so you know how it feels to push the middle of the race.' He ran the second mile in 4:04.5 and set the meet record at 13:31.8."

Detailed chart of Rono's record-setting 81-day journey from April 8–June 27 is included in the appendix.

Rono's remarkable outdoor season began in earnest on April 1 with a 5,000-meter race against Oregon State on a snowy day in Spokane, Washington. "There really was snow on the ground," Chaplin said. "But he ran 13:22.1."

Thirteen-twenty-two...point one!

It doesn't matter how that number is expressed. It is inconceivable that anyone would even attempt to run that fast in what amounted to a warm-up meet in March, much less on a track surrounded by the snow-covered playfields at Spokane Community College, but "then I knew he'd get the world record," Chaplin said.

Chaplin and Rono knew then that it was time to attack the world record of 13:12.9, held at the time by Dick Quax of New Zealand. The next opportunity would be the double dual meet with Arizona State and Cal in Berkeley, California. But the world record attempt would mean that the 5,000 was the only race Rono would run in the double dual meet against Cal and ASU. Who attempts a world record in an early-spring dual meet? "So, I got the team together and told them the other guys would have to pick up the slack. Josh [Kimeto] and Samson [Kimombwa] would have to go one-two in the mile and then run the 5,000 with Henry."

Chaplin's strategy was for Kimeto, a two-time NCAA 5,000-meter champion, to take the lead for the first four laps and for Kimombwa (the world record holder at 10,000 meters, at the time) to take the lead for the middle three or four laps. "At that point," Chaplin remembered, "the ASU and Cal runners were all spread around the track, and Henry just had to run them down one by one. When Henry went by the three-mile mark [at] 12:42.9 on my stopwatch, I knew that the world 5,000-meter record was going to be broken."

And it was. It would not be the first time Rono would set a world record in an obscure meet with only token spectators, but that race would set the stage for the rest of his remarkable season. He ran 13:08.4 that day, finishing far ahead of his WSU teammates Kimeto and Kimombwa. In the process, he sliced more than four seconds off Quax's record, which had been set in July the previous year. The record would stand until Rono himself ran 13:06.20 as a WSU senior in 1981, and that mark would hold up until David Moorcroft of Great Britain ran 13:00.41 in 1982.

Moorcroft himself has, at least implicitly, credited Rono with providing a measure of inspiration and motivation for his own record-breaking career. "Rono was, for my generation, the African [athlete] who had the greatest impact," Moorcroft explained during a broadcast on British television. "I mean, Kip Keino had an impact in the 60s and 70s, but Rono transformed things, breaking world records week after week, and winning championships and doing it from the front, using surging and negative splits.

"I had it in my mind that one day, I wanted to beat Rono," Moorcroft said. "So, part of my build-up as a youngster was that I wanted to beat Brendan Foster, I wanted to beat David Bedford. Then, as I was moving towards the 5,000-meter distance, in my mind, it was that I wanted to beat Rono. Rono was my yardstick." Fittingly, Moorcroft broke Rono's record in 1982.

"Now it was time to look at the 3,000-meter steeplechase," Chaplin said. The steeple was Rono's best event prior to coming to WSU, and after he set a WSU track record of 8:24.4, the stage was set for an attempt at Garderud's world record of 8:08.2. I told Henry we'd need another meet before we make a run at the world record," Chaplin said. The next opportunity would come in the now infamous dual meet against the University of Oregon in Eugene.

Remember?

Rono slowed down in the final lap and a half (600 meters) despite being on world record pace because Chaplin was certain the water jump did not meet the IAAF's specifications. Then the reporter's question about Rono's literacy or lack thereof. Then Chaplin's undiplomatic outburst about Oregon fans and excremental press. And then his promise that Rono would set the steeplechase record in Seattle rather than in Eugene.

"But I told him he could go for the collegiate record, which was around 8:21," Chaplin said. "Because no one would check the water jump for a collegiate record." Of course, Rono obliterated the collegiate record by running 8:14.75, (as mentioned previously) the fastest time ever run in the US at the time, despite a slow final 600 meters. Next up was the Northwest Relays in Seattle on May 13. The 8:05.4 world record he would run that day would survive more than eleven years until Peter Koech, a former WSU All-American and NCAA steeplechase champion, ran 8:05.25 in 1989.

The 10,000-meter world record held by teammate Samson Kimombwa was Rono's next target. In the fall of 1976, Rono (28:06.6) and Kimombwa (28:16.8) had finished one-two at the NCAA Cross Country Championships, with eventual world champion Craig Virgin at 28:26.53 in third. Those times remain the top-three performances in the history of the meet.

Then, on June 30 the following summer, Kimombwa broke the world 10,000-meter record when he ran 27:30.47 in Helsinki, Finland. I remember being surprised when the news of Kimombwa's record finally got back to the US (in the days before the Internet and virtually no media coverage of track & field in the US). I thought to myself that if the runner-up at the NCAA cross country meet could run the fastest 10k in history, how fast could the NCAA champion run?

But Chaplin did not wonder. He knew. "Henry already had the collegiate freshman record of 27:37.1, set in London in 1977," Chaplin said. "So, I knew he could get the 10,000 record."

"I decided to use the Pac-10 Track & Field Championships at Corvallis as a trial to see where all four runners were in their training," Chaplin explained. "Henry wanted to run the triple, which was a final for the steeplechase, and the 10,000 on Friday, and a final for the 5,000 on Saturday. This was fine with me since I needed to see where he was at that point."

Chaplin wasn't particularly worried about points in the 1978 Pac-10 meet because "there was also the possibility that Joshua Kimeto [with bests of 13:26.8 for 5,000 meters and 28:00.6 for 10,000 meters] or Samson Kimombwa [13:21.56 and 27:30.47], or my newest runner Joel Cheruiyot [13:34.8 and 27:50.3], could also win two races—in 5,000 and in the 10,000." Imagine how dominant a team with four guys between 13:08.4 and 13:34.8 for 5,000 meters and 27:30.47 and 28:00.6 for 10,000 meters would be in collegiate track these days.

The meet began with the steeplechase, but Rono had bruised his instep in the process of setting the world record in Seattle. "He was about 50 meters ahead on the third lap," Chaplin said, "when he dropped out." The meet physician examined Rono's foot and gave him the go-ahead to run the 5,000 and the 10,000 because it was pushing off the barrier at the water jump that had aggravated his foot injury. Without a steeplechase win from Rono, WSU would be unable to win the Pac-10 team title.

Even though he had clearance to run, Rono's injury changed Chaplin's strategy for his team in the 5,000 and the 10,000. "I said to the group, 'Let's run together for 4,000 meters [ten laps] in the 5,000 and until 8,000 meters [20 laps] in the 10,000. Then all bets are off, and may the best man win.'

"What I wanted was Henry to have a good, fast 10,000, and we would see what happened and where to correct if needed [before attempting the world record in a few weeks]."

Chaplin got exactly what he needed, both from a team standpoint and as far as assessing Rono's fitness was concerned. Rono won the race at 27:46.6, with Cheruiyot second and Kimombwa fourth. It took an athlete the likes of Alberto Salazar in third place to prevent WSU from sweeping the event. Bill McChesney of Oregon, who later ran 13:14.80 and was the Oregon 5,000-meter record holder until 2021, was fifth with a time that was better than Steve Prefontaine had run. In 1973, WSU did sweep the Pac-8 10,000 meters. John Ngeno won that race, with Dan Murphy second and Spokane native Phil Burkwist third. In the 1979 NCAA national cross country championship race, Rono sprained his ankle, opening the door for Alberto Salazar to win his only NCAA title.

The 10,000 was on Friday, and the next day, Rono would join Kimeto, Cheruiyot, and Kimombwa in the 5,000. "I got all four athletes together," Chaplin said, "and told them, 'I have a problem. If I pull any of you out, USC might not win the team title, but if I run all four of you, Oregon might not win the team title.' And I asked them, 'What do you think?'"

The four athletes were unanimous in their response, an answer typical of the Kenyans' attitude toward competition. First, they recognized that Chaplin's explanation of the scoring indicated that WSU did not have enough points to be involved in the race for the team title. Second, that fact did not matter. "They all said we should try to win as many points as we can. It's not our place to worry about who wins the title, especially since we don't have any chance to win it."

So, all four ran the race. Rono won in 13:20.2 with Cheruiyot in second, Kimeto in third, and Kimombwa in fifth. This time, Oregon's Rudy Chapa came in fourth, breaking up the Cougar juggernaut. Oregon was loaded at the time. In addition to Chapa, the Ducks had Don Clary in sixth. Matt Centrowitz Sr., who would win four US titles and run in the Olympics twice, was seventh. Oregon's Alberto Salazar, in eighth, would go on to set American records at both 5,000 and 10,000 meters. The Oregon runners were good, but Chaplin's preferred tactics—team running, surging, and negative splits—were on display in this race.

So, as Chaplin pointed out, it was not superior talent or toughness that made it difficult for the Oregon athletes to compete against WSU's Kenyans. It was simply a matter of where they were in their development. The Oregon athletes were, for the most part, younger with less elite racing experience. Chaplin insists that it was WSU's use of surging tactics and negative splits that allowed his athletes to dominate the long races in that 1978 Pac-10 meet. Don Clary of Oregon was the only non-Cougar to win a long race—the 3,000-meter steeplechase, after Rono had dropped out—in that meet.

"What the general public does not know is that the Pac-10 meet had a blind scratch entry system and an honest effort rule," Chaplin explained. In a blind scratch entry system, each team enters a specific number of athletes, but no one knows who those athletes are or what events they will compete in until the schedule is posted. "That means if you enter an event, you have to run or be disqualified from the rest of the meet unless the athlete was granted a medical exemption," he continued. "Even though 5,000 meters is the last distance race, it is still not ethical to take athletes out of the meet if they are physically okay to compete just to give another team a chance to win the team title. And it was not as if I added four guys at the last minute just so USC could win the conference title." USC did end up winning the title, outscoring Oregon 126-119, with UCLA being third with 114 and WSU in fourth with 109.5.

WSU's next meet would be the NCAA championships, to be contested over three days from June 1 to June 3. "And Henry wanted to run the triple again," Chaplin said. On Thursday, the first day of the meet, Rono won his steeple preliminary heat in 8:18.63 and then won his heat of the 5,000 in 13:21.79, both NCAA meet records. Bear in mind these were preliminary heats, and Rono was running faster than any other collegian in history. Rono remains the only athlete to set two NCAA Division I championship records in the same national meet.

But his foot was sore again after his preliminary runs. "So, I pulled him from Friday's 10,000. Saturday, he set another meet record [8:12.39] in the steeplechase final because his foot was still sore," Chaplin said, noting that since the 10,000 was a final, the honest-effort rule did not apply. "I didn't need another NCAA gold medal for WSU in the 5,000, especially when the future of maybe the best distance runner ever might be in danger. I told Bill Dellinger that Henry was not running the 5,000 final and it was Rudy's [Chapa] to take if he can, which he did, winning his only NCAA title, turning the tables from his fourth-place finish at the Pac-10 meet by beating all three Cougars in the race."

Smart move. Nine days later, on June 11, in Vienna, Austria, Rono won a special four-man race over 10,000 meters in 27:22.47, again with very few spectators in attendance, taking exactly eight seconds off Kimombwa's record, set nearly one year earlier.

The last of Rono's world records is, *in my opinion*, his best. At the time, the record was 7:35.2, set by Brenden Foster in 1974. The 3,000 is not contested outdoors in international championship events, but it is the longest race run at the world indoor championships. In the US, the two-mile was the standard indoor event. Rono won the two-mile and was third in the mile at the 1977 NCAA indoor meet at Detroit when the Cougars won the team title. During the 1978 indoor season, Rono ran 8:18.3, a WSU record for that distance, which is about 218 meters, longer than 3,000 meters, during the 1978 indoor season. Later in 1980, he lowered the WSU record to 8:15.9 in San Diego, California. Rono was officially timed at 7:39.2 for 3,000 meters in that race.

So, again, Chaplin was confident that Rono could challenge Foster's record outdoors. An opportunity presented itself on June 27 at what may be Europe's most prestigious annual meet, the Bislett Games, in Oslo, Norway, on June 17. Rono started the race (relatively) slowly with a first kilometer (two-and-a-half laps) in 2:34—about 61 seconds per lap. Then he surged, covering the next two-and-a-half laps in 2:30—60 seconds per lap. And then he surged again. He ran the last kilometer in an astounding 2:27.6. That's 59.0 seconds per lap. He covered the final four laps in 3:57.9 to finish in 7:32.1. Here again, Chaplin's preferred tactic of surging and running negative splits worked to perfection.

How good was Rono's time? Well, his record lasted more than nine years, and the world record in this event has improved by only twelve seconds in the forty-four years since Rono set the record. He averaged 60.3 seconds per lap, essentially running the equivalent of two back-to-back 4:01 miles. Forty-four years ago.

One of the interesting aspects of Rono's record-setting was that two other WSU athletes served as bookends for two of his records. Koech broke his steeplechase record, and as noted earlier, the 10,000-meter record Rono broke when he ran 27:22.47 on June 11 had been 27:30.47 by his WSU teammate Samson Kimombwa.

The culmination of Rono's season came a little more than two weeks after his 10,000-meter record. He ran 7:32.1 for 3,000 meters, a record that would last even longer than his steeplechase record and would take an athlete the likes of Said Aouita of Morocco to break it in the August of 1989.

I guess it is inevitable that with Rono's success, which, in the mind of some observers (whoever they are), came from virtually nowhere, his coach's involvement in his accomplishments would be scrutinized. Chaplin accepts that but insists that his participation in Rono's European success in the summer of 1978 was limited and extremely so.

"There are writers who say that I made Rono run all those races on foreign soil," Chaplin said. "Not true. I only interceded in one... his attempt to break the world record in the 10,000 in Vienna. I set up that 10,000 race, which was part of our original plan to try to break the world record in each of the three Olympic distance races.

"I'd heard that he was thinking of going to Bislet to run a flat 3,000 race from the Nike rep Pete Peterson, but I thought that it was just another race he wanted to run. I also knew that he had made the Kenyan national team for the Commonwealth Games, and he was scheduled to run both the steeple and the 5,000. But that was expected due to his world record run at the three Olympic distances.

"I talked to Henry when he was in Edmond, Alberta, and I was with the Australian Commonwealth Games team training in Pullman and getting ready to go to Canada. We discussed tactics.

Henry was to surge in the prelim of the Commonwealth Games steeplechase and run negative splits to make sure he could control the race in the final, which he did by taking the lead and pushing the pace lap after lap, finally winning in 8:26.54.

"He was just to jog along in the 5,000 prelim and qualify, then put the hammer down at the 3,000-meter mark in the final. He did just that and ran away from the other competitors in the final to win 13:23.04. These tactics were necessary because Henry was competing in two tough events and four races in total. Most of the other competitors had only one event. The results speak for themselves."

This, of course, was all part of the plan. The two-mile race against Steve Ovett was not.

"As for his September race in London against Ovett, I read about that in the newspapers and thought nothing about it since it was an imperial distance and not an official metric mark required for IAAF records. As a rule, I usually did not interfere with foreign athletes' summer competitions. I left that to their home country's federations to deal with.

"The next time I talked to Henry was when he returned to WSU for the fall cross-country season. I was never in Europe in 1978, so I could not have been controlling the schedule, nor did I take any monies from him or receive monies to manage his, or any other athlete's, schedule at any time in his career. That is true for every other athlete who went through the WSU program.

"Kenya, the IAAF, and others left unsaid had more to do than I did with Henry's 1978 summer running schedule after the NCAA. As for my private conversation with Henry Rono, that will stay private, notwithstanding some quotes and comments in his book. I have had many pleasant conversations with Henry over these past 40-odd years, and in June of 2022, he was thrilled and approved of WSU having a statue of him at the Mooberry Track facility."

Rono's book is titled *Olympic Dream,* in reference to the fact that he was prevented by the Kenyan government from competing in both the 1976 and 1980 Olympics. Rono's 2007 book is an interesting look at his difficult upbringing in Kenya and his challenges in adjusting to both life in the US and as an international track & field celebrity at a time when it was virtually impossible for an athlete to make a living from the sport, at least legally. In the book, Rono does acknowledge Chaplin's contribution to helping him adjust.

Records are nice, but in the mind of serious track & field aficionados, it's competition that defines the sport. One man against the clock is one thing, and few, if any, athletes have been able to match what Rono did in 1978. But the true measure of the sport is one runner against another. Competition tests not only an athlete's ability to run fast but also their understanding and application of the more subtle aspect of the sport and another benchmark of Chaplin's approach to training and racing: strategy and tactics—the ability to read your opposition and adjust your pace and intensity at the appropriate moment.

For that reason, it was a race Rono lost in September of 1978 that may best define the man as a competitor. But first, he would represent Kenya at the Commonwealth Games in Edmonton, Alberta, Canada, where he ran four races in seven days and won two gold medals. On August 3, he won the steeplechase preliminary, and then on August 6, he won the final in 8:26.54, with countryman James Munyala almost six seconds back in the silver medal position. On August 7, he won the 5,000-meter preliminary, and then on August 10, he won the 5,000-meter gold medal in 13:23.04, with Michael Musyoki almost seven seconds back in second place and Foster more than nine seconds behind in third.

Winning the Commonwealth Games gold medal in the 5,000 certainly established Rono's credentials as a competitor. In the final, which came nearly six weeks after his fourth world record, Rono faced a loaded field. With the likes of fellow Kenyan Michael Musyoki, Brits Brenden Foster and Mike McLeod, and Tanzanian great Suleiman Nyambui in the race, Rono's record-breaking bona fides and competitive mettle would be put to a stern test. But with about one kilometer left in the race, Rono surged, and no one went with him. At the top of the final turn, he took a quick look over his left shoulder and seemed surprised to discover that none of his world-class pursuers were close enough to provide a threat in the final stages of the race.

So, when he traveled to London on September 15 to take on Steve Ovett over two miles, it was the race between two athletes with such contrasting competitive styles that had the international track & field world paying attention. The latest in a long line of great British distance runners that included both Foster and Moorcroft, Ovett would later win the gold medal at 800 meters in the 1980 Olympics and set numerous world records at 1,500 meters, the mile, and, on that night at Wembley Stadium, a world best at two miles.

Foster was the world record holder for two miles at 8:13.7, set in 1973, and he was in the race, but it was Rono who took control with three laps to go and forced Ovett to hang on for three tortuous 60-second laps. Rono continued to increase the pace, and Ovett continued to hang on until the two runners swept off the final turn.

Rono reached down deep for one more big surge, but Ovett sprinted into the lead. Rono matched Ovett for about 30 meters before the British great's superior sprinter's speed finally overcame him. Ovett won in 8:13.4, a new world best, with Rono two strides back and less than a second outside Foster's previous record at 8:14.66.

Since 1976, the IAAF only recognizes world records at metric distances, except for the mile. So technically and officially, Ovett's time would have been considered a world best rather than a world record. But this is a distinction without a difference, and most track & field observers use the term world record. By January 1, 1978, Ovett's time would have been considered a world best by the IAAF and not a world record because the mile run became the only imperial distance that can be ratified for a world record. All IAAF world outdoor records in yards became unofficial at the end of 1976. IAAF world indoor championships world records became official on January 1, 1987.

What had made Rono's remarkable season to that point so, well, remarkable was the way in which he defeated elite-level performers. He never looked distressed. For example: shutting down in the last 600 meters of that steeplechase in Eugene and still managing a collegiate record of 8:14.75 by nearly seven seconds. Running the turns and cruising the straightaways in a preliminary heat of the 5,000 meters in the 1978 NCAA prelims, he broke another meet record. This tactic was Rono's answer to the racist remarks by Carl Cluff, who also suggested that Steve Prefontaine would have beaten Rono. Or breaking four world records with such apparent ease. But in that two-mile race against Ovett, he was tested and stretched, challenged for what may have been the only time that season.

But he lost, right?

Not the point. He had taken on Steve Ovett, perhaps the only runner in the world that year who could have stayed with Rono long enough to use his superior speed in the final agonizing meters of an eight-lap race and forced himself to run a world-best mark and win. I think this race, even more than the world records, sums up John Chaplin's philosophy of training and racing. It was possible to beat Rono and WSU's other great athletes, but an opponent would have to run very fast and suffer a great deal to do so.

The first question most people ask Chaplin is when the issue of the Kenyans at WSU comes up. "How did I get the runners from Kenya?" The answer is a combination of foresight and good fortune.

Rono, Ngeno, Kimombwa, and Kimeto were just the beginning, of course. During the next twenty years, Chaplin would take advantage of his growing international connections and the advice of some of his athletes to build an athletic pipeline to the African continent that has still not been equaled.

"*The* question that most people ask me is how did I get the runners from Kenya?" Chaplin said. "So, this is what happened.

"In the summer of 1971, I am sitting in my office playing with my paper airplanes with nothing to do," Chaplin explained, "when two Black gentlemen come into the office. One is a graduate student, and the other is a professor in political science at a small university in the Seattle area. Both gentlemen were from Kenya, and one was Dr. Jonathon Ngeno, who later became the Speaker of the House in Kenya and an advisor to the Kenyan president, Daniel Toroitich Arap Moi."

Dr. Ngeno told Chaplin he had a younger brother, also named John Ngeno, and his younger brother had a friend, also named John Ngeno. At first, Chaplin was confused, but he became intrigued when Dr. Ngeno told him a little more about the two young Kenyans. John Ngeno No. 1 was a 14.2 high hurdler, and John Ngeno No. 2 was a 13:45 5,000-meter runner. And both John Ngenos were looking for a place to go to school in the US.

By 1971, because of their performance in the 1968 Olympics, in which they won seven medals (two gold) at distances as wide-ranging as 800 meters and 10,000 meters, Kenyan athletes had launched themselves into the top echelon of the international distance running world. Chaplin had competed with international athletes during his time as an athlete at WSU. He had several Canadian teammates, along with John Bentzon, a 1:49.6 half-miler from Norway. And, of course, he had worked with John van Reenen, so he was amenable to having athletes from other countries on his team. But still, the prospect of adding Kenyan athletes to the program was a new and intriguing proposition.

"I then explain all the NCAA rules on recruiting," he said. "And say that I am interested." Interested, but not convinced, that a 13:45 5,000-meter runner could be dropped into his lap that easily. "After they leave, I toss the contact info into the trash, and I think to myself, John Ngeno is too good to be true."

Too good to be true or not, Chaplin remained intrigued.

"A little later, I think, I could contact Mal Whitfield," Chaplin said. Whitfield had won Olympic gold medals in the 800- and the 4x400-meter relay at the 1948 Olympics and won the 800 again in 1952. In 1971, he was working for the US State Department in a program to encourage young people from around the world to come to the US to study. "So, I sent a telegram to Mal," Chaplin said, "He is in Ethiopia and [coincidentally] is going to Kenya the next week and will let me know by telegram if these marks are for real."

The truism is that if something is too good to be true, it usually is. But after Chaplin's two weeks of waiting to hear back from Whitfield, it turns out that John Ngeno's 5,000-meter times was not too good to be true, but simply true. "So, I call Dr. Ngeno and tell him what he needs to get them into the university—test scores, transcripts, etc."

Chaplin discovered later that Dr. Ngeno had also contacted coaches at the University of Illinois, Cal, Washington, "and several others," he said, "but none of them followed up, so I get to look good for a great recruiting job when in truth I did not do much."

When the athletes arrived on the WSU campus, Chaplin, of course, realized there might be just the slightest bit of confusion over their names. Both kids were named John Kip Ngeno. "They are in my office with Dr. Ngeno," Chaplin explained. "I turn to the hurdler and tell him 'You will be called Kip Ngeno, and the distance runner will be John Ngeno.'"

Chaplin had, as usual, done his homework. He explained that all members of the Kenyan Kalenjin tribe have a middle name that begins with *K*, and that middle name could have several meanings—place of birth, for example. Most of the East Africans he recruited were from the Kalenjin tribe. None of the three Kenyans in Chaplin's office that day had any objections to the young hurdler's new name. I was with the local newspaper in Pullman at the time, and to my knowledge, Kip Ngeno was not known by any other name during his time in Pullman. But the young man's name was not the only thing Chaplin changed.

"That spring of 1973, we are in the field house, training," Chaplin remembered. "And I was working with the hurdlers on start drills, and something is not copacetic." Despite Kip Ngeno having run 14.2 in the 110-meter-high hurdles, Chaplin noticed something amiss about the hurdler's approach to the first hurdle. So, always willing to take advantage of the latest technology, "I get my Super 8 camera out and film the first two hurdles."

Chaplin had to wait a week for the *Super 8* film to return, but the movie revealed a technical flaw with a stunningly easy solution. "What do you know," Chaplin said. "He took a quick step [at the start] to switch his feet." So, Chaplin questioned his new hurdler and learned that Kip Ngeno had almost no experience with starting blocks before coming to WSU. "I tell him to reverse his starting pads, and he goes over the first two hurdles like a bat out of hell." That simple adjustment was the first step for a hurdler with relatively modest credentials to become a two-time Pac-8 champion, an All-American, and the African record holder at 13.49, set in Berlin in 1975.

John Ngeno's credentials were even more impressive when he arrived, and his impact on the Pac-10 and the NCAA was felt immediately. During his first indoor season, he set an NCAA freshman record over three miles at 13:08.2. Outdoors, he won the Pac-8 six-mile title, placed second to Oregon great Steve Prefontaine in the three-mile, and became an All-American by placing fourth in the NCAA three-mile at 13:13.0. Ngeno would go on to win three NCAA indoor three-mile titles (in three tries) and three outdoor six-mile/10,000-meter titles (in three tries), plus an AAU cross-country title and an additional NCAA title at 5,000 meters. He was an NCAA All-American eight times, and he remains third on the WSU all-time list at both 3,000 meters (7:38.6) and 5,000 meters (13:20.6).

Of course, African athletes had to adjust to cultural norms here in the US that were quite different from what they were used to at home. Chaplin explained, "An example comes to mind with John Ngeno," he said. "It was the second time that Ngeno competed in Modesto at three miles. John wins, and they give him another TV set. That night at the motel, I keep getting calls from the front desk. So finally, at 4:00 a.m., I go down to the office, and I pass a calf tied to a palm tree. The manager says, "One of your athletes brought this calf over to the motel and tied it to the palm tree. What are you going to do about it?" So, a little later, as we are getting ready to go to the airport, I ask, 'Do any of you know about that calf tied to the tree?' John says, 'Yes, Coach, I traded my second TV—one only needs one TV—to a farmer for the calf, and I want to take it back to Pullman.'

"I explain that United Airlines does not have the ability to carry the calf back to Pullman, nor did we have any other method to so do. So, I call Tom Moore, the meet director, and say, 'Can you pick up this calf that Ngeno traded to a farmer for the TV you gave him for winning the three mile and send it to WSU?' Tom laughs and says,

'Yes.' After talking to Ngeno, I realize that he figured if he could get the calf to Pullman and find a farmer to buy it, he can then take the money back to Kenya and buy himself a few cows with the cash. Rational behavior in a society in which cows are wealth. And just another day in the life of Cougar Track & Field."

The pipeline had been opened. John and Kip Ngeno were just the beginning of a long line of Kenyan and West African runners who would, often with the encouragement of former Olympic athletes and foreign national coaches, find their way to Pullman over the next 20-plus years.

Kipchoge Keino, who had beaten Jim Ryun at 1,500 meters at the 1968 Olympics and led his country's dominance of the long races at those games, alerted Chaplin to Josh Kimeto. Kimeto would come to Pullman and win two NCAA 5,000-meter titles. Ben Jipcho, who sacrificed his chances for a medal to set up Keino's defeat of Ryun, but who also won the silver medal in the steeplechase at the Mexico City Games, alerted Chaplin to Samson Kimombwa.

"In 1974, at a meet at San Jose State, Ben Jipcho tells me about this kid Samson Kimombwa, who was just out of high school and working as a prison guard," Chaplin remembered. "I ask about his time, and Ben says he runs 30:00 flat [for 10,000 meters]." Not bad, but Chaplin was also not overly impressed. "I say that's not real good, and Ben says, 'Yeah, but that was at altitude.'" Then, Jipcho adds that Chaplin would make this Kimombwa kid a world record holder. "I thought he was blowing smoke up my ass," Chaplin said with a laugh.

Ever humble, Chaplin concluded that Jipcho knew more about the potential of Kenyan runners than he did. "So, I scholarship the kid." Two years later, Kimombwa won the 5,000 and the 10,000 at the Pac-8 meet and the 10,000 at the NCAA meet. "And I send him to Europe," Chaplin said, "and what do you know, he breaks [Britain's]

David Bedford's world record of 27:30.80 with a 27:30.47, running negative splits." *More on that later.*

Chaplin added an element to this story: The Kenyans had been instructed to call him after a good race. "They call me in the middle of the night because they know I will be in bed, and they are not about to spend more money on daytime phone calls." Chaplin continued, "Samson calls at 3:00 a.m., and I ask him how he did, and he tells me he won the race. After a little conversation, I say, 'Oh, by the way, what was the time?' Samson says, 'It was 27:30.47,' and I say, 'That breaks Bedford's world record.' And then he says, 'But Coach, you told us all that if we were not the first to run under eight minutes for the steeple, thirteen minutes for the 5,000, or twenty-seven minutes for the 10,000, we would not go down in history as great runners.' My point was that I did not want a kid to think that he just did the greatest thing since the invention of water wings because I wanted him to keep everything in perspective and not make that one race the highlight of his life."

In 1976, Kimeto and John Ngeno were in Canada for the Olympic Games. In a pre-Olympic event, Ngeno beat Lasse Viren of Finland over 5,000 meters. It was Viren, remember, who won both the 5,000 and the 10,000 at the Munich Olympics four years earlier and who would win both the 5,000 and 10,000 for a second time in Montreal, albeit in the absence of Ngeno and the other Kenyans whose country, and twenty-seven other African nations, decided at the last minute to boycott the Games to protest the presence of New Zealand in Montreal. (New Zealand had recently participated in a rugby competition with South Africa, despite that country's apartheid policies.)

"But they call me from Montreal," Chaplin said. "They say, 'Coach, there's a kid here who made the [Kenyan] team as a steeplechaser. Do you want him?' By this time, I'd figured out that any time a good

Kenyan runner tells me about someone from their country, I am on it right now." Of course, he wanted him. That steeplechaser, of course, was Henry Rono, who enrolled at WSU in the fall of 1976, and the rest, as they say, is history.

By 1978, the Kenyan connection to WSU was fully and firmly established. "Henry tells me about Joel Cheruiyot," the coach said. Cheruiyot was one of the other three runners in Rono's 10,000-meter world record race. "Joel had a great career in the 5,000 and the 10,000." Indeed. Cheruiyot ran 13:34.8, which is the WSU track record, and 27:50.3 while at WSU.

In the spring of 1981, "Henry comes into my office and says, 'Coach, I have two good kids for the Cougars.' The two kids were Peter Koech and Richard Tuwei," Chaplin said, already planning ahead. "Peter ran the 800 and the 1,500, and Richard ran the 1,500. And I ask, 'Have either of you ever run the steeplechase?' Tuwei slowly raises his hand and says, 'I tried it once.' I ask about his time, and he says, '9:10, but Coach, it was at Kinjo, Kenya,' and I say, 'Isn't that one of the highest altitude tracks in Kenya?'" Chaplin then informed the incredulous Richard Tuwei that he would continue to run the 1,500, but he would also learn to run the steeplechase. "Peter [Koech] laughs," Chaplin said. "And I say, 'Wipe that smile off your face because you will be running the 1,500 but also the 5,000 and the 10,000."

As a freshman in 1982, Tuwei won the national title in the steeplechase by running 8:18.22. Then in 1983, Richard placed second in both NCAA indoor championships in the 1,000-meter race (2:19.15) and the mile (3:59.67). Koech had three runner-up finishes at the NCAA meet in the 5,000 meters (1982, 1984, and 1985), scored at 10,000 several times, and won the 1984 NCAA indoor two-mile championship and several Pac-10 titles, including 1,500 meters and cross country. Then as a sophomore, he ran 13:09.50 to become the second-fastest man in history at 5,000 meters. Rono had by then run 13:06.2. "Then his senior year, I moved him to the steeplechase," Chaplin said. Koech went on to win the NCAA steeple title in 1985, win a silver medal in the 1988 Olympics, and then in 1989, break Rono's world record.

Koech connected Chaplin with Julius Korir, a Commonwealth Games steeple champion in 1982, who would become the only athlete to win NCAA 5,000 and steeplechase titles. Korir would go on to win the steeplechase at the 1984 Olympic Games in Los Angeles. Chaplin recalled that in the 1984 Olympics, at his press conference, a reporter asked Korir, "Your coach must be overjoyed with your win today?" Julius replied, "I don't think so. I don't even have the steeplechase sophomore record at WSU." This is another example of Chaplin's attempt to have his athletes keep their accomplishments in perspective. Korir had won the steeplechase with the fifth fastest time in history, 8:11.80.

Next came Samuel Kibiri, who would win the NCAA 1,500-meter title and finish second in the steeplechase in 1991. And then, "Kibiri tells me about a kid named Joseph Kapkory," Chaplin said. Kapkory would win two NCAA 3,000-meter titles indoors and one national cross-country title. At the Pac-10 meet in Pullman in 1994, he won the steeplechase, 5,000, and 10,000. Kapkory had a good friend back home, Patrick Muturi. Muturi would place third in the NCAA 10,000 for WSU and set a collegiate freshman record of 2:12.58 for the marathon, the ninth-best time in the world that year.

That was the end of Chaplin's direct connection to Kenya, but he brought James Li to Pullman from China in 1984 as a coach so that Li could work on his master's degree and his Ph.D. After Chaplin retired, Li brought Bernard Lagat to WSU. Lagat has since become one of the sport's all-time greats. At one time, Lagat, who became an American citizen in 2005, was the second fastest miler in history, and his 3:47.28 still ranks as the tenth-best time ever run. He remains the collegiate record holder at 1,500 meters with a time of 3:30.56. He won Olympic silver and bronze medals at 1,500 meters. He was the world indoor 3,000 champion three times. And he is still the only man to win both the 1,500 and the 5,000 at the world championships.

Lagat now coaches distance runners at the University of Arizona. And in an ironic twist of the WSU-Oregon rivalry, he was filmed during an indoor meet in 2022, enthusiastically cheering for two former Oregon athletes as they teamed up in an attempt to break his American indoor record in the mile. He was then photographed with the Oregon kids after their attempt fell just short.

Despite bringing James Li to WSU and giving him a contact in Kenya, Chaplin stakes no claim and takes no credit for Lagat's collegiate and post-collegiate success. But it is clear that Lagat came to Pullman via the road map drawn up by John Chaplin.

CHAPTER 5

CHEMICAL MACHINES

A coach in charge of a well-organized collegiate track & field program needs to consider three primary factors: recruiting, training, and competing. When it comes to training programs, John Chaplin believes there are two types of coaches. "Coaches who believe the system is the solution," he said. "And coaches who understand that humans are chemical machines and that every athlete's system may not be the same during a training session." What Chaplin is getting at is the notion that even at the collegiate level, where virtually every athlete is experienced, fit, and motivated, there is a great deal of variability in what a particular individual can tolerate from one training session to the next.

"For example," he went on, "a certain type of coach puts up a daily schedule and requires each athlete to complete the workout in full, just as it's written." This is *"the system is the solution"* approach, he explained, and then suggested that this approach is often indicative of a program that can attract a large enough number of talented and ambitious athletes. Attrition due to injury, illness, or burnout will be the natural outcome of this rigid and aggressive approach to training. Without recognizing daily individual variability, Chaplin insists, an athlete's progress will be slowed or interrupted. A program like WSU, which relies on a limited number of athletes remaining healthy and available, cannot afford to lose even one athlete for even a short period.

A saner and more effective approach is to devise a training schedule that allows the coach to stop a workout as soon as the athlete is unable to continue at the prescribed intensity. "The problem is that after running, say, three of the five reps that the day's workout requires, an athlete may look tired or stressed." The implication here is that continuing the workout could put the athlete in jeopardy, either mentally or physically. "So, I put up a workout that says three-to-five reps, and then, at any time in the workout, I can tell the athlete that I've seen enough for that day. This is the variable reps training approach."

There is, of course, a sound physiological basis for this approach, and frankly, this methodology has become much more prevalent today than it was during Chaplin's years at WSU. But there is also, according to Chaplin, a psychological component. If the athlete forces themselves to finish a workout or extend it beyond what would be prudent on a certain day, "the kid may feel they are not living up to the coach's standards. Whereas, if the coach stops the workout after three reps and says that he or she has seen all they need to see that day, the athlete is less likely to be stressed or feel like the workout has been a failure."

With the kind of world-class athletes WSU was attracting to Pullman, this notion of training-session variability would be critical and nonnegotiable. It would be unreasonable for the coach to expect a recent high school graduate, no matter how talented or accomplished, to train at the same level of volume and intensity as the likes of Gerry Lindgren, Rick Riley, or…Henry Rono.

"To put it in a nutshell," Chaplin said, "I used max VO2 testing, which is a measure of how efficiently an athlete takes in, to determine how well an athlete metabolizes and uses oxygen." The assumption was that the higher the max VO2 number, the greater an athlete's potential in endurance events and workouts where one must push their anaerobic and aerobic thresholds in training. "I also used fartlek and interval concepts with drills if needed," he went on, "to make the athletes more efficient. Surging drills and learning how to run negative splits in a race are the foundation of the program, coupled with the concept of *quality over quantity* as a basic underlying philosophy of the program." As a final note, and Chaplin emphasized this point again and again during our discussions, "rest was also an important part of the WSU training and racing program."

By the time he was ready to take the reins from Mooberry in the fall of 1973, the success of Lindgren, van Reenen, and Gittins had suggested a model for how John Chaplin would develop the WSU program once he became the head coach. But even now, he wants to make sure people know the program's subsequent success was not the result of happenstance but instead, was based on a carefully considered and executed plan made necessary by a particular set of challenging circumstances.

The presence of Rono and other Kenyans, along with Chaplin's recruitment of other far-better-than-average foreign-born and American athletes to Pullman, is indicative of his response to those circumstances.

Chaplin explained, "As a caveat, a coach needs to know and understand how to find the best event[s] for each athlete and to train him mentally and physically to be able to make changes in his workouts. Or to select events that he may not have considered or had shied away from because those events may have been, in their minds, too hard to try." He went on the explain that the success his athletes had in the steeplechase over the years was at least partially the result of convincing athletes who had an aptitude for the event but might have been reluctant to give it a try.

"An example of a race that can be easily figured out is the 3,000-meter steeplechase," he said. "The ability to turn over your pace [change speed] quickly is paramount. If you tell me what time a kid can run for 800 meters, I will tell you in what range their steeplechase time will fall."

In the intervening years, this notion has become common practice at the collegiate level and is even trickling down to high schools. That is, more coaches have come to recognize that an ambitious kid's potential in a long race is determined to a large degree by how fast they can run in a shorter event.

"Let's say," Chaplin explained, "that a kid runs the 800 in 1:49.0, 54.5 per lap. A steeplechase time of 68 seconds per lap is walking [relatively speaking] for a 1:49 800-meter runner, but 68-second laps equals an 8:30 steeplechase time. Because of the hurdles and water jumps, in a short race of 3,000 meters, a surge strategy is no good. And you can teach almost any athlete to hurdle. In all other distance races, there is no good prediction formula, just trial and error."

This is where the ambition factor in the formula comes into the equation. There is certainly nothing wrong with a 1:49 800-meter time. Not many athletes at the college level can run that fast, but...

"So, you ask your 1:49.0 800 runner, 'Do you want to win a dual meet or place in the Division I Championships?'"

Chaplin made the point that all successful university programs must confront a set of limitations and advantages based on three factors—budget, geography, and tradition. The amount of money a coach has available has an obvious and profound effect on the number and quality of athletes they are able to attract; the financial discrepancy between schools, especially when it came to the number of scholarships available, was much more pronounced in 1974 than it is today, although discrepancies still exist. And, of course, issues like climate and population matter. Bear in mind Chaplin's earlier observation that the population of Los Angeles County is greater than that of the entire state of Washington. And the weather in LA, Austin, or Tallahassee is more conducive to year-round training than winter in Pullman or even Seattle, especially for sprinters, jumpers, and throwers.

I need to make the point here that Chaplin refuses to use WSU's financial or geographical situation as an excuse. He is simply explaining that because of WSU's specific financial and geographical situation, he had to take an approach to attracting, retaining, and developing athletes who, at the time, were unique to WSU and Pullman, Washington. But he also pointed out, correctly, that all successful coaches must figure out how to take advantage of their school's particular set of financial and geographical advantages and how to mitigate their disadvantages.

In Chapter 8, former Stanford University coach Brooks Johnson will make the point that WSU's unique situation and assumed disadvantages, especially the small-town atmosphere and even Pullman's relative isolation, are what makes the school attractive to a certain type of kid, particularly international athletes—many of whom would have come to WSU from remote, agricultural communities themselves. Johnson also makes the point that Stanford's prestige and difficult admissions standards could also be considered recruiting and retention disadvantages that he had to be creative to overcome.

Chaplin noted that he had five thousand dollars for his annual recruiting budget and ten thousand dollars for equipment during most of his tenure at WSU. A consulting contract with Nike and the generosity of the late Jeff Schwartz of UCS and Steve Chappell of UCS Sprint, the track & field equipment manufacturers, allowed him to stretch his university budget. In his role as a technical official with the International Amateur Athletic Federation, the international governing body for track and field at the time, and as the chief of mission for several US junior teams, Chaplin was able to travel globally to see and connect with plenty of talented kids anxious to receive an American education.

"I came to the conclusion," Chaplin explained, "that just because you get the job on Wednesday doesn't mean that you know what you are doing on Thursday. So, you damn well better have a plan. And I decided there were three things that had to be taken into consideration. One, the budget they were going to give you. Two, the plan better fit the climate in the area where you live. And three, you better hit the tradition at your school if there is one."

The financial issue, especially as it pertains to the amount of money WSU was willing to spend on scholarships for track & field, would determine both who Chaplin would recruit and how he would navigate the recruiting process. It was clear he was not going to be able to match the number of high-end domestic athletes at the larger and wealthier schools in the conference, especially those in Southern California or at the University of Oregon. And, despite the success of athletes like Lindgren and Gittins, he could not limit his search for athletes with elite potential to the state of Washington, the Pacific Northwest, or even the United States.

Pullman is the second highest incorporated city in Washington, at 2,339 feet above sea level, and is hard up against the foothills of the Moscow Mountains, just across the border in Idaho. The city is known for long, bitterly cold winters. Wind, rain, and even snow are not unusual in April, nor are spring snowstorms in May. WSU has had an indoor facility since 1931, but when Chaplin took over as head coach, he knew the 200-meter tartan track inside the field house was not ideal for the sort of high-quality training and racing that was taken for granted in the southern half of the conference.

"People probably think I just fell into this situation," Chaplin said. "But no. By the time I became the head track & field coach, after six years as the cross country and assistant track & field coach to Mooberry, I had figured out a plan based on a handful of things." In that handful was the recognition that the training year would have to be adjusted to fit a climate that for six months or more are among the most severe in the entire Pacific Northwest and certainly the most challenging in the conference. "One of the concepts was that I was going to have a limited amount of track time outdoors [because of the weather]," he said. "I have a lot shorter spring season, so I am going to have the eight or ten dual meets to race our athletes into shape and solve the weather problem that way."

But "racing into shape" does not mean running the races and hoping for the best. According to Chaplin, each race, especially those in the first half of the outdoor season, was run with a specific purpose in mind: to practice specific competitive skills and remove tactical weaknesses that might come into play when the championship season came around. "In their four-day mandatory workout schedule," Chaplin explained, "athletes were trained to take away their opponent's preferred style of running. That is to say, if he liked to lead, we would keep him from leading. If he liked to sprint, say, the last 400 meters, we would train to start our sprint with 600 or 700 meters to go."

Chaplin made sure to point out that his philosophy did not apply solely to distance runners. The same principles were used to develop some of the best sprinters and hurdlers for the Pac-10 and NCAA championships. "My program had to consider how to recruit some elite sprinters and hurdlers if we were to beat teams from northern California, Oregon to Washington in dual meets, and therefore my sprinters and hurdlers needed a program for their development," he explained. "But just as in the distance events, quality over quantity was the main ingredient."

But even with all that, it was surging that Chaplin believed was the most effective tactic to use against other college distance runners. "We were at will to surge," he said. "To surge whenever we wanted because very few college runners used surging as a tactic. If an athlete has not trained to surge and you drop a 2:23 kilometer on him, and he responds, the chances are he will go into oxygen debt.

"People often ask why we ran sets of 1,000 meters. This is because, in big meets, there are two running clocks, one at the start and one at the 200-meter mark. Our athletes were timed by the managers at all four corners, and in time they learned how to start surging from any of those points."

Today, I am not sure too many coaches would disagree with the basic set of assumptions Chaplin operated on here, but what I found curious was that he never mentioned "race pace," that element some coaches seem to obsess over when prescribing a specific workout to a group of athletes with various abilities and levels of fitness. Race pace is the ideal pace (usually measured in 400-meter increments) that an athlete will run to achieve a specific time. Ideally, a runner attempting to run a 4:00 mile, for example, would run each lap in 60 seconds.

But from Chaplin's point of view, it's more than likely that an athlete who runs a mile in four minutes will not run even a single lap in exactly 60 seconds. It happens, but it is rare because the dynamics of racing usually don't allow for perfect pacing (even if, from a physiological perspective, that would be the most efficient way to run a specific time). Chaplin made it clear that, except in rare circumstances, as with Rono's world-record attempts, time was not the primary issue anyway. Racing and winning races were paramount. So, in training, athletes would be encouraged (required, really) to work on aspects of their competitive character, racing skills, and tactics that they either did not like or were not particularly good at.

"So, in my workout system," he said, "if you did not like to lead, you led. If you did not like to surge, you got more surging drills. And if you did not like to sprint, you got more sprinting. I made you practice what you didn't do well or did not like to do, not what you already did well."

The emphasis on racing over running for time is common among coaches who manage elite athletes, so this is not a criticism, but I also believe it's the single factor that separates elite athletes from casual fans or recreational runners. Fast times are satisfying and exciting for spectators, but the bottom line for athletes and coaches—from high school to the highest levels of international running—is competition, not time. The time achieved in a particular race often depends on factors the athlete cannot control, like the weather. Records can and will inevitably be broken. But championships are forever. American great Matt Centrowitz Jr. won the Olympic 1,500-meter title in 2016 with the slowest time in more than 80 years, but he is and always will be the Olympic champion. The time was and is irrelevant. Despite Henry Rono's greatness, all his records have been broken (though his last *Track & Field News* collegiate record, 13:06.2 for 5,000 meters, stood until May 6, 2022, when another East African athlete from Somalia—Abdihamid Nur of Northern Arizona University—ran 13:06.32 at San Juan Capistrano, California).

Chaplin believes it is important to explain that *Track & Field News*, the most comprehensive and authoritative track & field publication in the US, and which essentially invented the concept of collegiate records in the first place, changed its criteria for recognizing collegiate records so a record could not be set after the NCAA championships. That was not the case during Rono's career when a collegiate record could be set during the long summer season. If that were in effect today, Nur's automatically timed 13:06.32 would be considered equal to Rono's hand-timed 13:06.2, which Rono ran as a redshirt senior in 1981 but after the NCAA meet. Rono's time was delisted by *Track & Field News* when the magazine changed its criteria, as was Rono's then collegiate 10,000-meter record of 27:22.47. The 7:32.1 for the flat 3,000, also accomplished during the summer, was also delisted. Today, *Track & Field News* will only recognize a collegiate record set in the US through the NCAA Division I meet. So, Rono's time would still be recognized as the fastest time ever run by a collegian, but it is not the collegiate record. The NCAA uses *Track & Field News* to keep track of collegiate records, a fact that I was not aware of.

All of this adds up to an explanation of why Chaplin preferred the smaller field in a dual meet to the massive number of competitors who would be present in an invitational meet with dozens of schools. More opportunities to practice more varied competitive skills for more kids.

"So, then I have to figure out how to use this plan during the dual meet season," he said. "I went to a three-tiered system based on how far a kid is able to go." Any track coach at any level knows that once the regular season ends and the championship or qualifying season begins, track & field teams get smaller at each stage.

The first stage is the dual meet. "Dual meets allow me to have more kids do more things and get more experience," he pointed out. "In the Pac-8/10 in [Chaplin's] time at WSU, athletes had to meet a specific time or distance standard and a squad limit [there were standards for all events except the two relays where each school had a single entry] to participate in the conference championships. There also was wild card entry and a rule that each team had one entry in all events, except the two relays, if that was the only entry. Then, if an athlete qualified for the conference meet, you've reached stage two, and if you get a qualifying mark for the NCAA, you've reached stage three."

Today, there are no hard and fast time or distance qualifying standards to qualify for the NCAA nationals. Entry into the national meet is based on an athlete's performance in either the East or West regional meet. The top 48 athletes—determined by time or distance—in each region compete in what amounts to the first round of qualifying for the national meet. Athletes advance based on their performance in preliminary rounds in field events and preliminary heats in running events. A problem with this format is that qualifying spots are not allotted equally in each event. Only the top twelve of the 48 regional qualifiers in the 5,000 and 10,000 advance out of the regionals because those events are contested as a single final at the national meet. In every other running event, 24 athletes qualify out of the regionals because there will be another round of qualifying at nationals. In the decathlon for men and the pentathlon for women, the athletes with the twelve best scores during the season advance to the NCAA meet, the same qualifying procedure employed for all events at the indoor championships.

The consequence of this system is that during the season, athletes are more or less required to run for a time or jump and throw for a distance that will place them among the top 48 athletes in either the eastern or western halves of the country in order to qualify for the regional. Then, advancing to the national meet is based on placing in the top twelve in the qualifying rounds at regionals, with time or distance a secondary concern.

Of course, a balanced track and field program includes much more than a handful of elite athletes in a select range of events. Some universities have succeeded by focusing on one or two event groups. Gonzaga University, for example, is best known for its perennially powerful basketball program, but track & field at Gonzaga, led by coach Pat Tyson, is an extension of a cross-country program that has, in recent years, established itself as one of the premier programs in a region of the country that includes Washington, WSU, and Oregon. But only dual meets require a balanced team with all the event bases covered—running, jumping, and throwing. The limited number of scholarships allowed—12.6 for men and 18 for women to meet Title IX requirements—is undoubtedly a factor in how particular coaches construct their track & field teams. "So, walk-ons are important," Chaplin said. But even the number of walk-ons (non-scholarship athletes) is strictly limited by the athletic directors who need to balance the numbers to comply with Title IX.

"Now, I have to decide which events I am going to do," Chaplin said, referring to his earlier observation about the type of athletes who would be available in his corner of the country. "I look around the area I live in," he continued, "and I see an area where distance running is good. And the field events are good. And, by the way, some of those were very weak events in the United States at the time. So, I am going to take the triple jump, the hammer, and the javelin." It is worth noting here that track & field teams in most states did not throw the javelin in high school, but the state of Washington did, and with considerable success; Rhode Island is the only state that offers the hammer throw in high school. And thanks in part to Chaplin's efforts during his Wapato High days, Washington was one of the first states in the country to incorporate the triple jump for high school athletes.

Chaplin was quick to credit Rick Sloan, who was Chaplin's associate coach in charge of the field events from 1973 until he replaced Chaplin as head coach in 1994, with the lion's share of the credit. His dedication to teaching fundamentals was second to none. "Rick Sloan usually came at a problem from one end, and I came at it at the other end. But we both knew that the solution was probably in the middle. That way, neither one of us drank the Kool-Aid about the program.

Sloan was especially effective coaching high jumpers, Chaplin explained, "because Rick Sloan liked the high jump." As well he should. In 1967, Sloan became the first UCLA athlete to jump 7-0 when he set a school record of 7-½. He also placed fourth in the NCAA pole vault and sixth in the high jump that year. The following year, Sloan represented the US at the Mexico City Olympics and set a decathlon world record of 6-11 in the high jump.

Eight of the top ten high jump performances in WSU history were achieved during the time Sloan was Chaplin's field event coach. Eventually, Doug Nordquist would jump 7-8¾ and Brent Harken 7-8¼ after college. Chaplin credited their post-collegiate success to lessons learned from Sloan. Harken was a local kid from just up the road in Spokane, and Nordquist was a junior college transfer from southern California. At one time, Nordquist ranked fourth and Harken fifth on the US all-time high jump list.

"Rich Sloan was the best all-around field event coach in the country, in my opinion," Chaplin said. "I want people to know that."

An interesting side note is that in 1972, the year before Sloan arrived at WSU, Cougar athlete Phil Walsh set an NCAA Division I meet record in the decathlon high jump when he cleared 7-0 on his way to placing fourth in the NCAA meet in only his second decathlon competition; he was coached by Chaplin.

"I recruited Phil from a junior college as a long jumper, high Jumper and high hurdler,' Chaplin explained. "But he bruises his heal in the triple jump, so I tell Coach Mooberry that I will make him a decathlete. What do you know he ends up an All-American in only his second decathlon competition."

Back to the running events. Chaplin continued, "I am going to take the 5,000, the 10,000, and the steeplechase, and those athletes would go all the way through to the NCAA level."

To make sure the Cougars were competitive team-wise in those dual meets, Chaplin indicated he'd search far and wide for at least one high-end competitor in the sprints, hurdles, and jumps to round out his squad. WSU sprint, hurdle, and jump stars have come from as nearby as Seattle (Lee Gordon), Tacoma (Kris Durr), and Spokane (Anthony Buchanan and Brent Harken), along with Jody Page, Jeff Bruce, and other in-state hurdlers, and from as far away as West Africa (Gabriel Tiacoh, George Kablan, Joseph Taiwo, and Augustine Olobia), Australia (Michael Joubert), Spain (Javier Moracho), and China (Tony Li) as a *stopper*," he explained. A "stopper" in an athlete who can place at least first or second against the other dual meet powers on WSU's schedule. "Remember, the dual meets count. And after that, I am going to take the best athlete I can get."

Again, geography and finances rear their inconvenient and unattractive heads. "There is no way, given my geographical area and a limited travel budget, I can take 25 to 45 guys to the Modesto Relays or 45 guys to the Mt. Sac Relays in California," he said. "So, I had to run dual meets so I can develop young kids from the state of Washington. I can redshirt them for a year because tuition was affordable in those days. I could develop kids in the intermediate hurdles. For example, eight of the top ten athletes on the WSU 400-meter hurdles list are Washington kids, and all six were Division I All-Americans in the event. So, I didn't have to recruit intermediate hurdlers outside of Washington."

Chaplin pointed out that track and field is still a numbers game. It takes a certain number of athletes to cover the seventeen individual events on the dual-meet program, plus the two relays. The 10,000 and the decathlon are only contested the conference and national championships. In an era of limited scholarships—12.6 for men's Division 1 track & field—a coach must get creative in order to fill out his team. That is, if dual meets matter. But the problem, according to Chaplin, is that in the current climate, dual meets are rare or even unknown in most programs, so there is little incentive for coaches to fill out their teams with walk-ons or with athletes who may require some time to develop, although some still do. In short, more and more, dual meets simply do not matter since most athletic directors don't demand head-to-head dual meet competition from their coaches. But many top schools do want them to win conference and/or national titles where teams are scored. American fans want a final score. Somebody needs to win.

One area of confusion for casual fans is the way track and field meets are scored, especially dual meets. In a dual track meet, whether at the high school, collegiate, or international level (dual meets between nations were once a regular fixture on the summer track & field schedule), each event is worth nine points: five points for first place, three points for second, and one point for third. Relays are generally scored 5-0. There are 167 points available in a typical college dual meet, so when one team has accumulated 84 points the winner is determined.

"If I hadn't had a dual meet system," Chaplin said, "I'd be down to twelve or thirteen people on the track team. Plus, I was only allowed by the athletic department to travel to meets in Oregon, Washington, Idaho, and rarely, California, Utah, and Montana. Plus, Arizona, but just a few times." Chaplin noted that dual meets today are all but non-existent, but he is convinced "they are coming back." The University of Washington-WSU dual meet rivalry that Chaplin's teams dominated for more than two decades is still a significant fixture for both schools, but these days, it's unusual for either the Huskies or the Cougars to have any other dual meets on their schedule. And there were only five other dual meets in the Pac-12 during the 2022 season: USC vs. California, UCLA vs. USC, Stanford vs. the University of California, and ASU vs. Arizona. And all are local rivalries similar to WSU vs. Washington. Washington and WSU have met in a dual meet 101 times since 1901, making *The Dual* one of the oldest and most consistently contested dual meets in NCAA history.

But, as Chaplin pointed out, other natural dual meet rivalries have all but disappeared from the collegiate schedule. Prior to the 2022 season, he noted, neither the University of California nor USC had competed in a dual meet against each other in 40 years, despite the presence of nearby conference rivals Stanford and UCLA. Chaplin clearly believes the renewal of these rivalries would go a long way in creating interest in the sport among casual fans, especially those tuned into the Pac-12 Network.

Today, most college track & field schedules consist of a string of large invitational meets involving dozens of schools. Chaplin implied that while he has no quarrel with large invitational meets, track races in those meets inevitably turn into an exercise in pursuing personal best times and distances because winning or even placing high is out of reach for most athletes, even in elite programs. He insisted that what athletes in the running events learn in those circumstances is how to run fast times, but not necessarily how to compete effectively against other elite athletes.

Such is not the case in dual meets. The final score is the object and winning or losing is often determined by the performance of athletes down the depth chart. It is that shift in emphasis to make track & field more of a team sport and the fact that "Americans want to know the final score" that leads Chaplin to believe dual meets may become a more common fixture in collegiate track & field.

His reason? Television.

Every major conference now has its own television network or streaming service. Their primary purpose is to expand the audience for high-visibility sports like football and basketball, but the Pac-12 Network and others cannot broadcast football and basketball twenty-four hours a day. They need other content, content that appeals to the niche audiences attracted to so-called minor or non-revenue sports, to fill the void.

"TV needs more content," he said. "And you're paying some track & field coach $750,000, you're going to run some dual meets that they can put on TV." Even the most diehard track & field fans are not likely to sit through a televised invitational meet that lasts four, five, or six hours, and the casual fan, as Chaplin correctly suggested, is going to be less likely to be interested in any sporting event in which there is no winning or losing team determined at the end. But a dual meet in which the running events and the field events can be concluded in a couple of hours and in which there is a winning and losing team will appeal to a wider potential audience.

There are those in the broader track & field community—coaches, journalists, and the most enthusiastic fans—who fear for the future of track & field, especially at the college level. But despite the recent administrative execution of a handful of men's track & field and cross-country programs, Chaplin believes financial realities, the money generated by enormous contracts for the rights to broadcast football and basketball, will only enhance the viability of track & field and other non-revenue sports if or when several big conferences leave the NCAA for a larger slice of the monitory pie.

For one thing, he explained, today's athletic departments that must maintain a certain number of men's and women's sports to be eligible to compete at the NCAA Division I level currently get a three-for-one from their track & field and cross-country programs. Indoor track & field, outdoor track & field, and cross country are one program for budgeting purposes but count as three separate sports that contribute to meeting NCAA rules. The fate of sports other than football and basketball, if we end up with three or four super conferences, is now in doubt.

Chaplin said, "Thunder clapped on June 30, 2022, when USC and UCLA bolted [from] the Pac-12 conference to join the Big 10. The experts say this will undoubtedly lead to a race to join maybe four super conferences. The Pac-12 is left with ten members for now, and the Big 12, with its current eight members, will have to join forces in some manner, or their conferences will be in monetary trouble."

And, of course, Chaplin, like all experienced observers of the NCAA's financial and competitive situation, noted that this development is not limited to the Pac-12. "These other so-called *observers* wonder what will happen to the four universities seeking membership in the Big 12," Chaplin said. "They speculate that one of the two conferences [Pac-12 or Big 12] might well disappear as a power conference." But the inevitable outcome, Chaplin continued, "could be that the NCAA might lose control of collegiate football and basketball altogether." But then he went on to suggest that the NCAA Division I conference commissioners' recent vote to expand the Division I football playoffs to twelve teams in 2024 just might save the day. The champion of the six highest-ranked conferences will qualify for the playoffs automatically, with the next six highest ranked teams filling out the twelve-team field.

"The question still remains, who will control the makeup of national championships for baseball, softball, track & field, and the other sports if the current makeup of all NCAA Division I championships is in doubt?" he wondered. "And will the monies that the NCAA gets to support non-revenue sports be severely diminished if the super conferences also gobble up the TV revenue from basketball?"

Chaplin believes there is a genuine danger that the NCAA as a governing body and regulatory agency may cease to exist altogether. If that happens—because of the NCAA's increasing reliance on television and streaming revenue—the fate of non-revenue sports in the major college conferences will be in jeopardy. "Will the NCAA go the way of the ICAAAA like the passenger pigeon? As the man says, only time will tell"!

And the bottom line for Chaplin is that serious fans of niche sports—like tennis, swimming, gymnastics, soccer, and yes, track & field—are turning to the Pac-12 Network, ACC Network, Big Ten Network, and the SEC Network, which are all discovering a latent interest in other sports. The Big 12 conference has a deal with

ESPN but not yet a full network like the other four conferences. And the University of Texas, which is leaving the Big 12 for the Southeast Conference, has a network of its own.

"Those two guys on the ACC Network, Packer and Durham," Chaplin said, "they used to talk about every kid in every sport and have them on their show, now called *ACC PM*. They're selling the conference's whole program. People are coming out to see the games, and interest [in all the non-revenue sports] is rising. If you go to a soccer, volleyball, lacrosse, or women's basketball game today, there's a decent crowd. Ten years ago, there was nobody."

Chaplin insists that *the* primary reason for that increase in interest is possible because each soccer, volleyball, lacrosse, and basketball game ends with a final score. He is convinced that if track & field adopts a similar model—that is, if coaches schedule more dual meets in which the purpose is to determine a winner and a loser—interest in the sport will experience a similar rise.

Of course, as is the case with any successful high school, collegiate, or professional programs in any sport, there was much more to Chaplin's system than strategic scheduling and recruiting and developing young athletes into high-end competitors. He also had a plan for what happened on the track as WSU athletes raced for conference or NCAA titles, a plan that aligned perfectly with his belief that track & field would be more attractive to general sports fans if there were a more significant and better-promoted team aspect.

His team approach extended beyond the idea of scheduling more dual meets into the very nature of competition in general. On three separate occasions—in 1976, 1977, and 1984—WSU swept the top two or three places in the 5,000 meters at the NCAA championships. And on six occasions between 1973 and 1994, Cougar runners placed three athletes in the top five at 5,000 meters, 10,000 meters, or the steeplechase in the Pac-8, -10, or -12 championships, including sweeping the top three places three times. The dominance of this sort in the running events at the NCAA meet was unheard of prior to 1976, when Josh Kimeto, John Ngeno, and Samson Kimombwa, all among the first class of Kenyans at WSU, pulled off a one-two-three sweep that year. In fact, Chaplin considers that performance to be indicative of the team-running philosophy that would characterize WSU's distance racing strategy for the next two decades.

One of the complicating aspects of distance running at the NCAA meet in those days was that athletes had to successfully negotiate a qualifying round in the 5,000 or the steeplechase on Thursday before contesting the 10,000-meter final the next day and then run the 5,000-meter or steeplechase final on Saturday. A preliminary round in the 5,000 and the steeplechase is common practice at major international track & field meets like the Olympic Games and world championships, but those events are usually contested over ten days, whereas the NCAA meet was generally contested over just three days. That means athletes who entered in the 5,000 *and* in the 10,000 had to race three times in little more than 48 hours. So, Chaplin noted, the object was to get all three WSU athletes through the 5,000 heats safely while conserving as much energy as possible for the 10,000 final, which would be contested the next day, and setting the stage for team success in the 5,000 final. Today, the NCAA meet is contested over four days, with the men and the women competing on alternate days.

Fortunately, NCAA rules at the time required that athletes from the same school not be entered in the preliminary round to race against each other. This allowed WSU's Kenyans to control what happened in each of their qualifying heats. To that end, Chaplin explained, each athlete—Kimeto, Ngeno, and Kimombwa—had specific instructions on how they were to race the preliminary round with the goal of qualifying for the final while saving as much energy as possible for the 10,000. Bear in mind that these were not ordinary college athletes. Had their country not boycotted the 1976 Olympics, Ngeno and Kimeto would have represented Kenya at the Montreal Games. Both were in Montreal preparing when the Kenyan boycott was announced at the last minute. It was also at that time that Ngeno called Chaplin to ask if he was interested in an up-and-coming steeplechaser named Henry Rono, who was also in Montreal for the Games. Additionally, Kimombwa would set the world record for 10,000 meters in 1977, and Kimeto was on the cusp of winning the first of his two NCAA 5,000-meter titles.

Ngeno was up first in Heat 1 of the 5,000-meter prelim. "He was told to run 63-65 laps," Chaplin said. "That's a 4:15 mile, and then back off to finish third, which he did in 14:01.0 to qualify comfortably. The top three finishers in each heat qualified automatically for the final, with the field to be filled out by the runners with the next three fastest times. That meant that athletes had to run fast enough to be in the top three but not so fast that they exhausted themselves for the 10,000 the next day. It's a delicate balancing act.

Next up was Kimombwa in Heat 2. "He is told to stay with the pack and finish at least third but no lower than fourth," Chaplin said. "But he might have to run under fourteen minutes." Which he does, to place fourth in 13:57.0.

Finally, Kimeto, who was only entered in the 5,000, was in the third heat. "I tell Josh I want a time of about 13:40.10," Chaplin said. His intention in having Kimeto run faster than the other two was to gain some measure of control of the 5,000 final. More on Chaplin's rationale is covered below. Kimeto won his heat in 13:41.02, and the stage was set with three WSU athletes in the 5,000-meter final. But first, the Cougars need to take care of business in the 10,000.

Ngeno and Kimombwa were heavily favored to go one-two in the 10,000. Ngeno did win the race in a meet record of 28:22.10, but Samson's chances were derailed when he was bumped off the track and sprains his back, apparently eliminating him from the 5,000 final the next day.

"Friday night [after the 10,000], all three athletes come down to my room," Chaplin said. "They tell me, 'Coach, we have to get Samson a medal [in the 5,000].' I say, 'Get a medal? Hell. He can barely walk.' But Joshua and John say, 'Coach, we know you can figure out a way to get Samson a medal.'" So, Chaplin sent John Ngeno to get the WSU trainer.

"I tell him I hope you have no plans for tonight," Chaplin said. "And he asks what I want him to do." The coach suggested an all-night regime of hot- and cold-water baths. The trainer told Chaplin that such a regime was not likely to hurt Kimombwa any more than he already was, "as long as he is honest with me if he can't continue." During the night, Kimombwa got to the point of being able to jog for 30 minutes, and after two or three hours of sleep and a 45-minute jog shortly before the 5,000 final, he was ready to attempt the race.

"Just before the 5,000 final," Chaplin remembered, "I say to all three, 'This is how it has to go down if we are going to pull this off.' I say to Josh, 'after that 13:41 Thursday, there is nobody in this field who will try to take the lead from you.'" This is why Chaplin wanted Kimeto to run a faster prelim, to make anyone in the rest of the field reluctant to take the lead in the final. "'So, I want you to go to the front and run sixty-eight, sixty-eight, sixty-eight, sixty-eight.'" But that was a pace that would result in a time over fourteen minutes and one that no one in the field would have any trouble maintaining for the entire distance.

"Then I tell him to drop a sub 4:20 [mile, four laps a little under in sixty-five], and if no one follows, maybe we can get away with this." Kimeto ran six consecutive laps under sixty-five seconds. That's a mile and a half at around 6:25.

Chaplin was operating on the assumption that because of the way his runners had been trained and because of the unique mindset that the Kenyans brought to their racing, the three WSU athletes were very likely the only guys in the race who could handle a twelve-to-fifteen-second surge inserted into the middle of a championship 5,000-meter race. But he was cautious as well. "If Samson can't keep up," he told Kimeto and Ngeno, "You guys will have to leave him."

But when Kimeto and Ngeno surged after six laps, Kimombwa did keep up, and "with two laps to go, the rest of the field made a run at us," the coach said. "But it was too late." Kimeto won in 13:47.6, and Ngeno finished second at 13:55.60, pulling Kimombwa, at 13:56.40, along in third place. Only the three WSU athletes were under 14:00 flat. Fourth place was four seconds back at the finish. Not only did Kimombwa have his medal, but this was the first time any school had placed first, second, and third in a running event at the NCAA national championship meet.

According to Chaplin, Kimeto was the *primary* runner in that race, suggesting it was no accident that he won. The very notion of "team racing" implies that a team goal takes precedence over individual accolades or accomplishments. This is anathema to the individualistic nature of track & field, which is generally (and increasingly) thought of in terms of a single athlete battling on their own against other single athletes, each waging a singular internal battle against the physical and psychological challenges inherent to hard, one-on-one racing.

This is especially true for the longer running events. Even with a group of athletes as talented as Kimeto, Ngeno, and Kimombwa, there can be only one winner. And given the depth of talent that was emerging at the NCAA level at the time, there was no guarantee that any of those three would be able to win either the 5,000 or the 10,000 simply by showing up. But in Chaplin's mind, the chances of any one of the three winning would be enhanced if the trio worked as a team by executing a plan intended to get the primary athlete across the finish line first.

The primary was the intended winner, in Chaplin's system. It was the responsibility of the other runners—secondary runners—to manage the race in such a way as to give the primary the best chance to win and for them to still pick up points. "Until the last 600 meters," he said. "Then all bets are off if there are other competitors still in the lead pack." In the final stages of a race, in other words, if the primary was vulnerable, the secondaries would pounce, especially if an athlete from another team was in a position to exploit a faltering primary. "We use a race strategy that exploits the weaknesses of our opponents by putting them in a position during the race that limits their tactical choices." It was the job of the secondary runners, then, to apply tactical pressure at predetermined and crucial 1,000-meter surges to upset the race plans of other prominent competitors.

This tactic did not necessarily originate with WSU's Kenyans, but it was almost certainly an innovation pioneered by Kenyan athletes, most significantly in the 1,500-meter race at the 1968 Olympics. That race was billed as a showdown between the American world record holder Jim Ryun and Kenya's tough and versatile Kip Keino, but the major factor in the race would be Mexico City's 7,349-foot elevation. In the thin air, the altitude-born and bred Kenyans would have a distinct (and scientifically based) advantage over the Americans.

When the 1,500-meter final began, Ben Jipcho of Kenya went directly to the front and led the pack through a lung-searing 55.98 first lap, sacrificing his own chances to win a medal in the process. Ryun was in last place for much of that first lap and was still in eighth place, with Keino far in front with a lap and a half left to run. Ryun launched a furious kick in the final 300 meters, but by that time, Keino was simply too far ahead to be caught. Ryun passed three athletes in that final 300 to earn a silver medal and almost immediately came under severe criticism by an uninformed press for carelessly succumbing to the Kenyans' tactics. The argument was that he should have gone with Keino and Jipcho from the start. The problem with that, of course, was had he done so, the lack of oxygen at that altitude would have put him in a very vulnerable oxygen-debt situation late in the race. The Kenyans knew this. It was Jipcho's job—as the secondary—to make the first lap so fast that Ryun would either run himself out early or be forced to make a Herculean run late. Either way, by sacrificing his own medal chances, Jipcho put Ryun in a very difficult position while putting his teammate in the best position to win the race. Despite his greatness, Ryun was at a physiological disadvantage in Mexico City's high-altitude environment, and the Kenyans teamed up to exploit this disadvantage.

By 1968, Ryun had the best finishing speed of any middle-distance athlete in history. The problem for the other 1,500-meter runners was that under normal conditions, no one could push the pace hard enough to take the sting out of his finishing kick. But the Mexico City Olympics were not contested under normal circumstances.

What Chaplin did was to codify and make specific a training plan that combined both aerobic and anaerobic elements that would reinforce the skills and abilities that would allow his athletes to race according to his preferred strategy—that is, to be able to disrupt the opposition's race plan. "One needs both aerobic and anaerobic workouts to maximize efficient racing," he said. "Our runners pushed their aerobic threshold on Monday and Wednesday during their longer runs and worked on their anaerobic threshold during Tuesday and Thursday afternoon sessions on the track," Chaplin explained, adding that his intention was for his runners to push those thresholds progressively throughout the season. "First of all, the program I devised," Chaplin said, "is about quality over quantity. I see no reason for an athlete to beat himself to death running multiple interval sets on the track. Every time you step on the track, you increase the chance of injury."

At the time, not everyone was buying Chaplin's insistence that his athletes were not running the same level of high milage as other world or national-class athletes. "The Kenyan kids would be asked [by a reporter] how much they run," he said, "and they would tell the truth." He implied here that telling the truth was a serious cultural value among the Kenyan athletes. "And the guy says, 'Oh, come on.'" People making inquiries about the Kenyans' training volume simply did not believe it when the athletes told the truth, citing mileage totals lower than others expected. "So, I tell the kids, 'Since they basically don't believe you anyway, tell them you're running 290 miles a week.'"

An in-depth description of Chaplin's training methodology is included in the appendix.

"There are three main types of race strategies that a good distance runner can use," Chaplin explained. "Taking the lead at the start and running a pace the competition cannot stay with. Surging during the race. That is dropping the pace for a prescribed portion of the race [surging], usually 800 for women and 1,000 meters for men, then returning to the original race pace. And finally, waiting to the end of the race and then outsprinting the competition with a better kick over a longer distance.

"We did not use the strategy of waiting until the end of the race and then simply outsprinting the competition with a better kick."

Chaplin did not cite the Mexico City 1,500 specifically, but it's clear that his philosophy of racing was to have his athletes disrupt what other runners would have considered normal circumstances.

"As a rule," he said, "if the athlete you are running against has real talent, you cannot shake them by running a steady pace, no matter how fast your run." Notice here that Chaplin acknowledged that certain athletes are so good that his athletes needed to employ drastic measures to disrupt their race plan (Steve Ovett, in his race against Rono, for example). "This is because you cannot put enough stress on very good runners to put them in oxygen debt. It takes a surge of at least 1,000 meters, often repeated several times, to break good runners in a 5,000- or 10,000-meter race. If it can be done at all in that particular race."

Thus, it is the job of the secondary runner or runners to wreak havoc with a talented opponent's race plan by creating an abnormal racing circumstance, even at the cost of their own success, to give the primary runner the best shot at winning.

"The ability to cope with surge running was the main tactical problem most distance runners faced," he said. "Surging is more mental than physical." Chaplin went on to suggest that the reason surging was so effective was because American athletes at the time did not train for it. It was Chaplin's intention to train his athletes to be able to make racing as uncomfortable as possible for the opposition. "We never let a less talented runner stay in the race until the final sprint," he said. "That will increase your chances of losing. This is their big chance, and they will probably make the most of it."

To execute surging in a race, athletes have to practice it. But, as we saw early on in this chapter, Chaplin was aware of the dangers of overtraining, and he knew that surge training was extremely demanding. "So, we never run more than five times 1,000 meters in practice," he said, adding that it was not uncommon for him to have an athlete cut a workout short rather run the risk of injury or illness brought about by overtraining.

"Quality over quantity," he insisted. As soon as an athlete was unable to complete the prescribed distance at the prescribed speed, the session was terminated. "To do this, we'd start with three times 1,000 meters at the beginning of the season, and by the end of the season, we'd be running five times 1,000 at a world record pace. All the time decreasing the rest period between 1,000s." (See the appendix for more detailed information on Chaplin's training philosophy.)

To complicate matters for his runners, the surging drills would often be done in the afternoon after the Cougar athletes had run the Snake River Canyon in the morning. "So, they are running surging drills when they are a little tired," he said, "which will be just like they feel at the end of a race." WSU used this type of training for every distance above 1,500 meters with the exception of the 3,000-meter steeplechase, which is too short to use surging effectively.

This brings us back to where Chaplin started: The purpose of training, beyond simply conditioning his athletes to run fast for a long time, is to eliminate deficiencies to make things as uncomfortable as possible for their opponents. So, in training, "if you don't like to lead, you lead. If you can't surge, you surge. If you can't sprint, you get more sprint work. What you do on the off days is your business as long as you're not trying to be the kid who runs the most mileage every week." In Chaplin's system, "all this is coupled with the idea that we do almost nothing in practice that does not have a direct connection to our racing philosophy. There is no place for an individual that thinks he needs to make the one-thousand-mile club."

Finally, Chaplin noted that in certain circumstances, even world-class athletes need to be allowed to do something the coach is certain will fail. "So, you can get back to a relationship in which the coach and the athlete are on the same page," he said.

"We had scheduled meet with Oregon, and John Ngeno comes to my office and says, 'Coach, it's a hard trip to Eugene, and I have to run [three miles] against Paul Geis.' Then I ask, 'How are you going to beat him?'" He says, 'I will just run 8:30 for the first two miles, and he will be gone.' Then I say, 'Okay, John, I will send you to Eugene on the plane, but if you lose, you ride back with us on the bus."

The outcome, according to Chaplin, was predictable. Geis followed along, biding his time, and then sprinted past Ngeno in the last 300 meters. Ngeno was scheduled to run the 10,000 on Friday at the Pac-8 championships and then take on a fresh Paul Geis in a rematch of their Eugene race the next day. "I say to John," Chaplin said, "okay, that race in Eugene did not go the way you thought it would, so let's try it my way this time.'"

Chaplin's plan was simple, practical, and based on what he saw the last time Ngeno raced Geis, who was the 1974 NCAA three-mile champion, a future Olympian, an athlete Chaplin and Ngeno held in high regard, and who had proven he could beat Ngeno under the right circumstances.

"I told John, 'Here is what you are going to do. You will wear your flats in the six-mile because no one will be near you, and when you finish, jog over to Paul and ask him to go for a jog with you. Then, in the three-mile, you will run sixty-four seconds per lap and then drop a 4:10-mile surge on him.'" Ngeno won the race in 13:16.0, with Geis seventeen seconds back. "The point is," Chaplin said, "to let an athlete try something that you know will not work to get them back into a listening mode."

And for the record, Ngeno did return to Pullman on the bus with the rest of the team.

CHAPTER 6

ENGLISH LESSONS

At about the time John Chaplin became the head coach at WSU, Phil English was a young athlete in Ireland, talented enough and improving fast enough to contemplate traveling to the US so he could run collegiately and study exercise science. In the years since, after a WSU career spent trying to run down the likes of John Ngeno, Josh Kimeto, Samson Kimombwa, and Henry Rono, English has combined the lessons he learned observing the great Kenyan athletes and studying in the classrooms and laboratories at WSU to become one of the most successful and highly regarded high school track & field and cross-country coaches in the state of Washington. And, like Chaplin at the college level, English has become an important figure in the growth and development of high school distance running, generally and more specifically, cross country in Washington. And as we'll see with other former WSU athletes, English's academic and social experience at WSU under

Chaplin's direction and inspiration were just as important, if not more so, than his own athletic experience.

"It's the early seventies," English explained, the cheerful lilt of his Irish homeland still evident even after living in the US over forty years, "we had kids coming back [to Ireland] from US colleges. Like Donie Walsh [and] John Hartnett out of Villanova. Like Eamonn Coghlan [once the world indoor record holder in the mile at 3:49.78], who was a couple of years older than me."

By the time he was finishing up high school in Ireland, English was considering how to follow the trail blazed by the likes of Walsh, Hartnett, and Coughlin, so naturally, the first school that came to mind was Villanova.

"A pipeline had already been built since the 1950s," English said. "And Villanova was the school the Irish knew most about because of Jumbo Elliott. But in the sixties and seventies, athletes [from Ireland] were spreading out to various schools across the country." Like the University of Arkansas. "John McDonnell [the long-time coach at Arkansas] was an Irish guy, and he'd begun to recruit in Ireland. Also, Providence College in Rhode Island was successfully recruiting Irish runners like John and Ray Treacy."

English then hinted at a couple of issues that will become important later. First, Irish distance runners had been racing and succeeding at the highest levels of collegiate track & field at schools like Villanova for years before John Chaplin arrived at WSU. Second, no one objected (at least, not loudly) or suggested that the presence of Irish kids on American campuses was unfairly denying American kids the opportunity for an athletic scholarship. Those objections would come later and apply to both Chaplin and to athletes from a much different part of the world.

Despite what was clearly a trend at places like eastern Tennessee and Villanova and later at Arkansas (and despite English's interest in pursuing an American education), WSU was not high on his list of options. Actually, he later admitted, he was not even aware that such a place as WSU existed.

"My great interest was in [the new and emerging field of] exercise science," English explained. "John Hartnett, who had run at Villanova and who had younger brothers that I knew very well, was a teammate of [WSU athlete] Dan Murphy in their junior days." Murphy had somehow found his way to WSU from Ireland, and Hartnett told English about the little-known school where Murphy was an athlete. He also told English about developing a world-class exercise science program under the direction of Dr. Phil Gollnick.

English explained that because of the type of athletes Villanova was recruiting at the time, he never did think he would be a good fit there. "I was a true distance runner. And they wanted milers, like Eamonn Coghlan."

From that realization, English's road took a sudden turn toward WSU, as would be the case with many athletes who ended up running for the Cougars under John Chaplin. English did not seriously consider WSU until "Hartnett contacted Dan Murphy [who had been third in the 1971 NCAA cross-country meet for WSU], and before I knew it, John Chaplin contacted me on August 14, 1973."

Some people make the erroneous assumption that Chaplin's pursuit of international athletes was a long, convoluted process of discovering some monumental talent hidden away somewhere in a remote part of the world. Then some sort of semi-shady backdoor deal got made. Or maybe there was an exotic journey to a far-flung location and a difficult (because of an assumed language barrier) sales pitch to get a super talented and budding superstar to commit to coming to an equally far-flung corner of the United States to compete for WSU before returning to the (assumed) primitive homeland (e.g., the reporter's query of whether Henry Rono could read and write).

Ireland is not Kenya, and Phil English, though undoubtedly capable, was not Henry Rono. However, the recruiting process was not unlike that which Chaplin used to get other international athletes to sign on to the WSU program.

"When John Chaplin contacted me, I didn't know there was a Washington State University. I honestly didn't," English explained. "A phone call was arranged, but we didn't have a phone at the time." English said he recalled taking Chaplin's call at the home of the chairman of his local running club, St. Anthony's A.C. "We talked for about forty-five seconds. That was mid-August of 1973, and I remember going home after that phone call and saying to my parents, 'I guess I'm going to Washington State University.' My parents never did understand that I wasn't going to attend a university right next to the president of the United States. The fact that New York would only be halfway to Washington State from Ireland was something they never understood."

As you might expect, long-distance phone conversations with kids half a world away were becoming commonplace for Chaplin. Of course, this was years and years before cell phones and at a time when many households in other parts of the world did not have a phone at all.

"Sean O'Riordan was an uncle of Dan Murphy, working in Dublin as a reporter," Chaplin said. "He had been a track athlete for Idaho State University, and he called me." Riordan told Chaplin about a talented young runner, Dan Murphy, who might be interested in coming to WSU.

Of course, Chaplin was interested. He secured Murphy's address and sent a telegram informing young Mr. Murphy that an admissions application would be forthcoming. "And I wanted a phone number to call him," Chaplin continued. "After I received his transcripts and the admission application, I sent an additional telegram telling him that his transcripts had been accepted, and a letter of intent was on its way."

But then a month went by, and Chaplin did not hear from Murphy, and no letter of intent had been returned. Chaplin needed to speak with his latest recruit, but making an international phone call in those days was a bit more complicated than it is today. "So, I get on the waiting list for an overseas call through White Plains, New York," he said. "Five hours later, the call goes through, and I ask to speak to Dan Murphy, and [say] my name is Coach John Chaplin from WSU. The lady on the phone says, 'Ah, you mean young Murphy. Just a minute."

Twenty minutes passed before Dan Murphy got on the phone. Chaplin picked up the story. "I say, 'And did you get the letter of intent?' and he says, 'Yep.' Are you going to become a Cougar and send it to me?' And he says, 'Yep.' 'Is there anything else you need to know?' He says, 'Nope.' That phone call with two *yeps* and a *nope* cost me $162."

Chaplin found out later that Murphy, like most people in Ireland at the time, did not have access to a phone at home, and that he was speaking to his future coach from the local pub.

This is a good place to point out some of the more subtle cultural difficulties international athletes who came to WSU had to face. The first problem was simply getting to Pullman. An athlete traveling from outside the US had basically two ways to get there (and the basics of traveling to Pullman haven't changed much in the intervening 50-plus years).

In the 1970s, most international travelers probably flew on a major international airline to Seattle and then got on a commuter airline for a bumpy 45-minute flight all the way across the state to the Pullman-Moscow Regional Airport, which even today has but a single runway and is literally in the middle of an endless expanse of wheat with few other apparent signs of civilization in sight. The only commuter air service to Pullman-Moscow at the time was Cascade Airways, known uncomfortably and with some cause in the region as "Crashcade" Air. The other most common route to Pullman for international travelers is the one English took after he finally located Pullman on a map.

"I knew about Oregon, and I knew about California," he said. "I knew the rough geography of the US. So, I start over on the East Coast, and I'm asking myself, 'Where is this Washington State place.' I'm going up and down on the map like a snake, and all of a sudden, it's in the last possible spot. In a remote corner of the most remote of the forty-eight contiguous states." English was lucky because, in those days, Pullman did not appear at all on some maps.

He began his odyssey from Shannon in Ireland and flew to Montreal, where he got on a flight to Calgary, Alberta. Then he got on a smaller plane from Calgary to Spokane, the only significant metropolitan area in Eastern Washington, and finally, a bus trip 80 miles south to Pullman.

Then came the next culture shock.

"I took a bus from Spokane to Pullman—a Greyhound." English laughed at the memory. "But I think they must be transporting greyhounds [racing dogs] because where I come from, greyhound racing is a common sport. So, I'm getting on this bus, and I say, where are the greyhounds? I want to see them. Aren't you transporting greyhounds?' I was disappointed there were no greyhounds on the bus."

The assumptions that underlie the greyhound incident, innocent as it appears, underscore a more serious fact of life for international athletes on WSU's campus. Imagine what kind of 18-year-old American kid it would take to travel unaccompanied to a foreign country (in English's case, through a *second* foreign country) in a distant part of the world and set up housekeeping on a university campus that was almost impossible to find on a map—clearly not an undertaking that the average contemporary adolescent would be comfortable with.

The implication? Kids like the 18-year-old Phil English, or especially athletes coming from places where the local culture was even more foreign than English's Irish homeland, were not average kids. They came to Pullman with a common set of ambitions and extremely high expectations.

The saving grace for English and other recent international arrivals?

"The [cross country] team was competitive from the word go," English said. The fact of a shared purpose, a shared challenge, and a shared set of difficult obstacles seem to have had a unifying and steadying effect on the athletes who came to WSU from such far-flung locations as Ireland and the Great Rift Valley (or from Seattle, Tacoma, or Spokane, for that matter).

In the midst of talking about the initial disappointment of discovering there would be no greyhounds on the Greyhound bus and that he later had no clue about the content of a class called Communications 101 in which he was expected to know the difference between a US senator and a senator in ancient Rome, English shifted gears seamlessly, as if doing so was an integral part of the assimilation process of talking about the 1973 WSU cross-country team.

"To be honest with you," he said, "I had no idea how we qualified for the NCAA meet." That surprised me. Ask any athlete on a competent collegiate team today and they will know precisely what must be done to earn a place at the starting line of the national championships. But English didn't think about it. "I just knew that we'd be at the NCAAs."

English did not say exactly when that realization hit him, but it must have been early. Imagine the new Irish kid's first day of training or the first time he perused the cross-country roster. Whenever our conversations veered into anything having to do with the history of WSU track & field during Chaplin's tenure, he all but insisted that the story of the athletes who passed through the program—regardless of whether they were foreign or domestic—be told in as much detail as possible. So, when English mentioned the kind of athletes he trained and raced with during his four-year track & field career at WSU, Chaplin wanted to make sure to reinforce the fact the that teams English ran on were indeed loaded.

The WSU track and cross-country teams during English's years were led by four extremely talented Kenyans, two Irish athletes, and four of the best American kids to ever compete for the Cougars. Of course, there was Rono and his four world records. John Ngeno was a seven-time NCAA champion on the track and the AAU national champion in cross country. Joshua Kimeto was a two-time NCAA champion at 5,000 meters, and Samson Kimombwa would, in 1977, produce a world record for 10,000 meters.

Who were the five American kids who contributed to WSU's impressive run in those days? Kurt Beckman, from nearby Richland, Washington, was a cross country All-American in 1975; Guy Arbogast would run 28:38 for six miles and was the top American finisher in the world cross-country championship in 1978; Dale Fleet would set a WSU record in the steeplechase (8:37.8); and two Oregonians: Dean Clark, who was third in the NCAA steeplechase in 1973, and Mark Hiefield, a sub-9:00 two miler and a cross country all-American.

All five American kids were consistent contributors on the track and to WSU's cross-country teams, which, in the years between 1971 and 1976, would place second at the NCAA meet twice (in 1971 and 1975). They would also place third twice (in 1973 and 1976) and fourth twice (in 1972 and 1974). The is, of course, that the WSU team was indeed loaded.

By 1976, Chaplin had turned WSU track & field into a program that would eventually contend for top-four finishes at both the NCAA indoor and outdoor meets. Indoors, WSU placed fourth in 1976, won the title in 1977, placed fourth again in both 1978 and 1984, and third in 1991 and 1993. Outdoors, WSU finished fourth in 1977 and 1978, third in 1982, and second in 1984, 1985, 1986, and 1991.

"In my own coaching career," English said, "if there is one thing I learned from Chaplin—and there have been more than a few—is that track & field and cross country were super important sports at that school. And [John Chaplin made sure] everyone on that campus knew it."

Phil English was certainly typical of the kind of athlete John Chaplin was attracting to Pullman in the early seventies: an accomplished distance runner (it didn't matter to Chaplin whether he came from Ireland or from Tacoma) who was also smart, professionally ambitious, and athletically aggressive. Remember Chaplin's insistence that his athletes leave WSU with a degree and with marketable skills. English was initially attracted to WSU's exercise science program, and while competing for the Cougars was definitely more than an afterthought, delving deeply into the scientific subtleties of human performance was his priority.

English went from WSU directly to Carroll High School in Yakima, Washington, to coach track and cross country and teach biology. In short order, Carroll, now defunct, was dominating the small-school division in Washington. English's 1982 Carroll girls team set a still-standing state record score of twenty points at the state meet. In cross country, a low score wins. A team's first five runners score, so a perfect score (finishing first through fifth) would be fifteen points. It normally takes anywhere from sixty to more than one hundred points to win a state meet, so a low score of twenty is almost unheard of.

English's best athlete at Carroll was future WSU All-American Robert Price (more on him later). Price was a 4:11 1,600-meter runner and won three straight small-school cross-country titles and twelve championships on the track at distances ranging from 800 meters to the two-mile.

When Carroll closed in 1986, the local Yakima school district made room for as many of Carroll's teachers as it could accommodate, and English moved right up the street to Eisenhower High School. The year before English arrived at Eisenhower, the school had fewer than twenty kids on the track team. After only three years in charge of the program, "Ike" had more than 100 athletes and won the big school district title. Then, in 1987, it won Washington's big-school cross-country championship.

English has also been the driving force behind Clear Lake/White Pass Cross Country Camp and Clinic (which attracts high school athletes from all over the Pacific Northwest to three one-week sessions each July) and a semi-annual coaches' clinic in which he and some of his coaching acolytes preach the benefits of a science-based approach to training high school distance runners. In short, the impact English has had on high school track & field and cross country is not dissimilar to the collegiate impact that John Chaplin has had on the sport—and for the same reasons.

Along the way, English has managed to ruffle the feathers of a few old-school coaches and administrators. But here is the crux of the matter: I remember at some point in the late seventies or early eighties when someone I knew said something along the lines of "John Chaplin is just too intense." I had a couple of similar conversations with coaching colleagues concerning Phil English as well. What I remember thinking was that if Chaplin and English had been football or basketball coaches, their intensity and insistence on the primacy of their sport would have raised no eyebrows.

English recounted an example of the lengths Chaplin would go to make sure everyone knew how seriously he took track & field. I can vouch for the veracity of his story of the WSU Sports Awards banquet in 1977 because I was there, covering the festivities for the *Pullman Herald*. Chaplin had informed members of the team that they needed to present at the banquet because they were to be recognized for winning the NCAA indoor track & field championship in the March of 1977.

"No one really wanted to go," English explained. But then Chaplin promised the athletes a free dinner, and they immediately changed their tune and welcomed the opportunity to be recognized.

"We're up in the Cub [the Compton Union Building at the center of the WSU campus]," he recalled, "and they've got all the trophies spread out on the front table. And the president of the university is there."

Also present at the banquet were a couple of WSU coaching legends, basketball coach George Raveling and baseball coach Bobo Brayton, along with football coach Jackie Sherrill, who was about to leave Pullman for the University of Pittsburgh. "Chaplin gets up there to speak, and he looks down the table in both directions, and he says, 'This is what an NCAA championship trophy looks like because I know you guys have never seen one.'"

What I remember about what happened next may be both clouded and enhanced by the passage of time, but I seem to recall Sherrill glaring up at Chaplin. Brayton closed his eyes and shook his head, and Raveling smiled ironically. But Chaplin had made his point: It is possible for small and frequently disregarded WSU to rise to the very pinnacle of collegiate sports. It should be noted that despite the dig at his colleagues, Raveling, Brayton, and Chaplin remained close friends.

I have been fortunate during my more than five decades in the sport to have worked with some excellent coaches, Phil English included. I had been an assistant at Eisenhower the year before English took over the program, and he generously allowed me to stay on, which I did for the next three years before moving on to my first teaching position at Pomeroy High School in the far southeastern corner of Washington. I'd known of Carroll High's success and was aware of some unique elements in the way English's athletes prepared and raced. The endless hopping and skipping drills were obvious and ostentation part of their warmup routine: the seemingly robotic arm movements. The taped wrists. The extraordinary similarity in the running style of the Carroll athletes.

This was at a time when conventional wisdom suggested that coaches not mess with a kid's running style, which was innate. It was apparent English had reached another conclusion. A few years prior, I helped the great British world record holder and Olympic medalist Gordon Pirie put together the beginnings of a book he was writing on training and racing. Like English, but years before, Pirie had become convinced that running mechanics were the key to running, in his words, "fast and injury-free." With that background in mind, I was probably less skeptical of what English was doing at Carroll than another coach might have been, but I was nonetheless curious about how his emphasis had come about and how he managed to get *all* his athletes to buy into the necessity of changing (dramatically, in some cases) the way they ran.

The evolution of English's thinking about the importance of biomechanics began with Chaplin's relationship with Gollnick and his research on the effects of an arcane and rarely discussed (at the time) physiological value called max VO2. Max VO2 is a measure of how efficiently an athlete takes in, metabolizes, and uses oxygen. The assumption was that the higher the max VO2 number, the greater an athlete's potential in endurance events. That is, an athlete with a higher max VO2 should win, all other factors being equal.

"There are two things I'll never forgive Coach Chaplin for," English said with a smile. "The first is giving me that class schedule when I first arrived at WSU." Remember the Communications 101 course? "The second is sending me over to Gollnick's lab right after I'd eaten lunch, and I was unaware I was going to be taking a max VO2 test."

A max VO2 test involves hooking an athlete up to various measuring devices, including a mask that covers the mouth and nose and electrodes taped to the upper body to measure heart rate and blood pressure. Then the athlete runs at a high rate of speed, aiming to get as close to complete exhaustion as possible. Chaplin had Gollnick test most of his middle-distance and distance runners so he could use the data to design the most appropriate training plan.

"So, I walk into Gollnick's lab," English said. "It was in Smith Gymnasium, in the physical education section of the campus, and there are cages with mice and a treadmill. And I've never seen a treadmill in my life."

English went on to explain that the treadmill was indeed a curiosity, but what caused him more concern was the mattress attached to the wall behind the treadmill. "And I think, *what the hell*," he said. The purpose of the mattress was to catch athletes after they collapsed in exhaustion when the test was complete. "So, he hooks me up, and he puts me through the VO2 Max test. And it is the hardest thing I've ever done in my life. Bar none. No race I ever ran. Nothing. Bar none. The hardest thing I've ever done."

Once the shock of the brutal effort wore off, English began to appreciate the value of the information the test produced. His max VO2 was extremely high, so high that he should have been running much faster than he was.

By this time, he'd also had the opportunity to observe the Kenyan athletes daily and up close. Like all runners, they came in a variety of shapes and sizes. Kimeto was short, a bit stocky, and barrel-chested. Kimombwa was slight, painfully thin, maybe 110 pounds. And Rono exuded speed and power. But, English observed, they all possessed an efficiency of movement that seemed to conserve energy. Light on their feet. No wasted motion. Efficiency. English concluded mechanical efficiency was the Kenyan athletes' secret. Well, one of their secrets, at least.

"I was training really hard," he pointed out. "But my *efficiency* wasn't where it needed to be." Then, the importance of running mechanics and their relationship to efficient oxygen use was driven home to English by another WSU runner.

"Kurt Beckman was a kid from Richland, Washington," he said. "Kurt usually finished in front of me, but his max VO2 wasn't nearly as high as mine. So as the race went on, over six miles, he'd beat me. And it all came down to efficiency."

It wasn't that Beckman wasn't capable. Far from it. He had contributed to a couple of state titles at Richland High School and had been successful at the University of Montana before transferring to WSU to "run with the best," according to Chaplin.

Of course, one way to interpret the data English had gotten from Gollnick's torture chamber and the insight he'd gained from recognizing that Kurt Beckman always beat him would be to discount max VO2 as a relevant factor in distance running success. But what English noticed was that Beckman shared one essential aspect of his running character with the Kenyans: sound and efficient biomechanics. Beckman's efficient running mechanics made it possible for him to overcome the physiological advantage English had due to his superior max VO2.

"This changed everything in how I approached coaching," English concluded.

Necessarily, science often tends to be very narrow. Gollnick preferred to focus on only one aspect of the energy utilization system in endurance athletes. But, as English pointed out, a coach must be able to focus on all aspects of advancing an athlete's capabilities to put everything together.

"Dr. Gollnick was one of my advisors for my master's thesis," he explained. "So, I asked him in class, but he's talking about muscle biopsies and…I loved him as an instructor. But I brought up biomechanics, and he said, 'Don't even talk to me about that. I know nothing about that. All I'm interested in is the physiological response.'"

Of course, English did not mean this as criticism of one of the genuine pioneers in the study of exercise science. But from a coaching point of view, English also knew he would have to think about biomechanics.

From the mid-1960s until Gollnick's death in 1991, nearly all of WSU's middle distance and distance runners were tested for max VO2 in Gollnick's lab, and some had muscle biopsies taken. However, only Gollnick himself, Swedish researcher Bengt Saltin, and Chaplin knew the max VO2 value and the muscle biopsy information for every athlete. At the time, Gollnick and Saltin were the top exercise physiologists in the world, and Chaplin was one of the first coaches to recognize the training implications of knowing an athlete's max VO2.

Chaplin recruited three-time Olympic gold medalist Peter Snell to study exercise physiology and silver medalist Ralph Mann to study biomechanics at WSU to pursue their PhDs during Gollnick's time. Gerry Lindgren and Boyd Gittins were still at WSU when Snell and Mann arrived.

High school and college coaching have much in common, but the most significant difference is that the great majority of athletes in any high school program are not exceptionally talented. They are usually average kids with a substantial work ethic and a profound lack of concern for the discomfort of training and racing. On the other hand, most of the athletes a college coach works with have innate physiological and biomechanical advantages over their less talented peers.

Since that is not the case in high school, English concluded, "I knew I had to incorporate biomechanics and motor development to get the best result." And the results speak for themselves. First at Carroll High and later at Eisenhower High, English designed a regime of strength exercises and technique drills that allowed his athletes to develop extraordinary efficiency and experience uncommon success precisely because of their improved running mechanics.

And those seemingly arcane drills that were such a curiosity when English was at Carroll? Thanks to the thousands of kids and hundreds of coaches who have been through the Phil English program at Clear Lake/White Pass Cross Country Camp and Coaching Clinic, using English's methods to improve running style and biomechanical efficiency has become standard practice in high school programs all over the Pacific Northwest.

All this might seem like an irrelevant aside when considering John Chaplin's impact on track & field and cross country. But nearly every former athlete I spoke with talked about Chaplin in terms of legacy. In every instance, they were far more interested in pointing out what they took from Chaplin into the larger world than they were in reminiscing about their Cougar glory days, of which there were plenty. Phil English is the perfect exemplar of that point of view.

But he is not alone.

WSU sprinters set relay world records (left to right): Harry Nettleton, Curt Ledford, Jack Orr, Lee Orr, and Loren Benke. Nettleton, Jack Orr, Lee Orr, and Benke combined to lower the world record in the one-mile relay to 3:12.3 to win the Pacific Coast Conference title in 1937. Lee Orr and Ledford later joined one athletes from Stanford and another from the University of Southern California to lower the world record in the 440-yard relay to 40.7 seconds.
(Photo Credit: Washington State Athletics)

Bernard Lagat - Five Olympic Games. Five World Titles (Two Outdoors
and Three Indoors). The only man to win both the 1,500 meters
and the 5,000 meters at the same World Championship Meet.
(Photo Credit: Washington State Athletics)

Boyd Gittins - 1968 Olympian and World Record Holder
(Photo Credit: Washington State Athletics)

Dixie Garner - World Record Indoor Two-Mile
(Photo Credit: Washington State Athletics)

Dominque Arnold - American Record Holder and
NCAA Champion in the 110-meter High Hurdles.
(Photo Credit: Washington State Athletics)

Gerry Lindgren - Multiple NCAA Titles, World Six-Mile Record
(Photo Credit: Washington State Athletics)

Henry Rono - The Greatest Cougar Ever
(Photo Credit: Washington State Athletics)

John vanReenan - World Record in the Discus
(Photo Credit: Washington State Athletics)

John Chaplin
(Photo Credit: Washington State Athletics)

Julius Korir - Olympic Steeplechase Champion
(Photo Credit: Washington State Athletics)

CHAPTER 7

UP AND DOWN THE VALLEY

John Chaplin wanted one thing made clear when the composition of his various WSU track & field and cross-country teams came up. He insisted when we began this project that the story of his time at WSU did not focus exclusively on international athletes. He made the point repeatedly that he was every bit as gratified with the development of American athletes as he was with the success of Henry Rono and other international greats, especially those in-state kids who came to Pullman with relatively modest credentials (and often without scholarships) and left with Pac-8 or Pac-10 conference or NCAA championship medals.

See the note in the appendix for an extensive list of in-state athletes who excelled at WSU over the years.

It is correct to say that every college track & field program can point to similar homegrown success stories. In fact, it is likely that, in these days of strict scholarship limits, the success of many collegiate track

& field programs relies heavily on athletes who have not been heavily recruited or who arrive on campus without world-beater high school credentials. However, it seems relevant and necessary to point this out in the case of WSU during the Chaplin years because so much of his reputation appears to hang on the eye-popping achievements of so many international athletes. Two of the best examples are Robert Price from Carroll High School, at one end of the Yakima Valley, and Chris McBride from Kiona-Benton City High School, sixty miles downriver.

High school sports in the state of Washington are divided into six classifications based on enrollment (and, since 2019, socioeconomic status). This makes sense for team sports in which it would be patently unfair, for example, to have a game between a school with 2,000 students and one with 200 students. Using student enrollment to determine participation at the state level in track & field also makes sense for deciding team titles. The evidence is clear that the opportunity for small-school kids to compete at the state level has increased participation in individual sports like track & field and cross country in those smaller high schools.

In Washington, like other states with large areas of sparsely populated rural countryside, more than half the state's high schools are in the three smallest enrollment classifications. The downside of the classification system is that the very best athletes in the smaller schools often do not get the opportunity to test themselves against the very best from the larger schools at the state-meet level. As a result, the best coaches in the small-school world of track & field must seek out big-school competitive opportunities for their best kids. Those competitive opportunities are provided by several important invitational meets, which are held around the state every spring.

In Eastern Washington, none of these meets is larger or matters more than the Pasco Invitational. Held every year in mid-April, the

"Invite" attracts more than 1,000 athletes from all over the Pacific Northwest and occasionally from Canada. It's no exaggeration to say that winning an event at the Invite is often more difficult than winning an individual title at one of Washington's six enrollment-classification state meets, because Pasco attracts the top athletes from across the state and the region irrespective of classification. Pasco offers top small-school athletes the opportunity to compete against runners, jumpers, and throwers from the big-school powers.

The list of Pasco Invitational winners and record holders reads like a *Who's Who* of Pacific Northwest track & field: Ja'Warren Hooker (10.44 for 100 meters and 21.40 for 200), who was coached by Price at Ellensburg High School; Calvin Kennon (46.88 for 400 meters); John Quade (1:50.43 for 800 meters); Michael Slagowski (4:05.71 for one mile); Rick Riley (9:00.1 for two miles, a national record in 1966); Vince Goldsmith (68-1 in the shot put); Ginnie Powell (13.79 for the 100-meter hurdles); Becca Noble (54.40 for 400 meters); Maddie Myers (4:49.02 for one mile and 10:18.46 for 3,200 meters); Corissa Yasen (6-0 in the high jump); Dory Reeves (160-3 in the discus); and Chinne Okoronkwo (41-9¼ in the triple jump).

In the 1988 edition of the Invite, Henry Hall of traditional track & field power Richland High School was the favorite in the 400 meters. Hall was an imposing athlete, tall and with the heavily muscled stature that epitomizes the physique of a great sprinter. He was known to be very fast and supremely tough. His imposing stature and reputation for competitiveness made him the kind of athlete who would make his opponents doubt themselves as soon as he stepped onto the track.

Also in the race was Chris McBride.

Benton City, Washington, is twenty-one miles up the Yakima Valley and a world away from the big-time atmosphere of the Pasco

Invitational. McBride was everything Henry Hall wasn't. Less than imposing (for a sprinter), even as a senior in high school. Thin and wiry. Looking more like he should have been in the two-mile at the Invite rather than in an event generally dominated by faster and stronger athletes.

It may have been more common back in the day than it is now, but high school (and many colleges) coaches still build their teams around 400-meter runners and hurdlers. Those athletes are versatile and determined enough to cover every event from the 100 to the 800. They can run both the 4x100- and 4x400-meter relays, and they are often competent in the jumping events. Nearly all of Chaplin's team roster included athletes who could race up and down the schedule, from 100 meters to 800 meters.

Chaplin went as far as to credit his most versatile athletes with being able to beat archrival Oregon. "Oregon and WSU would split the points in the field events and the distances," he explained. "But if I could beat them in the two relays with 400-meter sprinters and 110-meter and 400-meter hurdlers, I would increase our chances of winning the dual meets. As a rule, a team needs to be 15 to 20 points better than the Ducks on paper to beat Oregon in front of the supercharged Oregon fans in Eugene, but Chaplin is proud of his record (WSU 12, Oregon 10) against the Ducks, who were under legendary coach Bill Dellinger, one of his best friends.

Richland High's Henry Hall certainly fit the versatility bill. By the time he graduated, he'd run 10.8 for 100 meters, 21.6 seconds for 200 meters, and 49.4 for 400 meters. On the other hand, the night before he took on Hall and the rest of the loaded field in the 400 at the Pasco Invite, Chris McBride ran and won the 1,600 in another local meet. A miler stepping down into the 400 didn't figure to be much of a threat to the likes of Henry Hall and the rest of the nine-runner field.

The race began as you'd expect. Hall and the rest stormed around the first turn. McBride lost the stagger to the two runners on his inside by the time the field had reached the middle of the backstretch. He continued to trail as Hall took the lead with 200 meters to go and was firmly entrenched in last place—and not all that close to the leaders— as the field came out of the second turn with 100 meters left to run.

I've always been curious about the peculiar set of circumstances under which great athletes discover they have the capacity to become great athletes. For Chris McBride, it was a matter of a missed bus and a frustrated coach when he was in the ninth grade. I was hanging out in Benton City that year while my wife, Tina, taught physical education at the local elementary school. I covered high school sports part-time for the *Tri-City Herald* in nearby Kennewick, Washington, and was making a most feeble effort to reinvigorate my languishing and mediocre running career. I'd spent several years previously as an assistant track & field coach at Western Washington and Seattle Pacific universities, so to fill the hours during the spring of 1985, I volunteered to help with the Ki-Be track team. Time may have dimmed the particulars of the following incident in my memory, but I'm certain the gist is accurate.

As a ninth grader on that team, Chris McBride was a promising, if somewhat erratic, high jumper. The Ki-Be Bears had a midweek meet at Burbank High School across both the Columbia and Snake rivers in Walla Walla County, and Chris missed the bus. He eventually arrived at the meet with his dad but was too late for the high jump. The head coach, a delightfully patient music teacher named Linda Doria, was displeased enough to come up with a novel punishment. Ms. Doria took Chris aside and told him that since he'd missed the high jump, she'd entered him in the 1,600 meters (the high school version of the mile run).

Well, as you can imagine, Chris was not happy about the prospect of running the mile. He was, after all, a high jumper, and high jumpers are not known for their desire to run themselves to exhaustion. He protested and whined for a bit, but since he was a competitive kid, it wasn't long before he'd resigned himself to the task. He won the race and recorded a time somewhere in the 4:40s, respectable for a ninth grader at any level but remarkable for a school as small as Kiona-Benton. And, well, to co-opt a phrase, a star was born.

For the next three-plus years, McBride tinkered with running events, finally settling on the 800 as a nominal specialty. One of the advantages of being a very fast athlete at a very small school was that he had the luxury of experimenting with different events. And his coaches had the advantage of picking and choosing a limited number of meets in which a big effort would be required.

Which brings us back to the 1988 Pasco Invitational. With a little more than 100 meters left to run, McBride was close enough to the tail end of the field that moving up two or three places to earn a place in the top six seemed possible, but just as he came out of the second turn, he appeared to flip a switch. He moved swiftly through the field into second place halfway up the final straightway and caught Hall with twenty meters left. He won the race in 49.3 seconds. Hall was second, just three-tenths of a second back.

Six weeks later, Chris won the small-school state championship in the 800. His school records for the 400 (49.3) and the 800 (1:56.4) at Kiona-Benton remain intact to this day. McBride's next stop was Spokane Community College, where he won a couple of Northwest Community College titles. Then, it was on to WSU.

I ran track and played other sports at a very small high school, and I have coached at a school much smaller than Kiona-Benton, and it has always seemed to me that even the best small-school athletes, while not lacking talent or ambition, often develop a sort of athletic inferiority complex when it comes to competing against athletes from larger schools. If that's so, it would not be surprising to discover that an athlete from a small, somewhat insular farming community like Benton City, Washington, might find the atmosphere at a school with WSU's reputation for track & field excellence overwhelming—especially considering a coaching personality as intense and dynamic as John Chaplin and the school's history of international success, which included world-record holders, an Olympic gold medalist, and world champion.

"I was a bit intimidated [when I first arrived at WSU]," McBride said a couple of weeks before completing the 2021 Western States 100-mile trail race. (You read that right. One hundred miles! He placed 28th in 21:53:26. He was the first runner over fifty years of age among the 208 runners who completed the race.)

"But it wasn't because Chaplin was anything but nice to me. WSU was such a prestigious school with such a well-known coach and such a stacked team. I kind of kept my head down. I was kind of terrified. I *was* intimidated [at first] by the whole program."

Despite his initial unease, McBride made it a point to explain it was the program's reputation, the school's history in track & field, and Chaplin himself that led him to take the leap and enroll at WSU.

"I always wanted to race with the big boys," he said. Imagine a young Chris McBride, once he realized his athletic future was on the track and not in the high jump, logging training miles through the orchards and vineyards that surround his hometown or grinding out repetitions on his school's ancient five-lane 440-yard track. Like all reasonably talented young athletes, he no doubt passed the time dreaming of competing on the sport's biggest stages against the best athletes in the nation, or even the world. He quickly added, "And I finally got there."

Kapkory, Kibiri, Joubert, and McBride combined to run a WSU school record of 9:33.7 for the distance medley relay in Philadelphia in 1992. McBride contributed a 1:49.7 800-meter leg to that effort. How good were the other big boys on that record-setting relay team? Joubert ran 45.7 for 400 meters, Kibiri ran 2:48.5 for 1,200 meters, and Kapkory ran 3:59.7 for 1,600 meters.

And just how big were the *big boys* on that team? Kapkory won five Pac-10 titles at distances ranging from 1,500 meters to 10,000 meters, plus two conference cross-country titles and two NCAA indoor 3,000-meter titles. Kibiri was the NCAA runner-up in just his third 3,000m steeplechase and won the NCAA title at 1,500 meters in 1991. Joubert was an All-American at 45.89 for 400 meters in 1990 and would represent Australia in the Olympics.

Robert Price also came to WSU from a small school, but he had the benefit of having been tutored by Phil English, who was familiar with the "Big Boy" atmosphere of WSU track & field, had also been an international competitor for his native Ireland, and had experience racing the very best athletes at the highest levels of the sport.

When I suggested one reason for Chaplin's controversial reputation may have been that he was not recruiting the kind of athletes some observers with a microphone or a print media platform wanted him to recruit, English said, "I think that is probably true." But then he added it was the world-class nature of the WSU program that was most attractive to athletes like Chris McBride and Robert Price.

"When I called John for Robert," English explained, "the recruiting part took less than a minute. I told him what we needed [by way of a scholarship] for Robert, and he said, 'Yeah. We'll take care

of him.' And that was it. Robert was the best in the state at the time."
In 1986, Price had run 4:11.6 for 1,600 meters and placed second in
the 1,600 to future US Olympian Brad Barquist at Pasco. But here's
the clincher, according to both English and Price: A lot of athletes
even more talented than Robert Price and Chris McBride get to the
NCAA level but never thrive. Those who do manage to get better,
English suggested, do so because they share a common, essential,
determining characteristic—a singular desire to test themselves.

"The best Washington [high school] kids," he said, "want to
compete against the best athletes in the world."

Price added an example from his own experience as the parent
of a couple of talented kids. "After experiencing this with both my
sons and with what I experienced in high school," Price explained,
"when you get to college, you have to have this particular drive to be
great." Price's younger son, Jonas, ran under 9:00 for 3,200 meters
under English's tutelage at Eisenhower High and is now a promising
freshman at Oklahoma State University. His elder son, Ronan, is at
Eastern Washington University.

"Jonas is a perfect example," he went on. "In middle school, he's
asking if he can run to school in the morning. For Ronan, other
things were more important." Price gives a parental shrug at this
point, clearly fine with the choice each of his sons has made.

Robert Price's emergence as a force on the Washington high
school track & field landscape was dissimilar to McBride's in that,
even though it was the product of a small-school program, the
program was English's Carroll High juggernaut in the final years of
that Catholic school's existence. By virtue of three state, small-school,
cross-country titles, nine track & field championships, and that 4:11.6
1,600-meter time, Price may have been better known, with higher
expectations, by the time he enrolled at WSU. But he still had a lot

to prove to himself and to Coach Chaplin when he joined the team in the fall of 1987.

"[At the time] Some people asked me why I'd go to a school where I'd never set a record," Price said. "But that was not the issue. The issue was I wanted to get better. And the only way I'm going to get better was being [at WSU] and in that situation." "That situation," for Robert Price, was a powerful WSU team that would come within an eyelash of winning the NCAA outdoor track & field title in June 1991. By the time his senior year rolled around, Price had adjusted well enough to become an All-American in the 3,000-meter steeplechase, but like McBride, his initial impression of WSU track had the potential to set him back and even doubt his decision.

"You see all those pictures [WSU's gallery of international stars arrayed on John Chaplin's office wall]," he said. "It's very intimidating. You look at those Kenyans. You look at those records."

But then the work began.

"And then there's the first two weeks of cross-country training," he said. "I thought I was going [to be sent] home. I lived in fear of losing my scholarship."

By the time Price and McBride arrived at WSU in the late eighties or early nineties, the international flavor of the WSU track & field team had begun to change, but there was still an impressive collection of African talent from both sides of that continent in the program. "We had a lot more Americans on the distance side of things," Price said. "We did have a lot of foreign athletes, but they were in several other events." *See the appendix for information on specific athletes and their achievements.*

The counterintuitive saving grace for Price and, later, for McBride was that the coach was not particularly hands-on when it came to coaching, at least not on an everyday basis. I've since learned that this approach is still not uncommon in collegiate track and field today, but it can be a problem for athletes coming from high school programs in which every minute of every practice session, five or six days a week, is directed or overseen by a coach.

"This is something a lot of high school kids have a problem with when they go on to the next level," Price said. "Because I know in our system [at Eisenhower High, where he teaches social studies and serves as an assistant coach for English], we're pretty hands-on. But [at WSU] we only saw Chaplin twice a week [on the track and in the canyon]." Price was quick to add that he did not mean to say that Chaplin was disengaged on the days when he did meet with the distance runners.

Chaplin himself explained this approach. "Be present for key training sessions two mornings [Tuesday and Thursday] in the canyon and then that same afternoon with 3–5 x 1,000 meters on the track. Then leave the athletes to their own devices on the other days." He was at the track on Mondays and Wednesdays when the distance runners would run 300-meter or 180-meter sprints after their distance runs. The WSU staff consisted of only two coaches at the time, so Chaplin handled all the running events, including the relays and the two hurdle races. He would be present for the sprint drills, and then a manager would handle the actual workout.

Associate Coach Rick Sloan would handle all the field events and the decathlon. "Rick Sloan," Chaplin said, "was one of the best, if not the best, field event coaches in the nation. Rick was with me for twenty-one years, and when I retired, he became the head coach for twenty more."

Back to the training.

"You know, it's six of seven in the morning," Price said. "And we're running down the Snake River Canyon to Lower Monumental

Dam. And then coming out two miles up and then getting to the silos where [Chaplin had] dropped us off."

Chaplin, according to Price, did not simply drop off his runners and then drive away. No. This is where the coach was more hands-on than the athletes probably preferred. "And then you're running through four or five inches of gravel out this road, and he's behind you in his van honking the horn." Price smiled and chuckled a bit at the memory, but it was clear that at the time, and at first, he was not exactly comfortable with the training situation.

"And this is your first week at WSU, and he's honking his horn. If you're not running fast enough, he'd pull up beside you in one of those old 14-passenger vans, and the cattle doors [on the side] would open up, and he says, 'Get your ass in here.'"

Remember that Robert Price recalled this from the point of view of an 18-year-old freshman in his first week of cross-country training with the likes of Samuel Kibiri. It was not as if he was unfamiliar with training hard. English's program in the eighties was legendary for its day-to-day intensity, but for a youngster unfamiliar with John Chaplin's training philosophy and reputed impatience, the situation had to be daunting.

When the subject of training was broached with Chaplin, he explained his belief that when an athlete was unable to complete a workout at the required intensity, the best thing for that athlete was to end the workout. So, what a youthful Robert Price might have interpreted as a failure when Chaplin yelled, "Get your ass in here," was, in the mind of the coach, the best thing for that athlete on that day.

"He had a certain pace [you were supposed to run]," Price said. "You had to stay ahead of the van, but if the van pulled up beside you, you had to jump into a moving vehicle." Although somewhat distressed at first, Price did what Chaplin asked. "I wasn't the most vociferous person back then. He was the coach, and you did what he said."

Price continued to do what Chaplin said, and during his four years in the program, he progressed from being a scared freshman who was not sure he belonged at WSU to becoming an All-American steeplechaser with a personal best of 8:38.1 and who scored in WSU's near miss at the national title in the 1991 NCAA meet.

English himself had arrived at WSU in the earliest days of the Kenyan "invasion." His response to the likes of John Ngeno, Samson Kimombwa, Josh Kimeto, and Henry Rono was similar to McBride and Price's. The difference at the time was that the success of African athletes on an American college campus was enough to attract attention and, in the minds of some observers, suspicion.

"I learned a lot from training with the Kenyans," English said. "They were brought up in a tribal environment, and [in a tribal environment] you are an extension of the tribe, so they put themselves on the line, and they raced really hard. You could beat them, but if you did, then you better be prepared to beat them the next time.

"One time, I beat Samson in an indoor race, and he wasn't happy. So, we go for a run out Farm Road [into the rolling hills east of Pullman. And we're heading out toward the Lindgren Loop, and he starts picking up the pace. We're going like twelve miles, and he's trying to put me back in my box. He took it personally that I beat him three days earlier, so he just hammered that run."

According to English, this mindset, an unyielding approach to training and racing by the Kenyans and other internationals, was a problem for some American athletes. He hinted that some young American runners seemed to be beaten before they ever got to the starting line, almost as if they believed the international athletes at

WSU and elsewhere had some sort of innate or mystical advantage. Remember, despite the success of WSU's Kenyans, Chaplin never had a monopoly on international talent.

"I raced a few American kids before I ever came over here," English said. "[In Europe] the perception of them was that they were just not tough enough."

Chris McBride—an American kid who was undoubtedly tough enough—recounted a similar attempt to tag along with Kibiri on a training run during his early days at WSU. "I went on a 'tempo run' with Kibiri, early on when I first showed up," he said. "After a few miles, I thought, *Well, I'll never do that again.* They were out of my league." McBride went on to explain that his problem that day may have had less to do with the specific training exercise than it did with a misunderstanding of the Kenyan approach to training.

"I've since learned about this," he explained. "The Kenyans' fundamental training plan was to start very slow. They called it a tempo run, but it was really a progression. After a while, I was losing ground so bad that it was time to say goodbye. So, I never trained much with them."

Chaplin applied the Kenyan runners' approach to teaching his other athletes how to train to be able to surge and run negative splits (with the second half faster than the first half) in their races. Chaplin also used the tribal mindset of cooperative effort to encourage a buddy system of primary and secondary runners during a race.

Despite that early revelation, Chaplin made sure Chris McBride's training would continue to have an international flavor. Standing at just five-foot-five, Michael Joubert was pound-for-pound and inch-for-inch as powerful as any athlete in the world at the time. While at WSU, he became a legend for the intensity of his training and his single-minded determination to overcome his smallish stature and excel in the two events that favor taller, rangier athletes. Michael Joubert ran 1:47.0 for 800 meters while at WSU, was an All-American at the 400 meters, and was a member of the WSU school record sprint medley relay team that won the Penn Relays in 1991. He would eventually run 45.62 in the 400 and then represent Australia in the 1996 Olympic Games. Augustine Olobia (200 meters in 20.9), George Ogbeide (200 meters in 20.7), Joubert (400 meters in 46.3), and Samuel Kibiri (800 meters in 1:47.9) made up that Penn Relays championship team.

"I was exclusively locked into the 400 and 800, so I trained with Joubert," McBride explained. "I didn't get a lot of coaching instruction from Chaplin, but that is because he hooked me up with Joubert. He [Joubert] knew what he was doing, knew what he wanted to do, so I just kind of followed him around."

McBride's experience is an example of Chaplin's use of a "buddy system." Older athletes were charged with helping newcomers, and younger athletes understood the WSU system, with its emphasis on both education and track & field to maximize a kid's chances of success in the high-pressure atmosphere of major college athletics. Chaplin also allowed athletes a lot of freedom with their workouts as they matured.

CHAPTER 8

THE OLD
GUARD

A s you might expect, during his 70 years in the in the sport, John Prescott Chaplin came into contact and developed working and personal relationships with some of the most significant personalities in track & field. Coaches and athletes from all over the world. World record holders. Olympic and world champions. Administrators and organizers, some with the best interest of the athletes and the sport at heart, some with an inclination toward manipulating the arcane politics of intercollegiate and international sport in a direction Chaplin was either unwilling or reluctant to go.

It is not an exaggeration to say that Chaplin's career on the organizational and administrative side of the sport was as influential as his tenure as one of the most successful college coaches in the country. And, despite assumptions about his assumed conservative bona fides, it can be argued that John Chaplin was a motivating and enabling force behind USA Track & Field, making coaching and leadership opportunities available to minorities and women. (More on this later.)

"Let me put it this way," said Brooks Johnson, the coach at Stanford University during much of Chaplin's tenure at WSU. "John talked conservative, but his actions were very liberal." Chaplin himself concedes that he is liberal on social issues and conservative on monetary matters. "I'm a Rockefeller Republican, the type of Republican who is liberal on social issues and conservative on monetary issues. No poor man ever gave anyone a job."

"He would say things I would cringe at in terms of feminism," Johnson said, "but he was one of the first people [among male college coaches] to promote women's track." Johnson's statement calls to mind Chaplin's efforts on behalf of that handful of girls back at Wapato High School at a time when girls' sports at the high school level were all but nonexistent. "[I think] it goes back to his father," Johnson continued. "A radical in East LA. Two things [a conservative mindset and liberal action] combine to form a unique person."

John Chaplin, a unique person? Certainly. And as evidence, we can call on the testimony of three of the sport's most important historical personalities, all from Chaplin's own generation: Olympic Coach Brooks Johnson and Olympic gold medalists Charlie Greene and Mel Pender, all who credit Chaplin with nudging track & field in a more progressive and athlete-friendly direction. He had a plan to support female and minority coaches being considered for international positions by the USATF International Competition Committee and the Men's Track & Field Selection Committees.

Like Chaplin, Johnson moved from high school coaching to eventually presiding over one of the NCAA's most prestigious and most successful collegiate programs at Stanford University. After more than a decade of coaching at the high school level and stints at

Tufts University and the University of Florida, he became the head coach at Stanford from 1979 to 1992.

Green and Pender were both members of the US 4x100-meter relay team that won an Olympic gold medal and set a world record (38.24) at the 1968 Mexico City Games. Green also won the bronze medal at 100 meters at Mexico City. Both Pender and Green went on to serve with distinction in the US Army, and both served as coaches at the US Military Academy. All three of these track & field legends expressed unqualified admiration for and gratitude toward John Chaplin, but each had their own specific reasons for doing so.

Brooks Johnson's early life in Plymouth, Massachusetts, was nothing like John Chaplin's upbringing in Los Angeles. No radical politics, no arcane philosophical reading lists, no polemics for the adolescent Johnson. His father shined shoes and his mother was a housemaid. But despite early differences in their background, Johnson and Chaplin both became important figures in the development and growth of collegiate track & field during the latter years of the last century, and each remains an influential presence on the national and international track and field landscape today. Chaplin considers Johnson one of a handful of his best friends in the sport, and Johnson expresses a similar admiration and affection for Chaplin.

"I knew about John even before I got to Stanford in 1979," Johnson said. "Because of Henry Rono setting all those world records, I knew him by reputation before I knew him personally."

I expected a bit of pushback from his coaching contemporaries when the topic of Chaplin's legacy in the sport and his use of international athletes came up, but Johnson wasn't having none of that. "A lot of people were upset because he recruited a lot of overseas athletes," Johnson said, referring to the assumption common at the time that WSU's success under Chaplin was due to the presence of world-class African athletes. "I was not upset. Villanova was loaded with overseas athletes. The only difference was [skin] color and not the passport they had."

This is obviously a sore point for Johnson, who, like Chaplin, had considered a career in the law before he became a track coach. I wanted to make sure there was no misunderstanding, so I asked him directly: *Is it accurate to say race was an issue* in the criticism Chaplin received when the Kenyans and other African athletes showed up at WSU? "Very accurate," he said. "No one complained that Villanova had a pipeline to Ireland or that UCLA had athletes from Europe, as well."

Johnson is three years older than Chaplin, but he did not take over the Stanford University program until 1978, six years after Chaplin took the reins at WSU. "I am not sure what the perception was of what John was doing [in the years after he replaced Mooberry and before Johnson arrived at Stanford]."

Whereas Chaplin comes off as brash and sometimes impulsive, as if not wanting to give an adversary a chance to strike, Johnson speaks in carefully measured terms, as if wanting to make sure he is not misunderstood or his position misconstrued. Chaplin laughed at this description of his friend. "Hell," he said. "Brooks can get pretty radical himself when he feels an injustice has been done." From Brooks Johnson's point of view, Chaplin's success was as much a function of his coaching philosophy as it was his ability to recruit, both domestically and internationally, the type of athlete who would thrive in the remote environment of southeastern Washington.

"That was one of the first things John pointed out to me when I got to Stanford," Johnson explained. "[He knew and understood] there are a lot of things that make going to Stanford worthwhile. And he told me he would not recruit against me with athletes who have a chance to go to Stanford."

Johnson was not in any way denigrating WSU as an academic institution, but simply acknowledging that the university attracts and caters to a very different student clientele. He also noted there may not be two schools in the entire country more different from each other than Stanford and WSU. "There are plusses and minuses both ways," he explained. "A kid admissible to Stanford who is good at track & field probably had us on his short list anyway. I just went after kids who were acceptable [able to get in] and predisposed to think about Stanford."

By implication, Johnson suggested the same was true when Chaplin recruited a kid to WSU. Just as most kids are probably not suited to the academic rigors of Stanford, most kids are also not suited to the geographic isolation and severe climate of the Palouse.

"I think part of it [the reason Chaplin was successful at WSU] was where they were," Johnson said, speculating that geographic isolation can be a positive factor in the development of a certain type of athlete. "A kid really had to want to go to Wazzu [an epithet Chaplin does not like], distanced from a lot of distractions.

"At Stanford, it was a question of '*distracted by what?*' They may want to go into San Francisco [and take advantage of the opportunities for distraction there]. There are a lot more things that would stimulate their curiosity and interest near Stanford."

It is hard to dispute Johnson's essential point here. Options for entertainment and culture are certainly limited in the Palouse. What is a WSU athlete going to do? Head up to Colfax for entertainment and culture? Colfax, for all its rural charm, is not San Francisco. That's undoubtedly a good thing from the point of view of the Whitman County seat's 2,891 citizens, and in Johnson's judgment, may also be a good thing for a track & field athlete. That is particularly true for some international athletes who often came from small, remote farming villages, communities that have more in common with the rolling wheat country around Pullman than with the urban clang of the San Francisco Bay Area.

"It is easier to become monomaniacal," he said, "if you do not have other things pecking away at you." As in a place like Pullman. The result, in Johnson's judgment, was Chaplin's remarkable success at developing athletes who had often been overlooked by other collegiate programs.

"I'm not sure what my perception was of what John was doing," he said. "But he had a very high HIT rate." HIT rate is a measure of how much an athlete improves from the time they enter a program to the when they leave. "A lot of people can recruit, but his HIT rate was off the charts."

For Johnson, the most important measure of a collegiate track & field program is not necessarily winning individual titles or team championships, but rather, "does the athlete continue to get better? How much success does a coach have with the people they recruit?"

Interestingly, from Johnson's perspective, the Kenyan athletes Chaplin inserted into the US collegiate scene played a significant role in making that happen. To emphasize his point, Johnson told the story of Stanford 1,500-meter runner Jeff Atkinson. Atkinson had established himself as one of the Pac-10's most promising 1,500-meter runners, but like every other American collegian, he was overshadowed by WSU's Kenyans.

"We had a meet at Stanford," he explained, "when the Kenyans were running crazy [times], and everyone would quiver in their boots." Atkinson, however, was not willing to simply tremble in fear at the presence of the Kenyans. He decided to take them on. "With two laps to go," Johnson said, "Jeff Atkinson just took off." At this point, I expected Johnson's story to end with Atkinson's brave move producing a stunning upset of the indomitable Kenyans. But alas: "Of course, they ran him down, caught him, and beat him."

Well, a least Atkinson's teammates were impressed with his gutsy move, right? "His teammates told him what a dumbass he was for making that move," Johnson said.

Remember earlier when Johnson said that while some coaches objected to the presence of the Kenyans at WSU, Johnson himself was not upset?

This is why…

"I told him [Atkinson] that I needed to find a way to coach him so [that] when he made that move, he can make it stick." Johnson then explained the single factor that separated Atkinson from many of his American contemporaries: Atkinson admired the Kenyans, but he was not intimidated by them. "He had the courage to make that move. He just hadn't been coached to make it stick. My job was to coach him so that when he made that move, he could hold it."

This brings us to another aspect of coaching that Johnson shared with Chaplin and, indeed, with every other college coach who has had success over the long haul: an ability to recognize precisely what it will take to get a particular athlete to reach as much of his potential as possible. In the case of Atkinson, Jonson explained, it was a matter of finding a way to make him strong enough to outrun the best in the world over the last 400 meters of a 1,500-meter race.

"Atkinson's high school coach was a 5,000-miles-a-year guy," Johnson pointed out. "And the coach used his team to help him get in his 100 miles (a week)." The implication here is that as a young runner, Jeff Atkinson had not developed the requisite sprinting speed to become a world-class middle-distance runner. "The coach told Atkinson he could not run 55 seconds [for one lap] fresh. But I told him he needed to run 53 on the last lap of a 1,500-meter race."

So, Johnson and Atkinson got to work developing the latter's ability to sprint, or more specifically, the ability to sprint the final lap of a world-class 1,500-meter race. "He did two times 400 before the [1988 Olympic] trials," Johnson said. "He ran 48.5 and 48.3." For those unfamiliar, that is world-class speed for a middle-distance runner. "Then I told him he could run 54 and make the team, or he could run 53 and win the trials."

We can assume Atkinson's answer, given his earlier willingness to take on WSU's Kenyan superstars. "He said, 'I want to win the thing.'" Which he did, and then made the final of the 1988 Olympics. Atkinson still holds the Stanford University record in the mile (3:55.15), and he set a lifetime best of 3:52.80 in 1988.

Was Johnson suggesting that one significant reason Atkinson reached the competitive heights he did was because he had been exposed to the Kenyans from WSU? "One factor was that these foreign athletes—especially the Kenyans—were here. They trained and raced here. And as American athletes got closer and closer [to the Kenyans], they got used to being with them. And with a lap to go, they could beat them."

So, according to his coach, Atkinson's response to getting beaten by the Kenyans was an integral part of his athletic development. He saw what needed to be done and then went about working closely with an insightful coach to figure out how to accomplish it.

That seemed reasonable, so I asked Johnson if the success American runners have had more recently was part of the natural progression of training philosophy pioneered by Chaplin and others, engendered in part by the rapidly expanding presence of international athletes in the NCAA. "There was nothing natural about it," he said in response. "For example, John would take 1:48 800 runners and turn them into steeplechasers. Anyone else would try to coach 'em down to 1:46. John got them fit enough to run the steeplechase or some longer race."

Johnson is suggesting that Chaplin's background—his upbringing with a radical father, his early parochial school education, his success as a sprinter, his military experience, and his time coaching under Mooberry—adds up to a unique, sometimes controversial, and ultimately successful coaching philosophy. "John is a product of his background," Johnson said. "A lot of that came to manifest itself as a person and as a coach."

Along those lines, during one of our early discussions of training and racing, Chaplin pointed out that he believed most athletes train for and race at distances that are too short. He used the example of Tim Manson, a versatile athlete from Tacoma, Washington, who was a 1:48.2 800-meter who won the 1988 Pac-10 title at that distance. "Tim should have run the 1,500," Chaplin said, but then added he came to that realization too late.

According to Chaplin, the only event in which a time in another specific event can accurately predict success is the steeplechase. And that other event is the 800 meters. "In the steeplechase, an 800-meter runner feels like he's walking," Chaplin said. "He can't surge because of the shorter distance and because of the twenty-eight hurdles and seven water jumps. The steeplechase is all about turnover speed [stride frequency]." Historically, Chaplin explained, American coaches would put slower milers with limited turnover speed, or fourteen-minute 5,000 runners whose average lap times are slower, into the steeplechase with limited success.

"An example," Chaplin went on, "would be Henry Rono or Peter Koech or Julius Korir—two world record holders and an Olympic champion. They could all run 1:48 for 800 meters."

In order to assess an athlete's potential, Chaplin said almost all of his steeplechasers were required to run the 800 during the season in the same meet after he had run the 3,000-meter steeplechase and were still a little tired, "giving him the feeling of what it was like in a real fast race."

If there is a common characteristic that separates all great coaches (regardless of the sport) from their less successful contemporaries, it is that they see things a little differently and are willing to do things differently because of their unique point of view. Chaplin and Johnson began their lives in very different circumstances, but they each followed a strikingly similar path in coaching.

"I majored in history and English," Johnson said. "I went to law school. Got drafted out of law school. [With that experience] you see life in a different way. As a lawyer, it's your job to come up with information to cause the judge to rule in your favor. As a coach, it is your job to find the necessary stuff it's going to take [to make your athletes successful], and then apply it." Remember that Chaplin studied geography, history, and philosophy at WSU.

Both Johnson and Chaplin came to the coaching of middle-distance runners from a sprint background. Johnson competed in the 4x100-meter relay in the 1963 Pan American Games in Sao Paulo, Brazil. But, from his days as a competitor to his early years as the coach at St. Albans High School in Washington, DC, to his fourteen-year tenure at Stanford, to his service on the coaching staff of four Olympic teams (He was the head women's coach in 1984), Brooks Johnson, like Chaplin, has maintained a steadfast belief in the need to observe and evaluate and then adjust the way he coached a specific kid.

"Every track meet was like having your own library and research lab on the move," he said. "You look at movement through time and space. Speed is the essential component for endurance. The further you are from your maximum turnover [speed], the farther you can endure." A sentiment shared by Chaplin.

I asked everyone I talked to what they thought people should know about John Chaplin, and Johnson's answer was particularly intriguing. "It depends on your perspective," he said. "In the 1984 Olympics, John had a medalist in the 400 meters and in the 3,000-meter steeplechase." Chaplin also had two world record holders at 10,000 meters. "*Somewhere between the 400 and the 10,000,*" Johnson continued, "*is the touchstone of who John is.*"

When I was eleven or twelve and just beginning to become interested in track and field, my dad came home early from the farm near Granite Falls, Washington, where he worked with my maternal grandparents, and announced we were going to a track meet in Everett, about fifteen miles from our home, at the foothills of the Cascade Mountains. I knew my father was interested in track & field because two years earlier before we moved to Washington State from Santa Cruz, California, he measured out a stretch of pavement in front of our house on Lode Street so he could time me for 100 yards.

We had been watching the Rome Olympics on ABC, and I was particularly interested in the 100 because, as a nine-year-old, it was a distance I could realistically envision myself running. The winner, I remembered, had run 10 seconds, and I was curious to see how close I could come to that time. (Actually, the winner, Armin Hary from West Germany, ran 10.2, edging out American Dave Sime, who had run the same time.)

I don't remember if it was the next day or the following weekend, but we went out into the street, and I ran 100 yards, the first time in my life I would be tested against the clock. My dad got out an ancient stopwatch and shouted "Go," and I ran as hard as I could toward him. When I finished, he showed me the watch and told me I'd run 20 seconds for 100 yards. I was beaming. I told my dad that since I was less than half as old as the guys in the Olympics, 20 seconds was pretty good. He knew better but nodded and smiled and said we could try again next week. A week later, I was slower…and crestfallen.

We didn't talk much about running or track again until that afternoon on the farm. He'd read in the paper there was a pretty good sprinter running for O'Dea High School in the Western Conference Championships, and he thought I'd like to see him run. A couple of hours later, we were sitting in the stands at Everett Memorial Stadium, watching the finalists line up for the 100-yard dash. My dad pointed out a slender black kid who looked nothing like the powerfully built sprinters I remembered from the Rome Olympics on television. But when the gun sounded, he seemed to glide away from the other runners at a rate that was astonishing, even to my inexperienced eye. By the race's finish, he was so far ahead it seemed unfair.

Later in the 220, he again surged away from the field at the start, but what happened next is stamped into my memory as one of the most extraordinary things I've seen in several decades of observing track & field. Halfway through the turn, the strap on Greene's singlet slipped off his left shoulder. He slowed visibly, reached up with his right hand to replace the errant strap, and resumed running. He won the race in an even more dominant fashion than he had in the 100. Charlie Greene was just that good, and his relationship with John Chaplin went back to those days at Seattle's O'Dea High School.

"John Chaplin went to Washington State," Greene said. "And they selected him to give out the awards for the 100-yard dash [at the Washington State High School Championships held for more than sixty years in Pullman]. So, he gave me the award for winning the 100-yard dash, the little medal you get in high school. That was our beginning."

Greene won three state titles for O'Dea and then moved on to the University of Nebraska, where he won the NCAA title at 100 yards three times and tied the world record of 9.1 seconds. After college, Greene won the national title at 100 yards in 1966 and at 100 meters in 1968, tying the world record of 9.9 seconds in the process. After the 1968 Olympics, he entered the army and eventually became the sprint coach at the US Military Academy.

"I became the voting member for the military with USA Track & Field." Greene served on the thirty-nine-person International Competition Committee. That meant he'd be in a position to vote for who would be awarded the various coaching and managerial positions for teams representing the US in international competition and make decisions concerning where the USATF championships and Olympic Trials would be held. Chaplin was chairman of the International Competition Committee, a position he had been appointed to by then USATF president Leroy Walker.

"John came up to me [at the USATF convention], and he says, 'You're Charlie Greene.' I said, 'I was this morning when I looked in the mirror.' Then he said, 'Look, Charlie, do you remember when I gave you your medal at Washington State when you won the 100 in your junior and senior years?' I said, 'I don't remember but thank you anyway.'" And thus began a relationship of mutual respect and admiration that continued until Greene passed away in March 2022.

"John said he was taking over this position, and he needed a secretary. I had just retired from the army, so I became the secretary of the International Competition Committee, the committee that selects coaches for international teams." Greene went on to serve as the manager for several US international teams.

Greene suggested that Chaplin's new position was not one guaranteed to win friends in the coaching community. National team coaching positions are the most coveted jobs in the sport, and as with all institutional decisions, selections are often fraught with politics. From Charlie Greene's point of view, that made Chaplin the perfect person to guide those selections.

"The most significant thing about John is his honesty," Greene said. "That is what he is known for, and men like that are hard to find. He makes a decision, and then he sticks with it."

Greene pulled no punches when he described the inner working of the International Competition Committee, not that someone with his resume would need to. "All the snakes and vipers among the coaches, they will do anything to position themselves to be IAAF, Pan Am, or Olympic coaches. But John knew them all, and he guided the committee to select the best person for the job." Greene pointed out that the first time the committee met, Chaplin told the members he was making himself ineligible for any international coaching or managerial position as long as he was chair of the committee.

Chaplin remembered how Charlie Greene had been amused by his unorthodox method of getting a set of procedures through the International Competition Committee. He handed out copies of the proposed rule procedures, one copy on pink paper for the women's subcommittee and one in blue for the men's subcommittee. In the discussion that followed, there erupted a heated discussion about the color of the copies. Finally, Chaplin had someone stand up and call for a vote on the procedures so they could finally move on to other matters. The discussion of the colored paper ceased, the procedures were adopted, and the committee went on to other matters. It was only later that many members of the committee realized what was in the procedures they had just passed. And later, when he was chairman of the men's track & field committee, Chaplin put in place a rule that prevented members of the selection committee from being named to the staff of any national team.

When Chaplin speaks of his involvement with international competition, he recounts an interesting story. The staff of the US team for the 2000 Olympics was also appointed to lead the US team at the World University Games as a sort of administrative warmup for the Olympics. The World University Games were held on the Island of Palma de Mallorca, Spain, in early July 1999 and had an interesting system in which the coaches of each competing nation named one member of their group to the jury of appeal. Chaplin was elected as the jury member from the US team, and then the other jury members elected him the chair. This may not have been a vote of confidence on Chaplin's competence, but it was an indication of the high regard in which he was held by the coaches participating at the World University Games and by the larger international track & field community.

Mel Pender, as Charlie Greene liked to point out, is a real-life American hero. A certifiable badass. Movies have been made about athletes who accomplished less under less trying circumstances. Pender competed in both the 1964 and 1968 Olympic Games, but his journey from his boyhood in Atlanta to Olympic stardom was as unorthodox as his military career afterward.

Pender joined the army at age seventeen and took up track & field shortly afterward when his exceptional natural speed became apparent in intra-service football games. His precocious dedication also became apparent in other areas of army life, and he eventually entered Officer Candidate School. He was selected for the 1964 Olympic Games in Tokyo, and he made the finals of the 100 meters before an injury hampered his performance during the race. He placed seventh in that race, which was won by Bob Hayes, who ran what some expert observers believe to be the best 100-meter race ever run (given the cinder track and Hayes's limited preparation).

After the '64 Games, Pender returned to active duty and was eventually sent to lead a platoon in Vietnam. This is when the *legend* of Mel Pender should have begun. Qualifying for the US Olympic team in the 1960s and earlier was much different than it is today. Present day Olympians must endure a grueling trial competition that mirrors as much as possible the schedule of the actual Olympics. In the past, the team was "chosen" based on each individual athlete's performance over the course of a season. In fact, the 1968 Olympics, because of the unprecedented challenge posed by Mexico City's 7,382-foot elevation, was the first instance in which the US team would be chosen according to a two-qualifying meet formula.

The United States Olympic & Paralympic Committee (USOC) told all the athletes who had qualified for the 1968 Olympic Trials that they had to run in the AAU championships in Los Angeles. The winner would automatically be on the team and the remaining two places would be the top two from the Lake Tahoe Trials. Then, at Lake Tahoe, the USOC decided to ask the athletes if they agreed with this system or wanted to make it the first three at these trials! The athletes voted for the latter.

When I asked Chaplin about this, he said, "The AAU said you had to run the AAU meet in Los Angeles to be eligible to go to the training camp. I told Mooberry that this is not good for Lindgren. He had just won the 5,000 and the 10,000 at the 1968 NCAA meet in Berkeley, and he was still recovering from an injury prior to that meet. Gerry won the AAU meet in Los Angeles, CA, and thought he was in [on the Olympic team]."

But, as was not uncommon at the time, the AAU changed the rules.

"We had decided to let Gerry take some time off and heal up after a tough NCAA and AAU season because we thought he had made the team by winning the AAU 10,000," Chaplin said. "And we believed the results at the training camp Trials at Tahoe would not affect his place on the team.

"The short version of the story is that Gerry was not ready to compete at Tahoe since he thought he was already on the team from his win at the AAU meet. Lindgren did not make the team at Lake Tahoe," Chaplin said. "And I have never forgiven the AAU or the USOC for allowing that to happen."

For the Trials, the US Olympic Committee had carved out a state-of-the-art running track in the woods at South Lake Tahoe, California (elevation: 6,237 feet). So anxious was the USOC to match the thin-air conditions of Mexico City that they didn't bother to clear the infield of trees, making the South Lake Tahoe site perhaps the most primitive and picturesque venue in the recent history of track & field. Of course, because the Olympic Trials were being held there, athletes from all over the US came to South Lake Tahoe to compete for a place on what some expert observers still believe to be the best team the US would ever send to the Games. And no one traveled further than Mel Pender, but, if he'd had his way at the time, he might have preferred to forgo the opportunity.

"Mel Pender was a captain in the 82nd Airborne," Greene explained, making it clear he was among Pender's most fervent admirers. "He was special forces and a Ranger. If something was humanly possible, he could get it done." When the call came to compete for a spot in the 100 meters on the 1968 US Olympic team, what Pender was getting done was leading a combat platoon in Vietnam. And, as Greene explained, he was reluctant to leave the young soldiers in his platoon.

"Mel Pender was seventh in the 100 in the 1964 Olympics and sixth in the 1968 Olympics," said Greene, who, after his own Olympic career, would himself rise to the rank of major in the US

Army. "But the most important part of that [story] is that he was in Vietnam when a letter from a US congressman finally got to the army." The letter was an appeal to Pender's obvious patriotism and sense of duty and urged him to run for his country in the Olympics. "And they pulled him out of the field," Green explained, "right off the trail he was walking [with his men] and sent him to the army training camp."

Pender made the US team in the 100 meters along with Greene and eventual gold medalist Jim Hines. All three made the finals. Greene finished third, with Pender, who led the race early on, in sixth. Later, Greene, Pender, and Hines teamed with Ronnie Ray Smith to win the gold medal in the 4x100-meter relay in world record time, one of five world records set by American track & field athletes in the Mexico City Games. And according to Greene, it was Pender who was the linchpin for their relay success.

"He had just come out of the field in the Mekong Delta," Greene, who ran the first leg, explained. "And he just ate up the backstretch. Mel handed off to Ronnie Ray Smith, the young kid on the team. We knew that Mel would get him the lead, and he would just run with it."

Which Smith did admirably before handing off to Hines, who made a shambles of the rest of the field on the anchor leg.

After the Games, Pender returned to his men in Vietnam.

It's not too difficult to go online these days and find harsh criticisms of John Chaplin. Of course, I was aware of the criticism when I started this project. All sorts of assumptions about his methods and motivations have been circulating since the 1970s. As a result, there is some ambivalence and uncertainty about the precise nature of Chaplin's legacy. But a better measure when considering one's value is not uninformed ruminations from cyberspace, but rather the quality of the people who will come to his defense or express gratitude or admiration. People like Brooks Johnson, Charlie Greene, and Mel Pender.

"Everything John did as a coach and as an administrator, he was very professional," Pender said. "And he's still the type of guy who cares about people." For Pender, the measure of a coach and an administrator is how well he or she relates to and cares for athletes. "And as an athlete himself, he understands."

He understands. This is a refrain that was repeated by nearly every one of Chaplin's former athletes whom I spoke with. Chaplin understood their reasons for being at WSU, and he understood their expectations, both academically and athletically. He understood their needs in terms of what would happen after they left WSU, hence the emphasis he placed on getting a degree. There may have been some bumps along the way, especially early on, but his understanding grew as his coaching career flourished.

From Pender's perspective, what Chaplin understood was that former Olympians, especially those who had represented the United States before the current, ongoing professionalization of track & field, needed and deserved to be recognized for their contributions. As a high-ranking official in USATF, Chaplin made that happen.

"If you were an Olympian and had a medal," Pender said, his gratitude apparent, "he'd make it so you could get into the Olympic Trials. He would make sure we were taken care of. When he was a coach, and with the US Olympic committee, he was all about the athletes."

The 1996 Olympics were held in Pender's hometown of Atlanta. He even participated in the torch relay, bearing the Olympic flame from City Hall to the stadium, but when it came time for the opening ceremonies, Mel Pender, Olympic gold medalist, world record holder, and combat veteran, could not get into the stadium. That fact rankles him to this day.

"As an Olympian [myself]," Pender said. "And I live in Atlanta, but I could not get a ticket to the opening ceremonies. We [Olympians] didn't have a ticket and were told to go home. Can you imagine that?"

Pender is convinced that if Chaplin had anything to say about that situation, he and other former Olympians would have had a seat at the opening ceremonies. "John would have had a special area in the stadium for us. John understood the politics of track & field. He coached the Olympic team, and he understood the politics, and he still understands."

The 1968 Olympic Games were something of a watershed for track & field aficionados of my generation. We were just beginning to become enamored with the more arcane realities of this most basic of sports. I still have vivid memories of watching those Mexico City Games on our tiny black and white TV set. The heroics of those Games remain indelibly imprinted in my memory, but I wonder how well the exploits of athletes like Mel Pender, Charlie Greene, Jim Hines, Lee Evans, and Jim Ryun are recalled by today's remarkable crop of international superstars. Mel Pender probably wonders the same thing.

"[The way] former Olympians are disregarded still bothers me," he said. "I don't understand why administrators don't recognize or appreciate the contributions of athletes from an earlier time."

The final frustration for Pender is the fact that neither he nor John Chaplin is in the USATF Track & Field Hall of Fame. A situation he would at least partially rectify, were it in his power to do so.

"Anything for John," he said.

CHAPTER 9

YOU CAN'T EAT THE MEDALS

When I started this project, I had no illusions about what it would take to get John Chaplin to talk about track & field. I was reasonably confident that getting the coach to speak would not be a problem. All I had to do was ask questions. I was less sure about how to contact athletes who had subjected themselves to the Chaplin regime and worried a bit that they may not be all that interested in talking about their "glory days."

That was a major miscalculation. Enter Robert Price.

Price had compiled a spreadsheet with the names and contact information for several dozen WSU runners, jumpers, and throwers. He sent me a copy, and I started making phone calls and sending e-mails. I wasn't exactly shocked by the response I received, but the willingness of former Cougars to talk about Coach Chaplin and the effect he'd had on their lives after they left WSU was gratifying, if somewhat surprising.

No one turned down my request for a meeting, a phone interview, or an e-mail exchange. Every single WSU athlete I contacted, no matter where they were in the world, was not just willing to talk about John Chaplin, but anxious to do so.

Since I had a tenuous connection with one of the more prominent athletes on the list, I decided to begin with Kris Durr. Durr had been a standout sprinter, first at Clover Park High School in Lakewood, Washington, a Tacoma suburb, and then at Roger's High School in Puyallup. Puyallup is one of those small farming towns in Western Washington, which, at the time, was slowly becoming a bedroom community for Tacoma, just ten miles to the west. During the time Durr was at Rogers High, I was a reporter for a biweekly newspaper in Puyallup, the *Pierce County Herald*. I'd even written a feature story on Kris on the eve of Roger's annual dual track & field meet with rival Puyallup High. Puyallup was and is one of the preeminent athletic schools in Washington State, and it had been about ten years since Rogers had beaten their cross-town rival in track & field, so the meet was something of a big deal, at least locally.

The climate of the state of Washington—the typically late spring that can leave temperatures on both sides of the mountains in the 40s, 50s, and 60s until late May or early June—and the relatively small population, especially when compared to sprint-heavy states like California, Texas, and Florida, had never been conducive to the production of great sprinters. Distance runners? Yes. Lindgren and Riley are the best examples. Some remarkable jumpers and throwers. But not sprinters—at least, not in large numbers

But if quantity has not been the hallmark of sprint talent in the Pacific Northwest, there has been plenty of quality. From the old days, Charlie Greene, Forey Walter, Willie Turner, and Keith Tinner come to mind immediately, but then Chaplin noted WSU's sprint heritage goes back much farther than that. *See the appendix for more on WSU's history in the sprints.*

In 1982, Kris Durr placed second in the state track meet in all three sprints (the 100, 200, and 400). The caveat here is the winner of all three of those races was the best young sprinter, not just in the state of Washington, and not just in the United States, but in the world.

Darrell Robinson, of Tacoma's Wilson High School, won the 400 at that 1982 state meet in 45.76, with Durr way back in second place, despite running 48.28 and beating the third-place runner by nearly as much as Robinson had beaten him. That 45.76 was to provide the merest hint of what Robinson would accomplish once the high school season ended. Later that summer, he would run 44.69 to set the still-standing national high school record. Durr's best during his junior year in high school was 47.79, so after Robinson graduated in 1982, he entered his senior season seemingly poised to take his place among the small handful of Washington sprint greats.

Kris Durr emerged from Robinson's swift shadow in 1983 to produce one of the most dominant sprint performances in the history of the Washington State Track & Field Meet. His performance all but singlehandedly carried Roger High to the team title. Durr began that 1983 state meet by placing second in the 100. Then he won the 200 and the 400. That's 28 points, which he scored all by himself, more than all but two other entire teams. Then, with Rogers needing big points in the 4x400-meter relay, Kris anchored that team to a second-place finish, securing the team title.

During his senior year, Kris Durr had best times of 10.5 for 100 meters, 21.46 for 200 meters, and 47.10 for 400 meters. That level of performance made him an attractive target for Division I track & field programs from all over the country, but he was pursued with particular enthusiasm by both WSU and Oregon.

"My brother [Al] was at WSU," Kris Durr said. "So, I got a call from Chaplin. He was really engaged with me. I didn't see Dellinger that much [on his visit to Oregon]. Chaplin is who he is, and I liked his directness. His honesty." So, Kris Durr became a Cougar and, ironically, was again in the shadow of another great 400-meter runner. More on that later.

Durr not only agreed to talk with me about John Chaplin, but he also offered to organize a gathering of some of his teammates and other WSU athletes from the same era at his home in suburban Pierce County. But at the time, he was dealing with a serious health issue, so on the scheduled date of the gathering, he was not able to make it. However, he agreed to meet on the day before at the home of Ron Jenkins in West Seattle, and I would meet with the rest of the guys at the Durr home the next day.

So, on June 18, 2021, I met with Kris Durr, his brother Al, and Ron Jenkins, inexplicably nicknamed Beaver, at Jenkins's home in West Seattle. The next day, I met with several more former cougars at Durr's home. At around the same time, I met individually with 7-1 high jumper Lloyd Stoller and 27-plus long jumper and NCAA champion George Ogbeide.

Getting to West Seattle has always been a challenge. The Alki Peninsula, where Seattle was originally settled, is most conveniently accessible from the rest of the city by the West Seattle Bridge. But the bridge has been closed at various times for extended periods due to storm damage or construction. It has even been damaged by being hit by a barge.

When the West Settle Bridge is closed, the adverse effects on traffic ripple across the city, making getting from point A to point B, already challenging in the best of times, almost impossible. On the day I was to meet with the Durr brothers and Ron Jenkins in

West Seattle, the bridge was closed and had been for several weeks. After traversing several detours and navigating along an endless map of narrow side streets, I finally located the Jenkins home on a surprisingly sparsely populated, dead-end street. The house was separated from other residences in the area by an expanse of trees and underbrush, all watered and made lush by Western Washington's frequent—some would say omnipresent—drizzle. When I arrived, Jenkins's wife was just leaving, apparently with better things to do than listen to her husband and the Durr brothers recount the athletic exploits of their youth.

Since this was my first encounter with a group of Chaplin's former charges, I was not sure what to expect. But in the intervening months, I've discovered that what Ron Jenkins and the Durr brothers had to say about Coach Chaplin would be echoed again and again. The singular theme that emerged that day would become a steady refrain whenever any of his athletes talked about their time at WSU.

"If he said something was going to happen," Kris Dur said, "it was going to happen." We already know that Chaplin had little tolerance for his athletes not doing their job in the classroom. As Kris Durr would attest, "Chaplin would take you in his office and say, 'Goddammit, Durr.' His focus was on education. He was so big on education."

"Absolutely," Jenkins added. "One hundred percent."

Okay. We've heard this before. From Chris McBride and Robert Price, and from Chaplin himself. Brooks Johnson hinted at Chaplin's obsession (by now, I've concluded that no other word will do) with his athlete's academic success.

"He'd say, 'Beaver, you can't the eat medals,'" Jenkins said with a laugh. The occasion had been a meeting in Chaplin's office to discuss Jenkins's academic schedule and, apparently, his lack of progress toward a degree. "He said, 'I'm going to take this class away and this class away. Ain't no way you need to take these classes. No dummy classes. You're better than this.'"

Jenkins seemed to find the conversation humorous, but underlying the laughter was a clear hint of appreciation for the fact that Chaplin was not going to let one of his athletes sell himself short in the classroom. "You're going to get a major," Jenkins went on. "It wasn't about giving you a class like underwater basket weaving. 'You're getting a degree in business. Or you're getting a degree in sociology. Or you're getting a degree in history. You are not getting some basic degree in general studies.'"

The implication was clear and obvious. Chaplin intended for his athletes to perform well on the track and then get on with their lives. To get an education, in Chaplin's mind, was to become useful and be able to help others. Chaplin told me during one of our lengthy interview sessions, "Bruce, I can't even remember how many times I've said to an athlete, 'Listen, son, if you can't solve problems after you leave WSU, then I have wasted my money and your time, or you've wasted your money and my time.'"

Kris Durr was typical of one end of the WSU track & field spectrum: the highly regarded high school star with the best sprint credentials in that part of the country. I am biased because I knew Kris in high school and because I had been a sprinter/hurdler who labored mostly in vain to thrive in the damp and cold of more than twenty Pacific Northwest springs. But if Kris Durr had grown up in Texas or Florida, his personal bests out of high school would have been more in the order of 10.2, sub-21.00, and sub-46.00.

Ron Jenkins was at the other end of the spectrum. A decent athlete who transferred to WSU from Bellevue (Washington) Community College, he had no illusions he would ever perform at the same level as the likes of 400-meter greats from WSU like Chris Whitlock or Gabriel Tiacoh.

"WSU was always on my radar," Jenkins said. "But I wasn't ready for WSU [out of high school]. But I think Chaplin kind of took a liking to us local boys. He had his international athletes, and they had their own structure they brought with them, and then he had us local folks. Look at me. I wasn't a world-class athlete. I held my own, but I *was* running *with* world-class athletes and was honored to do so."

Despite his immediate connection to Chaplin, there was one misconception that he laughs at to this day.

"He wanted to see me excel," he said. "We wanted to see me run well, but he also wanted to see me graduate because I'm a local Seattle kid. He thought he pulled me from the *hood*. That's something Chaplin and I still laugh about. I'd say, 'Chaplin, I was never from the hood.' Both of my parents were engineers. But that's my point. He took a liking to us local kids. He took care of us. He made sure we were not going to be failures."

We need to remember that Chaplin's father was a left-wing radical, blackballed in the 1950s, and that he grew up in a lower middle-class white and Hispanic neighborhood in Los Angeles. As a result, he developed a personal knowledge of why it is essential to help all kids get an education, especially kids from a poor background. He knew then, and he continues to believe today, that a college education was the best way to move up in society.

Jenkins went on to explain, and with emphasis, that Coach Chaplin was determined to make sure the in-state kids were performing on the same level as the international athletes, because by the mid-1980s, the perception around the country, and even in much of the state of Washington, was that WSU consisted of just foreign athletes.

The number of WSU kids from that era who performed at the highest level proves Chaplin's point: Kris Durr placed second in the Pac-10 400 and ran 45.86 his freshman year. Brent Harken from Spokane is still the WSU record holder in the high jump at 7'7", Greg Jones is the school's indoor record holder at 7'6½", and James Cunningham won a Pac-10 title at 7'5". All-Americans Dwight Midles, Jim Jesernig from Kennewick, and John Billingsley are all still on WSU's top-10 list in the hammer throw. Forey Walter from tiny Odessa, Washington, Glen Wolf from Spokane, Clarence Williams from Seattle, and Tim Giesa from Spokane (who also ran 46.6 for 400 meters), all four ran 9.5 for 100 meters. Jeff Bruce, at 13.59, was a finalist at the Olympic Trials in the high hurdles, and Carl O'Donnell was the NCAA javelin champion. And remember, it was 26-5 long jumper Bill Ayears who won the bicentennial reenactment of the 1896 Olympic Games in Athens. Not to mention Boyd Gittins, the walk-on who set a world record in the 400-meter hurdles and made the 1968 Olympic team. And there are others. *See the appendix for more of WSU's track & field greats.*

Jenkins also pointed to the extra-educational value of being on what may have been the most diverse college track & field team in the country. He readily admitted that growing up in Seattle had limited his perspective somewhat, but "now I'm going to school [and running] with foreigners," he said. "And not just African foreigners. It was a learning experience, and I took everything in."

One of the unique and perhaps most useful aspects of being on an athletic team in college is that natural barriers that might separate people in a more *normal* social situation seem to crumble under the shared stress and anxiety that occur in the pursuit of common goals. An athletic enterprise simply will not survive in an atmosphere of racial, ethnic, social, or class division.

"What *was* interesting when it came to my African brothers and sisters was how much I learned from them. We made fun of each other. There was a lot of teasing going back and forth because they had their cultural thing, and we had a different cultural thing. We were black, but we came from different parts of the world.

"We had South Africans when South Africa still had apartheid. [We had] Carlos Gambetta from Argentina. He had to fight the war [in the Falkland Islands]. We had Big Ralph [a hammer thrower], and he came from Germany. We educated each other, and that's what made it so beautiful."

What Ron Jenkins described is a nearly perfect *university* experience. I don't suggest that the academic and social environment on the WSU track & field team was at the time unique, but it was rare. I also suspect that if you were to look for organizations on most modern university campuses that are most welcome to the open and unashamed sharing of diverse cultures, those organizations are most likely and frequently to be found in the athletic department. And to Jenkins, that fraternal feeling for the individuals with whom he shared his experience at WSU had not waned.

"I feel like I'm with my brothers right here," he said, indicating Al and Kris Durr. "There's a group of ten or fifteen of us, and we're still very close. We help each other's kids out. We help each other out. And we got that from Chaplin forty years ago."

What I found interesting in all my discussions with former WSU athletes was there were a few common threads, but each guy seemed to have one specific memory of some particular contribution John Chaplin had made to their college life and to their lives after college.

Al Durr's situation was much different than that of either his brother or Ron Jenkins. Despite setting numerous school records at Clover Park High School ("My record only lasted until Kris got there," he said), he was not heavily recruited for his track & field prowess, but fortunately, he was also a very good basketball player. "I went to WSU because they took all my credits," he explained, and because he could play basketball.

So, he was on campus and on the basketball team before his brother Kris arrived. "I would not have been able to stay at WSU if it were not for John Chaplin," Al Durr said. "Because I had used up all my military money early. He *happened* to see me in the hallway, but I think it was strategic because he wanted my brother." Apparently, Chaplin was somewhat familiar with Al's talent for both basketball and track & field because he offered Al a deal, probably with Kris in mind, but to Al, the result would be the same. "I was gym ratting in the gym, and he says, 'What's your name? You got any eligibility?'"

I am doing a lot of speculating here, but again I suspect that Chaplin did indeed have two simultaneous thoughts in mind as he talked with Al Durr. The Durr brothers offered a potential track & field twofer, Kris was a bona fide major league talent, and the addition of another solid 400-meter runner like Al to the team certainly would not hurt.

So, the deal. Al Durr could run unattached in a handful of meets, and if he attained a certain time, Chaplin would give him a partial scholarship. "I ran unattached in two meets," Al recalled. "And I come close, low 47s. But in the third meet, I hurt my hamstring. He said he felt bad about it, so he paid for my summer school and got me a job at basketball camp."

Chaplin's willingness to accommodate athletes like Al Durr paid off again and again. In this case, it was with the 1984 Pac-10 4x400-meter relay championship when Al teamed with brother Kris, Gabriel Tiacoh (the NCAA champion and eventual Olympic silver medalist), and Greek Olympian Sotirios Moutsanas. This was the second time a set of brothers from WSU had won the conference title in the four-lap relay. In 1937, a WSC team set the world record for the mile relay at 3:12.3. The team consisted of Jack Orr, Lee Orr (the NCAA 440 Champion in 1940), Loren Benke (who, in 1937, had also won an NCAA 440 title and set the American and collegiate records in the 400-meter hurdles), and Harry Nettleton (a PCC 440-yard champion who set the one-mile relay world record to win the PCC championship in Los Angeles). The Orr brothers lived in Washington but had dual US-Canadian citizenship.

"Some coaches don't like walk-ons," Kris Durr said. "But he [Chaplin] would give people a chance." He then noted that sharing that Pac-10 title with his brother was the highlight of his WSU track & field career.

One of the things Chaplin did that his athletes, no matter where they came from, appreciated the most was to establish a veritable United Nations of flags encircling the WSU track & field facility at the center of the campus. The national flag of each nation that had represented WSU in track & field was displayed, thirty-one in all.

"My biggest regret," Kris Durr said, "was when those flags came down. Because that was something we were known for." And took pride in. Interestingly, and ironically, a similar ring of flags now surrounds the newly renovated Hayward Field at the University of Oregon.

One of the ironies of Kris Durr's situation was that as good as he was, he only had one year with the spotlight all to himself—that senior year in high school when he led Rogers to the state title. Darrell Robinson was setting the high school world on fire during his junior year, and as a WSU freshman, he placed second in the 400 at the Pac-10 meet behind Gabriel Tiacoh of Cote d'Ivoire. How good was Tiacoh? In 1984, Kris Durr's freshman year, Tiacoh first broke Chris

Whitlock's WSU record of 44.80 in the 400 when he ran 44.64. Later that year, he ran 44.54 to place second in the Los Angeles Olympic Games. And then, in 1986, Tiacoh set a world-leading mark twice, running 44.32 at UCLA and then 44.30 to win the NCAA title.

It is simply not in Kris Durr's personality to hold a competitive grudge. In my capacity as a reporter for his hometown newspaper, I remember speaking to Kris after he placed second to Robinson. He was not even close to being disappointed. He seemed to realize, even as a college freshman, that he'd been exposed to greatness, and he appreciated greatness. The same can be said about the relationship that developed between him and Tiacoh. "For me, it was great," he said.

What Kris Durr possessed at the time was an uncommon level of maturity about his place in the hierarchy of track & field. Even as a high schooler, he had a sense of how good he was and of how good his primary competitors were. Darrell Robinson was the best high school 400-meter runner in the world, and by 1986, Gabriel Tiacoh was the best collegiate 400-meter runner, who ended the year as the No. 1 400-meter sprinter in the world. The fact that he belonged on the same track as the likes of Robinson and Tiacoh told Kris Durr all he needed to know about his own capabilities. "In any other country in the world, I would have been on the Olympic team." Track & field is largely about numbers. And the numbers indicate that Durr's modest claim is accurate. You can look it up.

But beyond fast times and conference titles, Kris Durr echoed Jenkins's sentiment about the value of being exposed to and influenced by the world-class athletes Chaplin brought to the Pullman campus.

"Chaplin set up two meets in the Cote d'Ivoire. I went with Gabriel Tiacoh twice," he said. "The first year Chaplin went, and we took four athletes—Dennis Livingston, Lee Gordon, Kris Durr, and

Tiacoh. The second year Chris Whitlock and Tim Manson went but not Dennis Livingston. Chaplin decided that we were mature enough to go on our own."

Chaplin sent several Black athletes to Africa, he said, because he knew what an impact the trip would have on their lives. The sports editor for the Daily Evergreen, *the WSU student newspaper, accused Chaplin of racism for taking only Black kids. "Sound familiar to what you might hear today," he said.*

To continue…

"Joseph Taiwo was a great mentor," Kris Durr said. "And Francis Dodoo and I were very close. At nationals my freshman year, I roomed with Peter Koech." Chaplin noted that he made room lists, "and over the years, I shuffled athletes around. They got to room with different guys from different cultures."

Taiwo was a 56-4½ triple jumper who was a two-time Olympian for Nigeria. His son Jeremy represented the United States as a decathlete in the 2016 Olympics. Dodoo, also a triple jumper, represented Ghana in the Olympic Games four times. Peter Koech was an NCAA 3,000-meter indoor NCAA champion and 3,000-meter steeplechase champion. He was also the silver medalist in the 1988 Olympics who would eventually break Henry Rono's steeplechase world record in 1989 and is WSU's all-time leader in points scored at the NCAA. Julius Korir was the 1982 Commonwealth Games steeplechase champion, the 1984 Olympic steeplechase champion, the 1984 NCAA 5,000-meter champion, and the 1986 NCAA steeplechase champion. He is still the only male athlete to win the steeple and 5,000-meter races in the NCAA championships.

Finally, I got around to asking the same question I ended each interview with. What is the one thing you think people should know about John Chaplin?

"I go back to caring," Al Durr said. "He genuinely cares about people. I was just some kid off the street. He just reached out and said, 'What are you doing? I did some things and said some things that he could have easily written me off [for]." But he didn't, and as a result, Al got to share a Pac-10 title with his brother.

"I'm going to piggyback off what Al said about caring," Ron Jenkins said. "Truth be told, he was a mentor, a father figure. Quite frankly, we had each other—the guys on the team—but Chaplin was the mentor. 'You're not going to eat the medals, Beaver. You are going to graduate.'"

Kris Durr then succinctly summarized much of what the other two had been saying. "He wanted his program to be special. He just wanted us to feel like we were special athletes and special people. It was the best program at WSU."

And then, at last, there is the single issue that I think John Chaplin would identify as the bottom line. Al Durr made the most direct reference to it, but nearly everyone I've talked to said something along the very same solid lines. "When I think of basketball," he said, "there were maybe twenty-five of us. Over a three-and-a-half-year period, maybe five graduated on time. You had guys who were there for four years, but they were still two years away from graduation. But the track team was different. There was a focus [on school]."

The track team's graduation rate during the Chaplin years was near 97%. Johnson even tells the story of one of their teammates, who Chaplin nagged for years to get his degree. "When are you going to get your degree?" Finally, after his son, who played basketball at WSU, graduated, Bill Ayears got his BA, and Chaplin was instrumental in helping him get a coaching job in Alabama.

"The common denominator was Chaplin," Kris Durr said. "I don't think you see that since he left."

CHAPTER 10

LEGACIES

Tim Manson was (and still is) one of those athletes to whom little things matter. Because he knows, after running 400 and 800 meters under John Chaplin at WSU and after a long career as one of the most successful personal trainers in the Pacific Northwest, those small things add up over time and turn into big things.

Manson came to WSU from the hotbed of prep track & field—especially for 400-meter runners—that was Tacoma and Pierce County, Washington, in the 70s and 80s. Lincoln High, Manson's alma mater, held the Washington high school record in the 4x400-meter relay for almost two decades. Erika Harris from Gig Harbor, just across the Tacoma Narrows, set the all-time state record of 51.54 in the 400 in 1979, a record that still stands. And Darrell Robinson is still the national high school record holder in the 400. He ran 44.69 in 1982 but was not even the best 400 guy on his own Wilson High School team until his senior year.

As a high school and college athlete, Tim Manson was cut from that same mold, a stellar 400-meter sprinter and the state champion in the 800 (once he turned his attention to the track from basketball, his first athletic love). But when he came to WSU after graduating from track & field power Lincoln High, he was nervous about the next four years under a coach with a reputation for being as intense and as demanding as any in the country.

"I was brought up by women," he said, referring to his childhood and youth in a section of Tacoma that was one of the toughest environments in all of Washington State. "I was not used to male authority." Manson soon realized he would have to get used to it, in the person of John Chaplin, if he hoped to thrive in the high-intensity track & field program at WSU or in the ultracompetitive Pac-10 conference. His new coach's focus on both schoolbooks and track meets would initially surprise Manson, but more surprising was Chaplin's encouraging manner when Manson faced a mostly self-inflicted academic crisis early on.

"I remember my first semester at WSU," he said. "I was a 3.5 [grade point average] student at Lincoln, but I got a 3.0 my first semester. I'd never gotten anything below a 3.5, so I was freaking out." This may seem like an unreasonable reaction by a freshman at the end of just his first semester of college coursework, but Manson's response is not uncommon. Good students are often dismayed when they discover their academic performance in high school is not immediately matched in college, even though it's true that most college freshmen would have been thrilled with Manson's 3.0 their first time out of the academic gate.

"Chaplin calls me on the phone in my dorm room," Manson continued. "He doesn't say why he wants to see me. He just says he wants to see me." What Manson did not know was that Chaplin had access to every WSU track & field athlete's academic records, and he kept track of each kid's academic performance and progress as closely as he did their athletic performance and progress.

"So, I walk across campus [to Chaplin's office], and I'm scared. I'm shakin'. I'm not used to authority. I sat down in his office, and he looked at me, and..."

I've mentioned this elsewhere, but one of the things that struck me about this project has been the willingness of former WSU track & field athletes to go out of their way to discuss their memories of Coach Chaplin. Not just to talk on the phone or to exchange e-mails or texts but to meet face-to-face, often at some inconvenience, and talk about the connection between their time with John Chaplin, their education at WSU, and the impact of both on their professional and personal lives. I think it also says something that these "kids" (as Chaplin still refers to them) focus on the good but are also willing to point out aspects of Chaplin's character and manner that made them uncertain or uncomfortable...at least initially.

Manson was part of a gathering of a half dozen former WSU track & field athletes, all of whom, except for triple jumper Joseph Taiwo, had gone to high school in the Seattle/Tacoma area. The gathering was organized by Kris Durr and took place at his home in the Seattle suburb of Black Diamond, even though Durr himself was unable to attend (see previous chapter as to why). In addition to Taiwo, the gathering included Manson, sprinters Lee Gordon, Bryan Johnson, and Dale Catlett, and long jumper Gerald Edwards. Gordon is from the upscale Seattle suburb of Mercer Island. Taiwo is from the West African nation of Nigeria, and the other three are graduates of Garfield High School, another of Washington's preeminent prep track & field powers.

Manson sat outside the main circle and listened during most of our conversation, apparently content to let others speak of Chaplin's virtues and the initial difficulty a couple of members of the gathering had with adjusting to the coach's...um...motivational style. When

Manson did speak, it was at length, with conviction, and with more than a little affection for the man he credits with not only his athletic success but also for laying the very foundation of his professional and family life.

He continued by quoting the coach. "'You know I was taking a gamble bringing you here,'" Manson recalled Chaplin telling him that day in the coach's office. "'Because there were other kids who came from Tacoma into the Division I ranks, and they didn't pan out. Some people told me not to bring you here.'"

Imagine where college freshman Tim Manson's mind must have gone at this point. He'd worried about the phone call from his new coach, stewed as he walked across campus about what awaited him in the coach's office, and now he hears that Chaplin had misgivings about bringing him to WSU at all.

But…

Again, Manson remembered Chaplin's words, recalling the conversation as if it had taken place yesterday rather than more than thirty years ago. "'I want to tell you that you are doing a great job and to keep up the good work.'"

Now, imagine the young Tim Manson's relief. In one brief meeting, one coach-to-athlete conversation, Chaplin had eased the young man's mind and set the emotional stage for his successful collegiate career, both in the classroom and on the track. Manson would go on to win the 1988 Pac-10 800-meter title and run on a 3:05.90 4x400-meter relay team (that included two other athletes from Pierce County. As we've already seen, Pierce County athletes formed the foundation for some of the best 4x400-meter relay teams in the history of WSU track & field.).

John Chaplin, or any other coach in any other sport for that matter, built his reputation with the broader public or within the bubble of a particular sporting community based on the performance of his best athletes. It's impossible to overlook the accomplishments of the likes of Henry Rono, Olympic silver medalist Gabriel Tiacoh, or Dominique Arnold, the NCAA champion and former American record holder in the 110-meter-high hurdles at 12.90.

Of course, there is another side to the WSU program represented by student-athletes with more modest incoming credentials. Dale Catlett, who came to WSU from Seattle's Garfield High School almost as an afterthought and with no intention of running track, is a prime example.

"I was *not* going to the University of Washington," Catlett explained, curiously echoing a familiar refrain by WSU athletes from Seattle. "It was too close." The campus of the University of Washington is less than three miles from Garfield High. "I thought about going to Western [Washington University], but then I got accepted to WSU."

By his own admission, Catlett's track & field career at WSU was anything but stellar. He had personal bests of 10.8 seconds for 100 meters, 22.4 for 200 meters, and 48.9 for 400 meters. Decent times to be sure, but far short of what it took to have an impact at the top of the Pac-10 or the NCAA. But for Dale Catlett, that was not the point. "I was able to get an education," he said. "It [the WSU track & field program] reinforced the ideas of working hard and achieving goals. It also exposed me to different cultures."

Once again, Catlett's experience underscores the fact that how an individual's future unfolds often depends on some unplanned, even unforeseen, development. "I wasn't going there to run track," he said. "I was an okay track athlete in high school. Not great. Not terrible." Catlett may have been demurring a bit on this point because to be *not great* at Garfield in the 1980s was to be pretty good.

"I went there to get an education. A lot of us came over together," he continued. "About halfway through the first semester, I think, we had a gym class, and one of the coaches, [Rick] Sloan, I think, was teaching the class." Apparently, Sloan was on the alert for athletes with sufficient enthusiasm and potential, so he encouraged Catlett to give track & field a try. "So, I went out for track. It was a whim. I hadn't really thought about running track at all."

Catlett had no illusions about what he might accomplish as a collegiate track & field athlete, but he was grateful for Chaplin's willingness to work with a kid who had not been recruited. "I didn't feel like I was great, he said, "because there were a lot of guys at Garfield who were great. But I did okay."

Bryan Johnson, another walk-on, interjected, "He was happy to have us [athletes who had not been recruited] on the team."

Catlett's track & field career did not last four years, but nonetheless, he credits Chaplin with having a crucial positive effect on his college experience away from the track & field program. "I red-shirted [sat out a season to preserve a year of eligibility] and then missed a semester due to a lack of funds," he explained. "I came back and wasn't running as well as I had the first year, and I was having grade issues."

Here, Chaplin's by now well-known and uncompromising emphasis on education steered Dale Catlett down a different path. "Chaplin thought I should focus on school," he said. "And he was correct." Today Dale Catlett is a senior project controls consultant for a consulting company in Seattle. "Currently, supporting Honeywell with their integrated division," he explained, "supporting Amazon fulfillment centers."

I made the point earlier that for students who come to WSU from the heavily urbanized Puget Sound region, particularly from Seattle and Tacoma, getting to and then arriving in Pullman can provide a certain measure of geographical and cultural unease. Driving east on Interstate 90, it doesn't take long (perhaps forty miles), for the urban and suburban sprawl to give way to lush and mostly unpopulated evergreen forests via a stretch of interstate highway that is among the most scenic in America.

But once Interstate 90 crests the summit of Snoqualmie Pass and begins the shallow descent along Lake Kachess and then down into the eastern Cascade foothills, the forest thins out, underbrush becomes sparse, and the verdant landscape suddenly gives way to the broad, flat, brown expanse of the Columbia Basin. The I-90 crosses the Columbia River at the gas-up and snack-up weigh station of Vantage. At this point, the road to Pullman abandons the interstate, and the bulk of the rest of the journey is a nearly straight, 150-mile, two-lane shot on Highway 26, past (but not through) Royal City, Othello, Hatton, Washtucna, LaCrosse, and Dusty, to Colfax, before turning southeast on Highway 195 for the last fifteen miles to Pullman.

I think what a prospective WSU student from the rainy and densely populated environs of Seattle and Tacoma would be struck by is that the further they travel from the lush green of the Puget Sound Basin and the Cascade Mountains, the browner, drier, and more sparsely populated the countryside becomes. In other words, *foreign*. The scattered municipalities along the sere 150-mile stretch of Highway 26 from Vantage to Colfax are home to fewer than 12,000 people, three-quarters of whom live in Othello.

When observers think of *foreign* athletes coming to WSU, they generally think of Africans or Australians, or even Canadians, but I'm not sure the word *foreign* should not, in some sense, apply to those hardy souls who ventured east from the urban hubbub of the Puget

Sound region into the comparative wilds of Eastern Washington and the Palouse.

Like Catlett, Bryan Johnson headed east to get away from Seattle. And, like Catlett, "I did not want to go to the University of Washington. It was too close," Johnson said. "But I did want to continue running track, and I had some friends over there. Actually, there were a lot of us from the [Garfield High] class of '82 who went to Pullman."

This is a point many observers of college athletics often miss. Bryan Johnson and, to a lesser degree, Dale Catlett, went to Pullman with an idea in the back of their minds of continuing collegiately a sport they had come to love while at Seattle's Garfield High, but their priority was, in the words of both, "to get an education." Garfield has long been the Seattle school district's flagship high school. The school has a reputation for high-achieving students, for sending kids to the best colleges and universities in the country (the University of Washington and WSU included), and for having those kids succeed.

But still, "it was definitely shocking," Johnson said of his arrival and first impression of Pullman. "I hadn't been to Pullman until my mother dropped me off there." At this point, the gathering broke out in good-natured laughter, led by Taiwo, whose first impression of the US and Pullman was even more dramatic (possibly even traumatic) and will be covered in the next chapter. "There was no visiting. There was no orientation or tour of the campus or any of that kind of stuff. It was, 'Well, this is where you are going to school.'"

Johnson was grateful that there were other former Garfield students already in Pullman. "A couple of other people from my high school were already there. I went on a whim, and it worked out." It worked out, according to Johnson, in part because of John Chaplin's attitude about *all* of the kids in the track & field program, whether they were national champions, All-Americans, or walk-ons.

"He let people be who they are," Johnson said, suggesting that Chaplin was interested in helping each kid pursue educational and professional goals that would make them useful once they left WSU. "Even though he was about winning, he wanted people to graduate. [Even] people like me, a walk-on. I mean, I scored some points, but he treated me like Joseph [he indicates Taiwo, the Olympian sitting across the table]. He treated everyone with respect."

Then Johnson made what I think might be the most astute and, in some ways, the most interesting observation concerning what motivated John Chaplin. "He wanted to win so he could show people he could do it a *different way*."

Don't misinterpret what Bryan Johnson was getting at here. He had no airy illusions about Chaplin's motivation or his singular focus on winning track meets, but "he cared about you *more* than *just* winning the race," he said. "A lot of coaches, they're just about winning, and they would chew you up and spit you out quickly. Coach Chaplin was about, 'Yeah, I'm going to use you, but you are going to get something out of it. A degree and something you can actually use when you leave here.'"

Gerald Edwards took a more circuitous route to Pullman, and given that he described his relationship with Chaplin as just a little bit contentious, it's surprising that he took the time to show up at this gathering of former teammates.

"I went to school with these guys," Edwards said, indicating Johnson and Catlett. "But I was Class of '80. And the U-Dub [the University of Washington] was too close." Sound familiar?

During the 1980s, I was covering high school sports for a succession of community newspapers in the Seattle/Tacoma area, and wherever I was, I paid more attention to the local high school track & field scene than most other reporters. The first thing that comes to mind when I recall those days was that Garfield High School track & field was good, *really good.* For example, Dale Catlett implied he was just average at Garfield, but what that actually suggests is that he was not *just* average. The same goes for Edwards.

"We won state my junior year," Edwards pointed out. "And we had one guy who was ahead of me in my event [the long jump], Lamar Hurd [the state champion], so there was nothing for me [at the UW]. I was in their own backyard, so I kind of took offense at that [that Washington did not show any interest]."

Despite the lack of interest from that big university just up the street, Edwards was determined to continue his track & field career at the college level. "I wasn't great," he said, "but I wasn't bad either." Not great, but not bad: This is a common assumption among athletes coming out of Garfield High in those days. "So, I thought I'd go two years to a junior college and hone my skills a little bit."

Community college athletics in those days could be something of a crap shoot for prospective student-athletes. There were programs across the country that had coaching and facilities equal to the best NCAA programs, but there were others that would not compare well to even a mediocre high school.

"I went down [to California] and ran for San Diego CC," Edwards said. "And found out I picked the wrong school. I got down there in 1980, but I think the head coach's best years were in, like, the late 60s." Like most competent long jumpers, Edwards was fast enough and athletic enough to run and jump in any number of events, but on a team with a limited number of capable individuals, athletic versatility can prove to be problematic.

"It was a joke down there," he said, disappointment bordering on disgust still evident in his voice more than forty years later. "Somehow, I became this utility kind of guy. I was trying to concentrate on the long jump and the triple jump, and they would come and get me for the mile relay or the 4x100 relay, and I sometimes wouldn't know what I was running."

So once again, imagine what an athlete coming out of one of the top high school programs in the state of Washington, a school known for being well organized and for taking a developmental approach to talented kids like Gerald Edwards, and finding themselves (in Edward's view, at least) in a slipshod, haphazard, disorganized track & field mess.

"We went to some great meets," he said, "like Mt. SAC." The Mount San Antonio College Relays were, at the time, and remain today, one of the best track & field meets in the country, attracting not only top collegians but also the cream of the crop among today's professional athletes.

"But he [the coach] had this thing about people in the field events. We'd get to a meet like five minutes before our event would start. I would literally have to run off the bus and run the long way over to my event, and they would be calling my name, and I wouldn't have any warmup."

So even before that first track season at San Diego CC had come to an end, Edwards was considering his athletic and academic options. It speaks well for the nature of the Garfield High program that even after his miserable experience in Southern California, Edwards was still enthusiastic enough about the sport to want to continue.

Once he had decided that "I am not coming back here," Edwards began to seriously look around for another place to hone his skills. "So, I thought, do I want to go to another junior college? But I went there because I wanted to [eventually] go to a Division I school."

WSU wasn't on Gerald Edwards's radar while he was in San Diego, but then his mother began to send him newspaper clippings with track & field results from the Pacific Northwest, and Edwards noticed that one name kept showing up again and again. "So, I started seeing this guy's name in the paper," he said, indicating Taiwo.

Slowly, the notion emerged that WSU might be a worthwhile destination for a prospective Division 1 long jumper/triple jumper. "It kind of dawned on me that Washington State was also a Pac-10 school," he said. "So, I'll be in a league with UCLA and USC."

The idea of competing against national powers like the two Pac-10 universities in Los Angeles was certainly attractive to Edwards, but also, "I saw the clippings, and all these guys [Taiwo and others] were going over 50 feet in the triple jump. And I'm like, I don't know what they are doing up there, must be something in the water or something like that. If they are jumping that well, I want to be part of that."

Like Johnson and Catlett, Edwards was a Seattle kid. He knew Pullman was somewhere over on the east side of the state, but that was about all he knew. And he recalled a certain level of trepidation the first time he traveled from Seattle to Pullman. "We stopped somewhere," he said. "I don't even know where, and I thought, *What the hell have I got myself into*? We were in the middle of nowhere."

When he finally arrived in Pullman, he did not find much to ease his mind. "It's like someone woke up drunk," he said while the others laughed, "and said, 'I think we'll put a school here.'" Remember Chaplin's initial impression at the gas station when he first arrived in Pullman from LA?

Since he was planning to walk on to the WSU track & field team, some of his former Garfield teammates directed him to Chaplin's office. "They told me I had to go talk to Chaplin," he said. "They said to watch out because he talks really fast. So, I went there the first day to talk to him…. [He talked] so fast my head spun. I remember him mumbling something about *Gerald Edwards* and *I'll see you on Monday*, and I was out of there."

By this point, and it goes without saying, Edwards eventually adjusted to Chaplin's style. He hinted that, at some point, he may have even begun to appreciate the coach's intensity. "He was a fast talker, but he was very honest. I didn't realize he was trying to make me better." A realization that, in time, began to merge with Edwards's own expectations for himself. "He challenged me a lot," he said. "I challenged myself, but he kept moving the bar."

In other words, Chaplin was raising Edwards's expectations.

"Yeah, but I didn't realize what he was doing," Edwards explained. "There were guys he could not always depend on. But I was always there and was like, *Damn. Does he see that or not?* It was a struggle, but it did make me want to be better, so I kept pushing and pushing and trying to be better."

The intensity and intolerance for nonsense are qualities Edwards shares with Chaplin, qualities evident in both men even today. He was, in time, able to see through Chaplin's bluster and recognize it for what it was—motivation. And even though he was not comfortable with Chaplin's approach at first, he persevered. His best mark in the long jump was 25-4 ¼, and he occupied a place on WSU's all-time top ten list until 2012.

As an example, Edwards recalled an indoor meet in which Chaplin had not entered him. Edwards's roommate told him he was not on the travel list for the meet. "So," Edwards said, "I think I better go see what this is about."

Apparently, Edwards was entered in the meet, only Chaplin "just told me, 'You better not screw it up.'" At this point, everyone around the table broke out in sympathetic laughter. After a slow start and trouble getting his steps right, Edwards ended up winning the long jump in that indoor meet. *All that scratching*, Edwards recalled Chaplin telling him. *You could have done a better job.* "And I'm thinkin', *Damn. I just won the meet.*"

The bottom line for Edwards?

Well, he did show up at the gathering, like the others, to have his say about the impact John Chaplin had on him. "It was a sort of pull-and-tug relationship with us," he said. "But when I got to be a junior or a senior, I thought he really cared about people. I found out that bastard really does care about people."

Near the end of Edwards's time at WSU, Chaplin told him as much. "He said, 'Gerald, If I wasn't on your ass all the time, that means I don't give a damn. I'm on your ass because I *do* give a damn.'" Hence, Gerald Edwards's presence at the gathering of his teammates. (Tragically, Gerald Edwards died suddenly on December 9, 2022. "And it was a shock to the entire WSU track & field family," Chaplin said.)

Lee Gordon was, in more ways than one, an anomaly in the insular world of collegiate track & field—a sprinter from a wet, cold, northern state who would become one of the very best sprinters in the NCAA. His background also did not fit the mold of what coaches and other observers might expect from an athlete who went to high school on the sheltered, high-income enclave of Mercer Island, which rests in the middle of Lake Washington, between Seattle and Bellevue. The only experience most people have of this seemingly serene community is when they speed across the island on the I-90 before the Mercer Island floating bridge deposits them into downtown Seattle about a mile or so south and a world away from Garfield High School.

At the time Gordon was attending Mercer Island High, the community boasted the highest real estate values in the state and was reputed to be home to many of the region's wealthiest citizens, as well as a significant number of the area's movers and shakers. Mercer

Island High was known in the prep sports world for great basketball teams, but few athletes who wandered the (assumed to be) gilded halls of Mercer Island High had as much success at the college level as Lee Gordon.

Of course, like just about everyone who ended up on the WSU track & field team, Gordon's journey to Pullman was through an indirect route. He explained that when an assumed scholarship offer from the University of Washington turned out to be much less than what he thought he'd been promised, he lost enthusiasm for the UW and began to look around for another place to run. Ironically, it was the connection he'd made with several Garfield High athletes, some of whom were present at the gathering, that caused him to look east.

"These guys were running for Garfield when I was at Mercer Island," Gordon said. Garfield was a member of the Seattle Metro League, which at the time included all the public schools in Seattle, plus Catholic high schools Seattle Prep, O'Dea (for boys), Holy Names (for girls), and Bishop Blanchet. Mercer Island was a member of the Kingco Athletic Conference, made up of the larger high schools in the suburbs east of Seattle. The distinction matters because there was really no reason for Lee Gordon to know any of the Garfield High athletes other than to occasionally face off in local invitational track meets.

Gordon got to know the Garfield kids by competing in what was, at the time, a very active summertime track & field program in Seattle. "It was easy to get isolated if you were in Kingco," he said. After the UW offer fell through, Gordon started to look around for another place to run.

"Robert Gary Jr. was running for CAYA [the Central Area Youth Association]," Gordon explained. "He told his dad about my situation. It was June, you know, time to decide. Mr. Gary [Robert Gary's father, a star sprinter at WSU] got in touch with Chaplin, and Chaplin called me."

Chaplin arranged a visit to the WSU campus, and Gordon flew east on "Crashcade" Air. "I just remember you land in the middle of a wheatfield. He picked me up, and that's when the first wave hit. The subject [being discussed] is *this*, and he's already two subjects ahead."

Gordon seemed less uncomfortable with Chaplin's demeanor or the rate of his conversation than some of the others. This could be due to the notion that Chaplin considered Lee Gordon to be one of the brightest and most intellectually thoughtful kids he had ever brought into the program.

So even though Gordon may not have been as overwhelmed by his first impression of Chaplin as some other athletes, the coach still needed something to say or something to show that would leave an impression and convince the promising young sprinter to return to WSU that fall.

"He brought me into that office," Gordon said. "And you see everything on that wall. Athletes from way back [someone mentions Rono], and I remember being really impressed. The UW had some really good teams over the years, but nothing like that."

Gordon knew WSU was in the Pac-10 and that the track & field competition in the conference was as good as any in the country. And like many of the Seattle kids who ended up at WSU, he wanted to be close to home. "WSU was my best last-minute choice," he said. "And then seeing all those plaques on the wall and all that history, that just cemented my decision."

As it turned out, it was the correct choice for Gordon and something of an athletic windfall for WSU. Gordon would go on to run 10.29 for 100 meters and place second in the NCAA meet. He also ran 20.83 for 200 meters and contributed a 47.8 leadoff leg to a 3:05.83 4x400-meter relay team, which, as of this writing, has been the WSU school record for thirty-seven years.

Each of the former athletes at the gathering came to WSU, and each experienced John Chaplin's unique approach to motivation in distinctive, though not dissimilar, ways. What each had in common—indeed, what everyone I spoke with insisted on—was that despite their initial misgivings, all were grateful for the role Chaplin played in their development at a formative period in their young lives.

Manson summed it up well.

"My daughter went to Utah," he said. "She's an 800-meter runner like me. In high school, she went to the junior championships, and Chaplin was there. And the contribution that comes to mind in regard to Chaplin is his legacy. The legacy. The legacy."

Then he said to Taiwo, "You have a son. He was an Olympian. All our kids. They're all coming up and excelling."

And expressing a sentiment that seemed to be missing in the relationship between too many kids and too many parents these days, Manson continued, "I tell her [Manson's daughter] that by all means necessary, you are going to meet that man. I'm thinking back twenty-five, thirty years. (But now) He's an old man, and it's 100 degrees, and he's trying to run up the stairs." Manson had already explained to his daughter that he'd met her mother while he was on the track team at WSU. "I told Chaplin to wait. I grabbed my daughter, and we walked down there, and we stand next to him, and I said, 'This man right here is the reason you are here.'"

A legacy indeed.

CHAPTER 11

OUT OF (WEST) AFRICA AND ON TO CHINA

There are two aspects of track & field that make the sport so intriguing to its most dedicated adherents. The first is that the sport is so simple. Who can run from here to there the fastest? Who can jump the farthest? Who can throw an object the farthest? *Citius. Altius. Fortius.* Faster. Higher. Stronger. It is basic. Track & field skills (running, jumping, and throwing) are foundational to every other sport.

The second is the extraordinary range of physical attributes that track & field can accommodate. Tiny distance runners: Many of the women in the 2022 world championship recently concluded in Eugene, Oregon, weighed less than 100 pounds. And enormous throwers: American shot putter Ryan Crouser, the world record holder, world champion, and Olympic champion, is six-foot-seven and weighs 320 pounds. World discus champion Kristjan Čeh from Slovenia is six-foot-nine.

But what does the wide range of body types apparent at a world-class track & field meet have to do with WSU and John Chaplin? Think back to 1968 when Chaplin first arrived at WSU as Jack Mooberry's assistant. Two of the world-class athletes he worked with at the beginning were Gerry Lindgren (nicknamed the Sparrow because, at five-foot-six and less than 120 pounds, he was small even by male distance running standards) and John Van Reenen (the massive South African shot and discus thrower). It's worth a reminder here that Lindgren set a world record in the six-mile run and that van Reenen set a world record in the discus.

This is the nature of track & field.

In his excellent book *The Sports Gene*, David Epstein makes an interesting observation concerning the American reaction to the emergence of African distance runners in the 1960s. To paraphrase, some Americans were shocked by the success of Black athletes in the longer races because, to the American mind, Blacks were sprinters and jumpers. They specialized and excelled in speed and power events. Distance running was a white sport dominated at the time by Europeans and a few Americans. Then along came Ethiopian Abebe Bikila. This marvel of a runner won both the 1960 and 1964 Olympic marathons, running barefoot on the cobblestoned streets of Rome in 1960. Then in 1968, Kenyan athletes dominated the long races in the thin air of Mexico City, leaving the likes of Jim Ryun (in my mind, the greatest American middle-distance runner ever) in their wake.

Epstein's book is a fascinating study of what, in some circles, might be a taboo subject: the notion that genetics and geography give athletes from certain regions of the world an inherent advantage in certain track & field events. Anyone paying even casual attention to international track & field events can easily see that black athletes from the Caribbean, West Africa, and the US has historically excelled in a different category of events than Black athletes from East African nations like Kenya, Ethiopia, and Uganda.

Epstein makes the case that it is more than culture or lifestyle or high altitude. Innate advantage is influenced by genetics combined with a multitude of biological adaptations and reinforced by local cultural norms. Those genetic advantages and those cultural norms have made it possible for East African athletes to excel in races above 800 meters and athletes who trace their ancestry to West Africa (like Black athletes in the Caribbean or the US) to excel in events below 800 meters.

Aha, a skeptic might say. What about Bernard Lagat, the American record holder of the 1,500 meters and the only man to win the 1,500 and the 5,000 in the same world championship meet. Or Britain's Mo Farah, who won the 5,000 and the 10,000 at the Olympics twice. Or multiple Olympic champion Sifan Hassan from the Netherlands. Or Mohammed Ahmed, the Canadian champion. All are Black distance runners competing and winning for European or North American countries.

Well...Bernard Lagat is a former Kenyan who came to WSU with average times and left in 1999 with the still-standing collegiate 1,500-meter record of 3:30.6. Lagat became an American citizen after his stellar career at WSU. Farrah was born in Somalia and illegally trafficked to Great Britain as a small boy. Hassan, an Ethiopian, came to the Netherlands at the age of fifteen. Ahmed was born in Mogadishu and spent his early childhood in Kenya before his family immigrated to Canada when he was eleven.

The point is that many of the best distance runners in Europe and North America have direct and very recent connections to the dynastic running traditions and the genetic predisposition for long racing in East Africa.

Conversely, as Epstein points out in *The Sports Gene*, American and Caribbean sprinters and jumpers (and increasingly throwers) can trace their ancestral and genetic heritage to West Africa. Epstein suggests that an aptitude for specific track & field events is much more a matter of geography and biology (that is evolution) than of skin color.

Chaplin agreed with Epstein's thesis to a point, but added, "Just having a genetic predisposition alone [specifically, high red blood cell count and slow twitch muscle fibers], which is common among certain East African groups, but certainly not exclusive to athletes from that part of the world, is not the sole factor in distance running success." He pointed to three factors: high max VO2, intelligent racing tactics, and effective training (including, of course, surging drills).

"And, he said, "the concept of putting the tribe first and the individual second, which leads to a willingness to engage in team running. All these factors have helped East African athletes ascend the distance running mountain."

On the other hand, "the formula for success for West African athletes with fast twist fibers is to train for explosive power and strength using plyometric-type drills and weightlifting," Chaplin explained. "Fast-twitch muscle fibers contain a low amount of myoglobin while slow-twist muscle fibers contain a higher amount of myoglobin. This means fast-twitch muscle fibers consume oxygen instantly, while slow-twitch muscle fibers consume oxygen slowly but in a very efficient manner.

"To put it in simple terms, fast-twitch muscle fibers contracts relatively rapidly. They are utilized in actions requiring maximum effort of short duration, such as sprinting. Slow-twitch muscle fibers that contract relatively slowly and are resistant to fatigue."

Which brings us around to the implications this would have for Chaplin and the WSU track & field program. Ask almost any longtime observer of collegiate track & field what comes to mind when the WSU program is mentioned, and the first name that comes up will likely be Henry Rono or Gerry Lindgren for the real old-timers. But I have a hard time separating the two because Lindgren is from my home state and was setting records at a time when I was first becoming obsessed with the sport. But in addition to Lindgren were athletes like John Valiant (who, in 1964, became the first WSU athlete to run under 9:00 in the steeplechase), and then Rick Riley, and later Rono, Kimombwa, Tuwei, Korir, Kimeto, Ngeno, Muturi, Kapkory, Koech, Kibiri, and later still Lagat—Kenyan athletes who kept the eyes of the distance running world focused on Pullman, Washington, during the last third of the twentieth century, some thirty-five years. *See the appendix for more on the Kenyan influence on the WSU program.*

But Chaplin was quick to point out another list of names and to insist that those athletes not get lost in the conversation over what it took for WSU to rise to the top of NCAA track & field.

Taiwo, Kablan, Dodoo, Tiacoh, Ogbeide, Olobia, and later, Hilary Mawindi—athletes from West Africa who occupy numerous spots on WSU's all-time top-ten list include a pair of NCAA champions (Ogbeide in the long jump and Tiacoh in the 400. Tiacoh also received an Olympic silver medal in 1984 and, as mentioned earlier, Tiacoh led the world in the 400 at 44.30 in 1986.).

I've dealt with the international flavor of WSU's top-ten lists and school records in the appendix, but suffice it to say for now that, though not as numerous, athletes from western African nations had a profound and prolonged impact on track & field at WSU.

While preparing this project, I spoke with three of these gentlemen—sprinter/long jumper George Ogbeide, triple jumper Joseph Taiwo, and sprinter George Kablan. And the difference between what I remember of the early Kenyans and the West Africans who came later is as pronounced as the events in which each group excelled. I hope I'm not dealing with stereotypes here, but the West Africans were, by and large, more forthcoming and more anxious to talk about Chaplin and the opportunity provided to them by WSU. I remember the Kenyans from the 70s being not exactly reticent, but more reserved. I wonder if the impression they left on me was a product of the time when African athletes were still a novelty in NCAA track & field or the result of some natural and culturally enforced tendency to keep their own counsel.

George Ogbeide, along with his American-born wife, Kara, was one of the first people to meet with me when this project was in its earliest stages. Ogbeide helped his native country Nigeria to a fourth-place finish in the 4x100-meter relay at the 1991 world championships, just a few weeks after winning the NCAA long jump title for WSU. George Kablan came to Pullman from Cote d'Ivoire. He was an All-American in the 4x400-meter relay for WSU in both 1980 and 1981 and is still the school record holder for the indoor 400 at 46.2. Taiwo was part of that gathering of former Cougars who met with me at Kris Durr's home in the Seattle suburb of Black Diamond. Taiwo was a four-time indoor All-American in the triple jump (from 1981 to 1984), an outdoor All-American three of those four years, the Pac-10 champion in '82 and '84 and remains the (official) school record holder at 56-4¾, a distance that would have ranked him as high as seventh in the world as recently as July of 2022

Australian Ian Campbell jumped 57-4¾ at the 1980 Moscow Olympic Games. At the time, Campbell's mark was ruled a foul, but a subsequent video has shown that Campbell's jump should have counted. Campbell had at least three jumps long enough to have won the gold medal, but all three were ruled fouls. Interestingly, athletes from the host country finished first and second. When Campbell's mark is verified and recognized (the Australian Federation has already done this), he should be awarded an Olympic gold medal. In the meantime, Campbell's mark should be recognized by WSU, making him the current school record holder. *As late as 2022, the discussion with the WSU Sports Information Director concerning Campbell's mark is ongoing.*

"The Pac-12 and WSU were not made aware of this change in Campbell's mark until 2017, a year after the conference named its all-century team in the triple jump," Chaplin said. "As a result, Joseph Taiwo was named athlete of the century for his overall competitive record, and rightly so."

An interesting side to all this is the central role Chaplin played in getting a former University of Washington athlete's world record recognized. Several errors led to UW long jumper Phil Shinnick not being recognized for his world record mark of 27-2, which he set in 1963. It took Chaplin and others until 2021 to get the IAAF to recognize Shinnick's record.

When I met with George Ogbeide, I was immediately struck by the notion that even though it had been more than thirty years since he won the NCAA long jump title for WSU, he still looks athletic enough to not appear out of place on a collegiate long jump runway. He strikes an impressive figure, tall, still lean and hard, with the regal carriage and confident demeanor of an athlete who knows what he is about.

There is no direct route to Pullman, Washington, from most other places in the world. But Ogbeide travelled to WSU by an even more circuitous route than normal due to a brief side trip to the University of Idaho in Moscow, just eight miles east of WSU.

Like the Kenyans who had paved the way for African athletes to come to the US, education was at the top of young Ogbeide's priority list, but first, he had to convince a skeptical father that it was a good idea to travel halfway around the world to compete and study in a section of the US that was virtually unknown to the majority of people in Nigeria or the rest of West Africa.

"I had a coach in high school who was one of the best combined jumpers in the world in the 70s," Ogbeide explained. "He went to Illinois. He's, like, you've got talent. You could get a scholarship and go to America."

But Ogbeide was a first son, and he pointed out that in Nigerian culture, a first son bears an enormous responsibility to set a proper example for younger siblings. And from the point of view of his traditionally minded father, the United States was not an ideal place to spend the early years of his young adulthood.

"My dad had reservations about me coming to America," Ogbeide said. "Because I was a first son and because we never heard anything good about America. Just like if you listen to the news here [in the US], you never hear anything good about Africa. The only thing we heard about America is people shooting people, and everyone is a cowboy."

When Ogbeide showed up in Moscow, Idaho, in the late 1980s, I do not think the "shooting" situation was much of a problem, but the "everyone's a cowboy" part was probably close to the truth. In any case, his coach convinced Ogbeide's dad that Moscow, Idaho, was nothing like the chaotic version of America he had in his mind. Young

Ogbeide needed to long jump twenty-two feet to earn a scholarship. He did so and was off to the rugged mountains and frigid winters of northern Idaho.

"It was cold," he remembered. Nigeria, of course, is a tropical nation smack in the middle of the continent's west coast and just north of the equator. By the standards of the inland Pacific Northwest, Nigeria does not have winter. "I wanted to go to Arizona. I came in the winter, and I had never seen snow. We had a track meet spring break in Tempe, Arizona, and it was still snowing in Moscow."

It's a story we've heard from Potential WSU athletes before. The weather and the isolation provide a daunting challenge to kids from Eastern Washington and Idaho who already know what they are getting into when they come to Pullman. But for a young man from a tropical climate who had never traveled any farther from home than neighboring Ghana, adapting to life on the Palouse was almost too much to bear.

"It was a struggle. I did not want to stay," he said. "This was not the America I envisioned. Not the picture in my mind of what America was going to look like."

Imagine the following scenario from the point of view of an untraveled Nigerian teenager after he landed in Spokane and was picked up to travel to Moscow, Idaho, by car.

"Spokane looked like a city," he said. "We kept going and going, and I fell asleep. When I woke up, we were in Colfax, and I'm like, where are we?"

For those unfamiliar with that part of the country, there is nothing except scattered settlements and empty fields between Spokane and Colfax. "Even though I wanted to leave, we had people around the University of Idaho who wanted to do great things in track. [I thought] maybe I should give this place a chance."

The University of Idaho is one of the best-kept secrets in American higher education. It is home, for example, to one of the finest music schools in the country. But it suffers somewhat from an athletic identity crisis. An original member of the Pacific Coast Conference (the forerunner of today's Pac-12), Idaho has also been a member of the Western Athletic Conference, a football independent, and is now back in the Big Sky, which, these days, is in the NCAA football division, one step below Division I.

This uncertainty and the fact that the U of I is only eight miles (but a world away) from the Pac-12, has made it hard for the Vandals to keep athletes from transferring across the Washington-Idaho border. Such was the case for George Ogbeide, with a nudge from a fellow West African, Francis Dodoo.

Francis Dodoo was from Ghana and was also a triple jumper at Idaho. Since we've brought up the topic of body type, especially as it relates to the difference between athletes from the two sides of the African continent, it's worth pointing out that Dodoo was a significant anomaly in the world of world-class triple jumpers. The triple jump requires speed and power, which usually come from the application of force by long levers. World-class triple jumpers are rarely less than six feet tall. What made Francis Dodoo unique was the fact that he jumped beyond 55 feet after transferring from Idaho to WSU (taking Ogbeide with him), despite standing only five-foot-five. The triple jump was not the only area in which Dodoo excelled. After WSU, he graduated near the top of his class at the Wharton School at the University of Pennsylvania with a Ph.D. in economics.

Anyway…

Dodoo (and Ogbeide) began to recognize that, despite not having any dissatisfaction with the University of Idaho, there were certain athletic advantages to competing in the Pac-10 against programs like

UCLA, USC, Stanford, and Oregon, rather than in the Big Sky against schools like Montana and Montana State.

So, Dodoo and Ogbeide made the eight-mile move across the Washington-Idaho border to compete for WSU.

"I didn't even know WSU was eight miles away," Ogbeide said, admitting with a laugh that even after spending time in Moscow, Idaho, he still did not know much about that part of the world. "I knew about New York. That was my entire knowledge [of the US]—or California."

But he did know that "WSU was a great school with a great program."

And he must have known at least a little about WSU's mercurial head coach. By the time Ogbeide arrived in the US, Chaplin's reputation as a blunt-spoken advocate for WSU track & field had been well established. In the early days, when he called out the Oregon press for an unflattering (even offensive) question about Henry Rono's literacy or lack thereof, Chaplin was something of a novelty. But by the early 80s, he was known for speaking out whenever he thought his athletes or the sport of track & field had been maligned. What struck George Ogbeide was that John Chaplin was an authority figure who fit in perfectly with a young Nigerian's expectation of what an effective authority figure should be.

Ogbeide became acquainted with Chaplin while he was still running at Idaho. With its unique 300-meter track, the Kibbie Dome, the University of Idaho's then state-of-the-art indoor track & field facility, was a common venue for collegiate teams from all over the Pacific Northwest during the winter months. And, of course, WSU was just up the road, only eight miles from the Kibbie Dome. Ogbeide must have had some inkling of Chaplin's reputation for intensity.

But "my first impression of John Chaplin was that he was friendly to everyone. Another thing I noticed was that he was about the same age as my dad." On the surface, that should not be much of a concern. An American kid would consider Chaplin's age an advantage. But "in Nigerian culture, you do not talk to elders," Ogbeide explained. "So, I was very apprehensive about how to deal with him. But then he comes at you with so much ease, he makes you feel comfortable."

This ability to recognize when a young person is uncomfortable or apprehensive, especially young people from other parts of the world for whom American culture is foreign, and then put them at ease is, without doubt, Chaplin's greatest strength as both a recruiter and as a coach.

"He saw my apprehension," Ogbeide said. "But he treats everyone with respect. He's fatherly. He does not have a favorite. [It doesn't matter if] you don't do well or if you do well."

Over the years, I've had conversations with teaching, coaching, and reporting colleagues concerning the relative merits and real-world value of athletic programs in colleges, universities, and high schools. The conversation inevitably comes down to a debate over whether the time, the money, and the energy expended on sports are worth it when academics are, by definition and by necessity, the primary mission of schooling. Ultimately, any discussion would always come down to whether athletic programs exist to enhance a school's athletic mission or whether athletics in school have an intrinsic value of their own—that is, benefits that exist separate from the classroom.

The answer to both questions is yes. Sports programs do indeed enhance a kid's chances of succeeding in the classroom, and yes, athletic competition has intrinsic value entirely separate from academics. My attitude, of course, is based on a unique American perspective and experience with the connection between school and sports. But a *student*-athlete like George Ogbeide—and others whom we've already met—the two are inseparable. One makes the other possible.

"My dad tells us, 'I don't have anything for you.'" In saying this, Ogbeide was not in any way criticizing his father. He was simply pointing out the reality that young people in much of the world grow up with no concept of the options that young Americans have. "He said to get an education. 'Education opens doors.'"

Then he cited John Chaplin's pledge, the promise Chaplin made explicitly to every athlete in his program for more than twenty-seven years. "He promised two things. You'll get great training, and you'll get an education," he said. "He gave me an education. Everything he promised actually happened. I had an athletic career, and I got an education. This is a debt I owe."

I am certain that from Chaplin's point of view, Ogbeide's debt was paid in full by his performance, particularly the NCAA long jump title he won in 1991. I've spoken to several members of that 1991 team, and all insisted that was the best WSU team ever. In 1991, WSU was the favorite to win the team title, but Tony Li, the national leader in the high hurdles, hit a hurdle while leading the final and failed to finish. The Cougars ended up in second place, nine points behind national champion Tennessee.

"I think our team was the best," Ogbeide said. "But Chaplin was a diplomat. We always said ours was the best team, but he would never deny or confirm it. He says '77 was good or '84 and '86 were good. 'Yeah, those guys were good, but we were well-rounded.'"

That '91 WSU team came away from the national meet with eight All-Americans in events as wide-ranging as the 100 meters and the 10,000 meters: Augustine Olobia in the 100 meters, Robert Price and John Hill in the steeplechase, and E. J. Gou from China in the 10,000.

Both George Ogbeide (in the long jump) and Kenyan Samuel Kibiri (in the 1,500 meters) won national titles. (Kibiri was also the runner-up in the steeplechase.) The 4x100-meter relay also scored.

The 1977 team, as was discussed earlier, was the NCAA indoor national champions.

The '84 team might have been even better with twelve All-Americans. Julius Korir, who would go on to win the 1984 Olympic gold medal in the steeplechase, won the NCAA 5,000. Peter Koech, who would eventually break Henry Rono's world record in the steeplechase, was second in the 5,000 meters. Mercer Island High School's Lee Gordon was runner-up in the 100 meters, and there were still others.

That 1986 team was the last of three WSU straight teams to place second at the national meet, losing the national title to Southern Methodist by a single point, just as the 1968 team had lost to USC when Chaplin was still a WSU assistant. The team included two national champions—Gabriel Tiacoh in the 400 and Julius Korir in the steeplechase. Both had been Olympic medalists in 1984. (Tiacoh won silver in the 400 meters in 1984, and of course, Korir won the gold in the steeplechase.) Then there was *The Viking*, Tore Gustafsson, and NCAA Champion and the collegiate record holder in the hammer throw.

Even though he was part of WSU's cadre of international superstars, Ogbeide remains impressed by the names arrayed on the wall of Chaplin's office. "Lindgren. Rono. It overwhelms you. If you hang around here long enough, you want your name on that wall too. You think, *'I want to do more.'"*

Joseph Taiwo, another Nigerian, was a member of two of the WSU teams that placed second at the national meet. Taiwo and Kablan were both steered toward WSU by Lee Evans, the 1968 Olympic 400-meter champion who was the first athlete to run that distance under 44.00.

"Lee Evans was the one who talked to Chaplin about me," Taiwo said. "Chaplin would go anywhere to get athletes, and I was supposed to be this up-and-coming guy in Nigeria."

Taiwo met Chaplin in Senegal for the African Championships in Athletics, and Evans introduced him to the WSU coach. Despite Evans's endorsement, Taiwo did not apply to WSU initially. "I was going to Missouri. The majority of Nigerian athletes were going to Missouri."

That was in 1979, the same year Taiwo injured his ankle badly enough that his entire athletic future was in jeopardy. "Nineteen-seventy-nine was the first time I made a national team to Senegal. The first time I ever traveled outside of Nigeria," he explained. "I did not do very well. I was trying to impress everyone there. I took off, and my hop [the first phase of the triple jump] was about this high off the ground." In other words, he was too high in the air in the initial phase of the jump. "And I'm like, '*Oh my God. What are you doing?*'" And when I came down, my ankle was gone." And with it, potentially, his collegiate future in the US.

"After that track meet, we went home to take care of my ankle, and a month or two later, I got this letter [of intent] from Washington State University, and I'm [thinking], '*Hmmm. I did not even remember I had applied to Washington State at Coach Evans's request.*' So, we opened it up, and I looked at it. And my brother looked at it. And my dad looked at it."

Not sure what to make of an overture from a school he had never heard of in a part of the US he had never heard of, Taiwo and his family sought input from a friend who had studied in the US and was working at the time for the Pepsi-Cola Company. "We showed him the letter," Taiwo remembered. "And he says, 'Grab your passport and take this letter to the U.S. Embassy.'"

"So, I go there, and I give my passport to the guy. He doesn't ask me a single question. He hands me back my passport and says, 'Have a nice life.' *Have a nice life.* That is what he said. So anyway—getting into the US was easier in those days…the first plane out of Nigeria to the US, I was on it."

Of course, Taiwo's first stop in the US was New York Kennedy International Airport. It was midwinter, and the kid from the tropics saw snow for the first time. "When we flew into JFK," he recalled, "and saw this white stuff on the ground as high as the airplane, I thought, *What the hell is that?* It was indeed snow. Which I had never seen in my life."

Chaplin's response? "Joseph, coming to WSU was the best decision you ever made in your life."

Then it was on to Pullman…in late January. "And it was freaking cold," Taiwo said. Not to beat a thematic dead horse, but just imagine… Young Joseph Taiwo had never been out of Africa. He had only been out of his home country once for a brief and injury-marred trip to neighboring Senegal, and his first impression of the United States is Pullman, Washington, in late January, in the snow. "It was freaking cold," he reiterated. "I [later] told Chaplin he was one lucky son of a gun because I had a one-way ticket. If I had a round-trip ticket, I'd have gone back home."

When Taiwo finally arrived in Pullman, Chaplin met him at the airport, and the young athlete settled in almost immediately. "That afternoon, I went to practice and was so happy to see a bunch of Black faces, and they were really nice."

Here is where the culture shock rubber meets the determined purpose road for athletes who came to WSU, whether from Seattle, Spokane, Kenya, or West Africa. "It was a shock," Taiwo said of his first impression of Pullman. "But I didn't let that affect me because I knew why I was there. This is what I had to do. Go to school and run track." And if he did those two things with diligence and determination, "they were going to take care of me for four years."

And in that winter of 1980, for a young athlete like Taiwo—a kid from a foreign land with diligence and determination—WSU turned out to be the perfect landing spot, and John Chaplin turned out to be the perfect stand-in father figure. "You go to school. You work on your degree. You get the grades because that is what [Chaplin insists] you have to do to run track," Taiwo explained. "It does not matter how good you are. You have to maintain certain grades, or you can't compete."

At this point, Taiwo made a point that might surprise some of Chaplin's more ill-informed critics. His reputation for intensity in pursuit of team titles was well-known and well-founded. But Taiwo wants it known there was much more to the relationship between Chaplin and his athletes than scoring points or setting records.

"If you can't compete," he said, "then you redshirt." Redshirting is the practice of holding an athlete out of competition for one or more seasons to preserve a year or more of eligibility. "In 1983, I wasn't sure what was happening. I told John I needed a break. And he was fine with that."

Losing an athlete like Joseph Taiwo for a year would be an enormous setback for the WSU team. But "I'm glad I took that break because the next year, 1984, was incredible." In 1984, Taiwo placed seventh in the triple jump at the 1984 Los Angeles Olympics. He was an NCAA All-American both indoors and outdoors, won the second of his Pac-10 titles, and set the then-WSU school record in the triple jump at 56-4¾. "I just needed that break."

In some ways, Joseph Taiwo and the other West African athletes provide a perfect example for critics of Chaplin's recruiting practices. The Kenyans were one thing. Distance runners of that caliber were not plentiful in the US at the time, and those who were available were not interested in a place like Pullman. Gerry Lindgren and Rick Riley were obvious exceptions.

But sprinters and jumpers were plentiful in the US (though maybe not twenty-seven-foot-long jumpers or fifty-six-foot triple jumpers), so why not recruit athletes who grew up close to home? "He is what he is, and he does things the way he does them," Taiwo suggested, "because he has no choice. I remember in 1984 in Eugene, Oregon, we're all in the room, and he says to go out and compete because [on some level] this is all about him. The school didn't help him at all. [He felt like] he was doing everything himself."

I want to clarify something. I did not at any time feel like Taiwo was suggesting Chaplin's motives were selfish. He was simply making the point that the more successful the athletes were, the more seriously the university might take their coach and his program.

"Look at that program," Taiwo said. "Look at what he has done. You would think the administration…" Taiwo's voice trailed off, and he thought for a few moments before shaking his head.

George Kablan's story should by now be familiar. A talented young West African sprinter, recruited by a couple of warmer weather schools (New Mexico and San Jose State, in this case) and confused about the location of WSU, ending up in Pullman at the behest of a track & field icon. He did know more about WSU initially than Taiwo did. "Henry Rono and Samson Kimombwa," he said, "were teammates on the African team [that competed in the IAAF world cup], and coach Lee Evans recommended WSU to me."

Kablan was a 4x400-meter relay All-American in 1980 and 1981. He still holds the WSU school record for the indoor 400 at 46.2 and is third on the school's all-time 200-meter list with a best of 20.61. Remember his earlier comment about Chaplin "hunting cougars"? It is performances like 46.2 and 20.61 that Chaplin had in mind.

"Do not laugh at me, please," he said, laughing at himself at the beginning of our phone conversation. "When I was in contact with John Chaplin, I thought WSU was in Washington, DC. I had a cousin working at the Ivory Coast embassy in DC, and I was happy to join him."

So again, the familiar journey from the other side of the world to the other side of the state of Washington. "I flew Air Afrique and landed in New York," he said. "John Chaplin had someone meet me at Kennedy airport to take me to Northwest Airlines."

Kablan assumed the flight from New York to DC would be short. But "over three hours later, we are still in the air. But my map shows Washington, DC, very close to New York, and it shouldn't take more than one hour. Panic. I contacted the airline lady. She checked my ticket and told me I was going to Washington *State*. Where is that?!"

Fortunately, there was another passenger on that flight headed for WSU. "She found someone on the flight going to WSU. It was Samson Kimombwa, a long-distance runner from Kenya who I knew." Then, typically, "Here we are in Pullman, and the trees are white...[as] snow."

George Kablan graduated from WSU in 1982 with a degree in communications. He worked for a time for the Special Olympics International as the organization's regional director for Africa. "I met many great people," he said. "Mrs. Kennedy and Sergeant Shriver, African politicians and political leaders." But none, he suggested, were any more remarkable than John Chaplin.

"Pullman has been on my mind," he said, summing up his recollections of his time at WSU. "And John Chaplin is in my heart. No problem can beat John Chaplin. He has a solution for every problem. If John Chaplin was the problem solver in Heaven, believe me, there would never be wars on Earth."

When Chaplin heard this, he noted that Kablan's statement might have been more than a little bit over the top, "but it probably fits the attitude, if not the rhetoric, of most of the young men I had the privilege of working during my twenty-seven years at WSU."

Just as Chaplin had turned East to Africa to find athletes, he now looked west to China. With the help of coach James Li, he found two gems in hurdler Tony Li and distance runner E.J. Guo. But again, as with the two John Ngenos there was a problem with their names. Chaplin pointed out that Li's name was Tong Li, but word *Tong* has a dubious connotation in the US. So, Chaplin told him is new name was Tony Li, a name that students would understand. Li came to WSU as a sprinter/long jumper (10.5 for 100 meters and 25'0" in the long jump with little experience in the hurdles. But he blossomed into a Pac-10 high-hurdle champion and would become a two-time NCAA champion and collegiate record holder in the 55-meter-high hurdles indoors.

Li's development into one of the best hurdlers in the world is another example of Chaplin's penchant for finding just the right event for an athlete, whether he had any previous experience in a particular event. Tony Li would eventually set Asian and Chinese records in the 110 hurdles and was on the Chinese world championship and Olympic Teams.

Chaplin went on to explain that Guo's problem was the spelling of his name. "It had so many letters, it would have been impossible for Americans to pronounce," he said. "The press would have screwed it up every time that they tried to say it or spell it. But it sounded like *E.J.* so I decided to tell him that his new names was *E.J. Gou*. Succuss. All the students loved Gou's name."

Gou became an NCAA All-American in Cross Country, indoors at 3,000 meters, and outdoors at 5,000 and 10,000 meters. He was also a two-time Penn Relays 10,000 champion, and he won Pac-10 Conference titles at 5,000 and 10,000 meters.

Gou's second Penn Relays win in 1991 was something of a surprise. "Gou had a thyroid problem, and in a race at Eugene, he could barely break fifteen minutes," Chaplin explained. "So, in Pullam the next week I had Kibiri run with him, and he let Guo beat him in the sprint in 14:25. So, now Guo thinks he can run the 10,000 at Penn because he just beat Kibiri in the sprint. [assistant coach] Rick Sloan says 'You're not going to send him to Penn. Are you crazy? The kid can't even break 14:20 for 5000 meters. He will never win the damn 10,000.' So, I sent Sloan to BYU with the team, and I took a few kids, including Guo, to Penn." Long story short, Gou won the 10,000-meter race at Penn in 1991, defending his 1990 title.

Chaplin noted, with considerable satisfaction, that with the addition of the two Chinese athletes, that the WSU track & field program during his tenure had included athletes from every continent represented by the Rings on the Olympic flag.

"With the addition of the two kids from China" he said. "WSU became a genuine world power [in track & field]."

Today Tony and his family live in Pacific Palisades, California and he has business interests in Asia. Gou and his wife live in Pullman and their daughter who was a triple jumper at Brown University. Both men still go by the names Tony Li and E.J. Gou.

CHAPTER 12

AN ABRASIVE SOFTIE

W hen I was a very young coach working for the inimitable
Doris Brown Heritage at Seattle Pacific University, I
was sent with a single athlete to the NCAA Division II
Regional Cross Country Meet at San Luis Obispo, California. This
was in the days immediately after the implementation of Title IX,
the federal statute that, required colleges, universities, and high
schools to upgrade women's athletic programs to the same level as
the men's programs.

This had not been an issue at SPU because under Ken Foreman,
the women's head coach for the 1980 US Olympic team, the school
was among the very first (if not *the* first) schools in the country to
offer a full-scale track & field program for female athletes. In 1977,
SPU had a six-foot-four high jumper, a 21-11 long jumper, and three
of the best shot and discus throwers in the country (including Lorna

Griffin, who would become the first American woman to throw the discus 200 feet). The SPU team that year was good enough to go to Eugene and beat Oregon in a dual meet at Hayward Field.

Alas, finances forced SPU to drop down to Division II the following year. Most of the top-end athletes left, Foreman resigned, and Doris Brown Heritage took over as head coach. I got a job as a graduate assistant and was sent off to Southern California to supervise that single athlete at the regional cross-country meet.

Two things struck me about that experience. The first is interesting, if irrelevant, to the topic at hand: The meet organizers had laid out two courses for the meet, one on the immaculate seaside golf course in nearby Morro Bay and the other a "rain course on the cart path and nearby service roads. They didn't want anyone running on the golf course if the grass was wet. We had just arrived from Seattle, and in Seattle, wet grass is a way of life.

The second thing that struck me was both surprising and, in retrospect, significant. There was a coaches' meeting held the night before the meet, and one of the topics that came up was the impact Title IX was about to have on men's sports in the NCAA. Several coaches were convinced the addition of women's teams would stretch their already meager resources to the breaking point, with the result that Title IX would sound the death knell of college sports.

The coaches' concerns seemed reasonable back in the day, but the passage of time has also proven such concerns to be unfounded and quite the contrary, really. Nonrevenue sports for both men and women have thrived since Title IX, and the most obvious benefit for coaches is that the number of coaching positions available in college and in high school doubled overnight. But Chaplin pointed out that one of the consequences of combining men's and women's programs at the college level had been to further limit head coaching opportunities for women (because many of the new women's head coaching positions often went to men). He noted that there are only about a dozen schools where the head coach of a combined program is female. Whether this consequence is intended on unintended, he did not say.

The most significant benefit of Title IX, without question, is the virtual explosion of athletic opportunities for young women, but the fortuitous fact that the federal law was also an enormous works program for track & field coaches should not be overlooked.

And, of course, it was a lawsuit by a group of female athletes at WSU, aided by testimony from John Chaplin, that helped break up the legal log jam that, for decades, had been holding back high school girls and college women with athletic aspirations. Once the log jam was broken, a veritable flood of great athletes, made up almost entirely of newly liberated female athletes from American high schools, inundated college campuses.

This leads us to recall John Chaplin's experience back at Wapato a decade earlier. When those girls approached the young coach and told him they wanted to have a track team, the administration told Chaplin that girls didn't do sports. Chaplin insisted that girls do, indeed, do sports, so at Wapato, they did. Chaplin also suggested that, ironically, it was female coaches and administrators who were most resistant to adding events to the women's track & field program. In the early decades of Title IX, for example, women and girls were not permitted to compete in certain field events and in the longer running events. I remember a meeting of high school coaches who were discussing adding the triple jump to our league schedule. The only objection came from one of two female coaches in attendance. Her rationale was that most girls were not strong enough to handle the extreme physical demands of the triple jump.

Similar arguments were made against the addition of the marathon and other events to the Olympic and world championship programs. In 1968, when Doris Brown Heritage was in the prime years of her pioneering career, the longest distance women were allowed to race in the Olympics was 800 meters. And, of course, the marathon was not added to the Olympic program until 1984.

Chaplin added the triple jump for boys and to meets at Wapato High School in the early 1960s. And at WSU, he included the women's steeplechase and the hammer throw in a dual meet with Oregon, held in Pullman in 1982. *(Note: Tony Tensci constructed a women's hammer that weighed the same as the women's shot because no woman's implement even existed at the time.)* Then, as the head of the International Competition Committee for the old Athletics Congress and the present-day USATF, he insisted that the women's steeplechase, hammer throw, pole vault, triple jump, and heptathlon be included in the Olympic Trials and national championships, even though those events were not to be contested at the Olympic Games or the IAAF World Championships. "And I insisted that those events be televised," he said, "and I tell Peter Diamond, the NBC producer, that the announcers and commentators were *not* to refer to them as *exhibition* events, and he agreed."

In addition, "I told the women's chair those events were going to be a twelve-person final, and they were going to be in the television window." The result, of course, was that the female athletes in the steeplechase, hammer throw, pole vault, triple jump, and heptathlon demonstrated on national TV that they were fully capable of performing in those events. That national TV exposure at the Olympic Trials and the US national championships, both of which were viewed by track & field athletes, coaches, and officials from all over the world, was a factor in those events eventually being included in the national and international programs for women.

What all this is pointing to is the behind-the-scenes impact John Chaplin had, if not on the concrete development of women's track & field in the US, at least to the role he played in encouraging several women who have become essential figures in the development of the sport for both men and women.

Stephanie Hightower's initial interaction with Chaplin involved a decision he made that did not turn out in her favor. Hightower was *the* dominant female hurdler in the US for much of the 1980s: She won four USATF outdoor titles in the 100-meter hurdles and five indoor championships in the 60-meter hurdles. She won the Olympic Trials in 1980 (the US boycotted the Moscow Games), and she won a silver medal at the 1987 Pan-American Games.

Unfortunately, and despite her nearly unparalleled accomplishments, Hightower is best known for coming up as the odd runner out in what may have been the closest race in the history of the 100-meter hurdles. After not being allowed to compete in the 1980 Olympics, Hightower was among the favorites to make the team in her event in 1984. But in the final, four women finished in a virtual dead heat, which meant one of the four athletes would not qualify to run in the Olympics.

After examining the fully-automatic-timing photo of the finish, Chaplin, who was the meet referee, determined that Kim Turner had won the race in 13.12, Benita Fitzgerald-Brown was second in 13.13, Pam Page was third in 13.13, and Hightower was fourth—though also in 13.13—and off the Olympic team. Hightower had some consolation in being named as an alternate to the Olympic team.

"My first real interaction with John was in a negative light," Hightower said during a brief break from her busy schedule as the president of the Columbus, Ohio, Urban League. "He was in the booth looking at the photo finish. I thought they should have run the race over because of the closeness. And they didn't have the technology they have today." Today, in a race that close, timing systems will produce a time accurate to one one-thousandths of a second, but in 1984, fully automatic timing was accurate to only one one-hundredths of a second, and officials had to examine the photo to determine a winner, or, in this case, the last spot on the Olympic team.

Ironically, that disappointment at the '84 Olympic Trials was not to be the end of Hightower's relationship with Chaplin. She credits his encouragement and support as a major component in her eventual rise as the chair of the women's track & field committee and the president of USATF, and to having a seat on the IAAF Council.

Rose Monday was one of this country's best middle-distance runners in the years after Title IX finally and forever altered the landscape of intercollegiate and interscholastic sports in the US. Racing in Europe in 1987, she ran 800 meters in 2:00.17 and 1,500 meters in 4:08.65. She was an athlete at precisely the time when the need for additional female participation in the administration of national and international track & field had become urgently apparent, and in the years since, Monday has become one of the movers and shakers in the development of track & field in the US and a tireless advocate for rule and policy changes that benefit athletes. And she credits John Chaplin with nudging her in that direction.

"I met John at the Eight-Nations Meet in Tokyo," she said. "He was the head coach. I didn't even know who he was before that."

A few months later...

"In 1984, at the national meeting of TAC [The Athletics Congress, the forerunner of USATF]," Monday remembered, "I was twenty-three or twenty-four years old, and I was on a mission. Because we didn't have any drug testing. And I knew there were athletes on drugs."

Like Hightower, Monday credits Chaplin with steering her in the direction of a more active role in USATF. While still an active competitor, she was elected to USATF's Athlete's Advisory Committee. "From that point, he became a mentor," she said. "He encouraged me to run for other committees, and I've been elected to key roles with USATF ever since."

The culmination for Monday came in 2022, when she served as the head coach for the US team at the Tokyo Olympics. "She is currently the chair of the USATF Women's Track & Field Committee," Chaplin pointed out, with a note of unabashed pride at how far Monday has risen in the USATF hierarchy. "That committee is responsible for the conduct of all USATF women's junior and senior championships and the selection of international coaches for women."

The issue that initially motivated Monday, of course, was the use of performance-enhancing drugs by track & field athletes. Chaplin noted that during the 1983 Pan-American Games, where drug testing would be required, the International Competition Committee was kept in a meeting for more than four hours until the committee agreed that drug testing would be required for athletes to make the 1984 Olympic Team.

"The USOC keeps telling us that we could not test because of *athletes' rights*," he said. "There was sometimes a little hanky-panky with drug testing, so we decided that athletes had to be tested at the national championships and/or at the Olympic Trials to be eligible to compete in international competition starting in 1984 for the Los Angeles Olympics. The reason we made this rule was because we felt that since the Games were in the US, we could not afford a drug scandal."

Under the USOC drug rules at the time, athletes could compete in the championships or the Trials even if they had a positive test, as long as an appeal was still active. "The problem," Chaplin continued, "was that the TAC/USATF was not allowed to tell anyone other than the appropriate individuals in the federation. After 1984, I was one of those people, as Chair of the ICC, Chair of the Men's Track & Field Committee, and Chief of Mission."

What all this means is that an American athlete could compete in the Olympics with a positive test if his or her appeal had yet to be adjudicated. And neither the International Olympic Committee nor the USOC nor the general public would know anything about it. "So," he went on, "I had a number of conversations with coaches and agents that the particular athlete needed to remove himself or herself from whatever team they had qualified for. If they did not, I would tell the press that they had failed the drug test. And in every case, that is what happened. No problems."

As you might expect, Chaplin's (and later Monday's) insistence on a *clean* Olympic team was not met with universal approval. But he was undaunted and undeterred. "There were those that did not want me to do this. My answer was, 'Let the lawyers handle it.' But I can say that no athlete with a positive test competed in international competition on my watch.

"Once, the USADA told me that they could not get the testing done by the time the team was going to compete in the world indoor championships in Budapest, Hungary. So, I told them, I am here, and you are there, and as the Chief of Mission, I am in charge, so no one will compete unless or until I am sure that they have a negative test. Period! What do you know, they worked overtime and got me the results. All's well that ends well, as the man says."

Did Chaplin care what the drug-testing naysayers thought? Of course not. Monday and numerous other point athletes, coaches, and administrators told me, *John Chaplin does what is right and damn the consequences.*

(The next chapter will deal briefly with the perspective of someone in a unique position to understand the complexity of the issue of performance-enhancing substances.)

Linda Lanker had been a successful hurdler in the days before Title IX. As an ambitious high school athlete, she was told by officials at her public high school in Phoenix, Arizona, that she would not be allowed to use the high school track until after the boys were finished. Then later, as the successful track & field coach at a small Christian high school in Spokane, she was told by the head coach in another sport that rather than coach both girls *and* boys on the school's track team, she should be home baking cookies.

The problem for that other coach was that Lanker came from a generation of female athletes who had been told repeatedly that they did not belong on the same track or even in the same events as the boys. I am married to a woman from that same athletic generation. So, believe me when I say *they are not easily dissuaded.*

Lanker became acquainted with John Chaplin as a result of the way she handled a situation involving two young men at an indoor meet in Moscow, Idaho. Neither Chaplin nor Lanker recalled the particulars of the situation, but Chaplin did remember that it left an impression. "At an indoor meet," he recalled, "I saw this woman with two young men in a corner. I don't know what had happened, but she had their full attention. The only thing they said the whole time was, 'Yes, Miss Linda. No, Miss Linda.'"

As the head of the International Competition Committee for USATF, Chaplin was on the lookout for coaches to send on international trips with US national teams. The obvious respect and attention the two young men were paying Linda Lanker led him to believe she might fit the bill.

Lissa Olson is much younger than the three women already introduced, but her early and subsequent experience with Chaplin is eerily similar. Olson was a standout high jumper on the WSU women's team, when the women's program was completely separate from Chaplin's men's program. Then she coached at WSU after the men's and women's programs were combined under Rick Sloan after Chaplin retired in 1994.

"As a student-athlete," Olson said, "I didn't know him all that well. The men's and women's teams did not have a lot of interaction. I had a high level of respect for him, but he was a little intimidating." But, despite her early timidity, once Chaplin learned Olson was interested in continuing in track & field on the coaching or administrative side of the sports, "he suggested I go the sports management institute in North Carolina run by Dr. LeRoy Walker.

"I got into the summer program on John's recommendation, and that connected me with so many avenues of athletics. I got into coaching, and from that point, we've always stayed in contact."

Chaplin recalled that "Every time her husband, a professional football coach, moves, I'd contact schools in the area where they moved to recommend her as a coach."

Olson very nearly became WSU's second female high jumper to clear six feet when she jumped 5-11¼ in 1988. That mark remains tied for the ninth-best jump in the school's history. As a coach, she was even more successful. "At Purdue," Chaplin said, "she was the first female head coach of a combined program to win a men's title in the Big Ten Conference. She was also the men's head coach for the NACAC [North American, Central America, and Caribbean] under-twenty championships."

"It's funny because when I got to be a fifth-year senior," she said. "I can't remember how we started talking. We'd see each other in the hall, and it would be, 'Hey, how're you doing.' I just felt like there was something about him. He was so kind to take me under his wing. I was honored and shocked that he'd taken the time to talk to me. I remember thinking, *Gosh. Coach Chaplin talked to me.*"

This is where some people may become confused about Chaplin. Is it possible that his most significant contribution to the sport he has devoted his life to is all but unknown to all but a remarkable cadre of determined women whom he nudged into positions of leadership within USATF and beyond?

To someone unfamiliar with the inner workings of national and international track & field, it would not seem unreasonable for Stephanie Hightower to harbor some latent ill will toward Chaplin for the role he played in the decision that kept her off the 1984 Olympic team. Hightower freely admits that she was not happy with the decision at the time, but she has come to understand that the man at the center of the decision-making process based his decision on a sincere and well-informed reading of the rules.

"He was always the person who stood up for the athletes and the integrity of the sport," Hightower said. "He knows every rule. Every article of the rulebook. He knows everything, so when he makes a decision, it is grounded in fact, grounded in process and procedure, and so it is hard to dispute."

It is fair at this point to draw a distinction between John Chaplin, the flamboyant, confrontational, outspoken college coach, and John Chaplin, the legal eagle of the track & field rulebook. Track & field officiating presents a different challenge than officiating other sports. Rules are often enforced after the fact and behind closed doors. It is rare when track & field officials are thrust into the limelight or under the harsh scrutiny of the camera and the TV commentator.

Chaplin found himself in just such a situation when, as the head referee at the 1996 Olympic Games in Atlanta, he was called onto the track to escort a visibly upset and understandably disappointed British sprinter Linford Christie from the track after a second false start. Christie, the defending 100-meter champion, insisted he was not guilty of a false start, but both the starter and the automated system that determines if an athlete has left too early said that he had. After a brief discussion with Chaplin, Christie left the track.

A difficult moment, to be sure, for both the athlete and the official. It is difficult for an ordinary mortal to fathom the disappointment Christie must have felt at not being able to defend his Olympic 100-meter title. But from Stephanie Hightower's point of view, there was no one else in the sport better equipped to deal with the situation.

"I would say he [Chaplin] is a compassionate advocate for the sport," she said. "He is unwavering in his commitment to excellence." As an athlete, a coach, and, later, an official. "That gets him in trouble from time to time, but at the end of the day, he has always been about the athlete, about process and procedure. No one can question his integrity or his commitment to elevating track & field."

Which brings us back to the 1984 Olympic Trials: how a decision that did not go Hightower's way and a disagreement with that call were the springboard to a lifelong association with the man who made that call. "I think he recognized my passion for women in sports," Hightower said, referring to Chaplin's later advocacy for her advancement on the administrative side of USATF. "We became allies and colleagues."

Hightower drew a distinction that separates Chaplin from some other strong personalities. He could be confrontational, sure, but according to Hightower, he was never a bully. "It wasn't always wonderful. There was tumult at times because that's who John is," she said. "But I never felt like I had to stand down. I could express the passion I had." And Chaplin would listen, and "he could compromise and make changes."

One of the most significant changes Chaplin wanted to happen (and started) was a movement to have more women placed in administrative and coaching positions on men's national teams. And Stephanie Hightower had made it clear that she was interested in pursuing those positions.

"Once I started down that pathway," she explained, "there was a movement toward diversifying [the administration] of the men's teams, and that was brought to John's attention [as the head of international competition for USATF]." Hightower pointed out that historically, men frequently coached women, but women almost never coached men. This is still true. "There were no women in coaching or in administration for men's teams," she said.

The result? Stephanie Hightower was the first woman to be selected as an administrator for a US men's national team.

"John was a trailblazer in track & field," she said. "Because he is so outspoken and because of his demeanor, he was the perfect person to lead this movement, to start the momentum. And that is one reason why it stuck."

Rose Monday was a freshman at California State University at Northridge in 1977. Like SPU up north, Northridge had made an institutional decision to prioritize women's & and field, which by then had become the school's flagship athletic program.

"Our program was Division I," she explained. "And the rest of the school was division II. Because we had a different sponsor, we had better uniforms than the men. And we didn't notice that we were less than the men." Which would have been the case at nearly every other major college and university in the country at the time. Oregon was an obvious exception. That dual meet with the Seattle Pacific women's team was held in conjunction with a dual meet between the Oregon men and UCLA's men's team and was attended by more than 10,000 typically knowledgeable and enthusiastic Eugene fans. And my recollection suggests that the University of Washington was making a sincere effort to increase support for all its women's programs.

Monday's collegiate experience had shown her that there was no reason men's and women's track & field could not thrive side-by-side and on an equal footing. Later, after her international competitive career had ended, her husband's work brought the couple to San Antonio. At the time, she was training for the 2001 world masters championships. She got permission to train on the University of Texas at San Antonio (UTSA) track, and then after she won the world masters 800-meter title, she was offered a job coaching the school's women's cross-country team and the female distance runners during track season. Her coaching was so well received that after just one year, she was asked to coach the men's team as well.

Monday has indicated that she and her husband had only intended to spend a couple of years in San Antonio, but she was grateful for the extended stay. And she has said the opportunity to coach both men and women brought her John Chaplin's attention.

"Because I had coached both men and women," she said, "John said, 'I can see you getting selected [to coach] on the men's side.'"

But like other women in track & field in those days, at a time when the female side of the sport was still struggling to get an equal share of the resources and attention, Monday was reluctant to step away from her campaign to raise the status of women's track & field in the US.

"I felt obligated to the women," she said. "There were not enough women role models and women leaders." At this point, Monday makes a startling (in today's terms) admission. Women of her generation were often left on the outside looking in when it came to their desire to be involved in decision-making about the future of their half of the sport. What it took, she said, was the involvement of prominent male personalities to shake up the staid and ridged hierarchy of the TAC.

She singled out Stanford's Brooks Johnson, Lance Harter of the University of Arkansas, John Babington from all-female Wellesley College, and not surprisingly, John Chaplin as being particularly active in support of the inclusion of women in the TAC (again, later known as the USATF) administrative hierarchy.

"Look, if it weren't for the men in my life, I would not be where I am today." John Chaplin was one of those mentors. With the support of Chaplin and the others, Monday eventually was named to the coaching staff of the 2004 world indoor championship team, the World University Games, and the 2016 Olympics. Further, she was named the head coach of the women's track & field team at the 2020 Olympic Games held in Tokyo in 2021.

Even with such prominent support, Monday notes that the rise of women like her—former athletes with a particular passion for the advancement of women—included missteps and detours along the way.

"I wrote legislation for drug testing on a napkin," she said of her early experience at the TAC convention. "It passed the athlete's advisory committee. It passed on the floor of the convention. Then in the board of directors, the athletes got up to go outside and caucus."

And while the athletes were absent from the meet, "Ollan Cassel [the long-time and controversial executive director of both the AAU and TAC] said this will never pass."

The drug-testing legislation was tabled, and Rose Monday, who had majored in political science at Northridge, got a lesson in the ways and means that athlete-centered progress was frequently "tabled" at the highest levels of the TAC.

"I was speechless," she said. "I thought, *What the hell just happened.*"

But as I said earlier, female athletes of this generation had spent much of their sporting life battling. Battling for facilities. Battling for resources. Battling for recognition. And they are not easily dissuaded.

"I knew this was a chess game," Monday said. "To be able to affect the change, you might have to lose a battle, but we were not going to lose the war."

I have always been mystified about why a sport that is so simple, so direct, and so fundamental to all other sports has been so infected with politics for so long. Monday recognized that if change were to occur, it would take individuals who were as hardcore in their willingness to play the political game as they had been in the training and racing days.

"I was a poli-sci major, and I had wanted to be a lawyer," she said. Sound familiar? "So, I got involved in the sport in a way I could affect change."

And this is the point at which Chaplin's influence became most useful to Monday. "He was definitely a hard case. But he was almost always right. He stood up for athletes and coaches. If there was any kind of inequity that was not in the best interest of the athletes, he'd fight against it. I admired that. He was a no-nonsense man. He was extremely intelligent and was not a hard ass against women." (Is there an implicit suggestion here that other male coaches and administrators were "hard-assed" against women?)

Linda Lanker's impression of Chaplin's willingness to work for the advancement of women was similar to Hightower's and to

Monday's, but she was more interested in making her own impact felt in the up-close-and-personal world of age group, high school, and college coaching.

These days, Lanker is as comfortable coaching nine- and ten-year-old age groupers at one of the summer track & field camps she offers in Spokane every summer as she is coaching the hurdlers at Spokane Community College. And, of course, it does not matter if the athletes are male or female. Each gets the same level of attention from Lanker, and she gets the same type of response.

"So, I was at one of the indoor meets at the U of I [Idaho] with my guys in the hurdles for Spokane CC," she remembers. "He [Chaplin] is watching me coach, and my boys are doing great and competing quite well against the bigger schools."

This was a point that Lanker referred to several times. She is clearly proud of the fact that her athletes at tiny Valley Christian School and at Spokane Community College consistently fared well against kids from larger, better-known, and better-resourced programs. I did not get the impression there was even a trace of braggadocio in Lanker, however. She was making the point that given quality coaching and high-end competitive opportunities, athletes from smaller high schools and colleges can compete with anyone.

"And he says, 'Hey, what's your name? And I have the same name as his wife, *Linda*," she said. "So, we start talking, and I can't get away from him because he was telling me about himself and what he does, and he asks me what I've done."

Prior to beginning her coaching career in Spokane, *what Lanker had done* qualifies her as a true pioneer of women's track & field. "I'd competed in the 1970s," she said. "In the 400-meter hurdles and in the 100-meter hurdles. We were the first women to run the 400-meter hurdles in 1973."

Several events (the 400-meter hurdles, the triple jump, the pole vault, the hammer throw, the steeplechase, and the heptathlon) were late additions to the women's track & field program, and in each case, some of the most vocal resistance to adding these events came from female coaches and administrators. Safety was the stated concern, and there were some worries over whether women were even able to competently perform in those events. Now we know those concerns and worries turned out to be unfounded because, in each case, the athletes proved they were not to be limited by such assumptions.

"So, I shared a little bit of what I'd done," Lanker went on. "And he said, 'You're really good. I've been watching you [coach], and I need a woman who can coach men.'"

The implication, of course, was that Chaplin had been actively on the lookout for a first-class female coach he could place with one or more US national men's teams. This sort of behind-the-scenes activism is typical of Chaplin's administrative approach, even if it seems at odds with his more recognizable, confrontational persona.

"Well, I've been coaching boys for a long time," she said. "My own son was the regional champion for the Junior Olympics. When you're the head coach, you have to coach both."

Chaplin stunned Lanker with his next statement. "I need a woman coach on a national team. Stephanie Hightower has done it as a manager, and you're really good."

At this point, Lanker said she did not know what to think. She had just met John Chaplin, and here he was, suggesting she might be selected to coach on the staff of an international track & field team.

"And I thought, *Well, we'll see*," she said. "Then I hadn't seen him for a while, and all of a sudden, my son gets on the computer at home, and he says, 'Mom, you're going to China.' I say, 'What?!'" and he says,

'It says you're going to China.' And I was like, *Oh, my God!* I thought he was just blowing smoke."

What Lanker didn't know at the time was that when it came to his duties as the head of the international competition and men's track & field committees for USATF, he didn't *blow smoke.*

"And I get on the phone," Lanker continued. "His number was easy to find. He's only an hour and a half away. And I go, 'What did you do?' And he says, 'I told everybody you're one of the best coaches,' and blah, blah, blah. 'And you are going to China and coach those boys at the World Juniors.''

There were two significant facts that made it even more flattering that Chaplin would even consider Linda Lanker for such an assignment. First, female coaches had never been sent with men's teams, even junior men's teams. And second, she was not a member of the somewhat inbred international coaching fraternity. "I feel like he really wanted to find quality women and had somehow found out that I had been a boys' coach of the year," she said.

Lanker's first impression of Chaplin may have been confusion due to the rapid-fire nature of his introduction and his fast-tracking her on to the staff of a national team. And since her home in Spokane is less than eighty miles from Pullman, she had to be aware of his reputation of controversy during his time at WSU.

"I knew he was an Olympic coach and was well respected," she said. It's worth noting here is that a crucial aspect of Linda Lanker's character is that whenever she speaks of other people, she begins by assuming the best and by stating something positive. So, she did not mention the assumed controversy at first. "I'd heard he was extremely intelligent and had a lot of knowledge. All that.

"I'd hear a lot of positive, not a lot of negatives. Some controversial things, but he loves the sport so much, and that's what I love about him."

But of course, there were people who chose, for whatever reason, to have another view of Chaplin, and those opinions also found their way to Lanker. "I'd heard bits and pieces, people saying he was a male chauvinist," she said, and then immediately discounted that assumption. "People would say that about older men. And I've had my share of coaching as an assistant where I'd get an athlete really good, and then a head coach comes and takes him. That's kind of commonplace for women in this business."

But that, to Lanker's great relief, was not the case with Chaplin. "First of all," she said, "the best thing about John is that he's someone women and female athletes can trust."

Lissa Olson hadn't seen Chaplin for several years when they ran into each other at the recent world championships in Eugene. But, as is typical of Chaplin, "he immediately came up and gave me a hug," Olson said. Her twins had just graduated from high school, and Olson suggested she might be interested in getting back into coaching. "He says, 'What do you want to do? Who do I need to call?' There is no doubt that if I wanted to get back into it [coaching], he would be the first person I would talk to."

And like everyone else I spoke with, I asked Olson what she thought people should know about Chaplin, and like everyone else, the answer depended entirely on the context in which he had entered their life.

"From my perspective," she said, "he is a woman's advocate. That's something people would be surprised about."

Then Lissa Olson offered a nearly perfect summation of the man's character, forged by his early Catholic school education and his radical father, his high school career in a tough section of Los Angeles and his time in the army, his track & field career at WSU, the Wapato years, his coaching apprenticeship under Jack Mooberry, and his nearly seventy years in track and field as an athlete, coach, official, and administrator.

"From the outside," she said, "he seems unapproachable and intimidating. But he has the kindest heart, and he wants to help people."

We'll just leave it at that.

CHAPTER 13

DOCTOR IN THE HOUSE

D r. Dick Strand, who had been an All-American 440-yard sprinter at the University of Nebraska, has known John Chaplin for more than thirty years. After serving as the chief medical officer at the 1992 US Olympic Trials, he was hand-picked by Chaplin to serve as the head of the medical team for the 2000 Sydney Olympics.

Prior to those Olympic Games, "I had to go to the USOC to get two more medical individuals and a weight coach, who was Olympic discus champion Jay Silvester," Chaplin remembered. "And I basically informed them exactly who I wanted on the medical team."

Who Chaplin wanted were Dr. Dick Strand, Dr. Dean Clark (a chiropractor and a former WSU distance runner who had been an All-American in the steeplechase), and Cheryl Parker (as head trainer. Parker later became a physician's assistant.).

"I first met John in 1988 at the Olympic Trial in Indianapolis," Strand said. "And he would find little jobs for Charlie [Greene] and I to do." Strand and Greene had been teammates at Nebraska, and of course, Chaplin's relationship with Greene had been established earlier. "John Chaplin was totally integral to what went on [for me] from there."

What Dr. Strand is referring to is his eventual participation on the medical side of USATF administration, including the evolving movement to get performance-enhancing drug (PED) use among US athletes under control. To be fair, PED use by American athletes at the time was anything but unique in international track & field. It is safe to say, in my view, that US runners, jumpers, and throwers were no more or less culpable for their use of performance-enhancing substances than athletes from other nations.

What may have been unique (or at least unnoted) was the behind-the-scenes work of people like Strand and Rose Monday (and the out-front presence of John Chaplin) to ensure that US track & field was as clean as possible. Complicating the issue was the notion that American athletes (unlike their counterparts in most other countries) had a right to privacy when it came to their medical histories. That policy, or more particularly, the athletes' privacy rights, created a situation at the 1992 Olympic Trials in New Orleans: John Chaplin was forced to sit and wait for a phone call from the US Supreme Court.

"Butch Reynolds had a dispute with the IAAF and the US Anti-Doping Agency (USADA)," Strand explained. "He'd had a positive drug test, and they [the IAAF] were going to ban anyone who competed against him."

At the US Olympic Trials, the IAAF was attempting to enforce a draconian anti-drug policy that seemed to violate US law. Even someone like Chaplin, who believed in doing everything (legally) possible to clean up the sport, would have had a problem with the IOC banning athletes for simply competing in the same race as someone who had allegedly tested positive for a banned substance. Also, Reynolds had appealed his positive test, and according to USATF and USOC policy in force at the time, he should have been allowed to compete while his appeal was adjudicated. But apparently, the IAAF was steadfast and insisted on its stringent policy. "They said they'd ban anyone who ran with Butch," Chaplin explained.

"So, John is sitting next to the fax machine," Strand said, "waiting to get a message from the US Supreme Court ordering [the USOC to either let] Butch run in the trials [or not]. How many times at a track meet are you going to get a message from the Supreme Court?

"John said to me, 'To hell with this. I'm not going against the US Supreme Court,'" Strand continued. "John called Primo Nebiolo, the IAAF president at the time, and told him that since the IAAF was not going to contest Reynold's suit, the outcome would be that when he [Nebiolo] and his bag man Simpson came to Atlanta in 1996 for the Olympic Games, the US Marshall would take what the courts had awarded and give it to Reynolds. Then Primo said, 'That can't happen,' and John said, 'Talk to your lawyers.'

"John has the speakerphone on, so Charlie Greene and I can hear. He then gets a call from Primo thirty minutes later, and Primo says to John, 'Let them compete,' and he hangs up," Strand continued. "John then tells Charlie Greene to let the athletes know that they will run the 400-meter trials. Then the marshals came to the track and handed Chaplin an order from the Supreme Court that Reynolds was to compete in the 1992 400-meter Olympic Trials."

The Supreme Court decision did not put an end to the issue. "This, of course, was big news," Strand explained. "A reporter asked

John, 'Let me ask you a hypothetical question.' But John replied, 'F
- - - hypothetical questions, we have a track meet to run.'"

"I called a meeting of the USATF Board of Directors," Chaplin
added. "And I told them to either support me in following the court's
order, and I would handle the logistics running of the two races on
the rest day, or they could get a new chairman. I had no intention of
going to jail in New Orleans for refusing to obey a court order from
the Supreme Court of the United States. The board agreed to support
my request."

Of course they did.

"The gist of all this is that John had to organize two races," Strand
said. "The first round and the quarterfinals, on a rest day, June 23.
Then he had to open the stadium [free] to the public, get the officials
back, and pay for security and all other staffing so the athletes could
compete. The semifinal was run the next day, and the final on June
28. For the record, Reynolds placed fifth in the final and did *not* make
the team."

It should also be noted for the record that Reynolds won his
lawsuit and, in Chaplin's words, "putting an end to the issue.".

Eight years later, at the Sydney Olympics, drug testing was still
an issue, and the Australian Anti-Drug Agency was determined to
make sure the games were clean. But, as Strand pointed out, Chaplin
had determined that safeguards that had been put in place to guard
athletes' rights were routinely being overlooked.

"Fast forward to the Olympics in Australia," Strand said. "What
was happening then was that drug testing was coming to the forefront."

As an example, Chaplin explained, "The IOC was embarrassed
by the fact that at the Winter Olympics in Nagano [Japan in 1998],
they had banned an American snowboarder for testing positive for
marijuana."

That does not seem unreasonable, until... "Then they discovered they didn't have a rule against it [marijuana use]. So, then they made marijuana, a social drug a lot of young people used, illegal. And they made sure they were going to be tested for it." Strand pointed out that his own research indicated that no American athletes at Sydney had a positive test for marijuana.

Strand then noted that the IOC began to demand blood tests from the Australian Anti-Doping Agency for athletes competing at the 2000 Olympics. A blood test is the most accurate way to determine if performance-enhancing drugs are in an athlete's system, but it is also the most invasive testing method. But there were other problems with drug testing by the Australian Anti-Drug Agency at Sydney. As stated earlier, procedures had been put in place to protect American athletes from being singled out.

But...

"In 2000, they started doing blood tests," Strand said. "And we had to address that with our people. But the Australian Anti-Drug Agency was all over everybody. They wanted to make the point that *We're in charge and the hell with everyone one else.* They were drug testing people arriving at the Sydney airport. They were really intense about this." So intense, in Strand's mind, that the Australian drug testing officials were willing, even eager, to ignore internationally agreed-upon protocols.

"One day, the drug people show up to test Abdi Abdirahman," he said. "They picked him out for *out-of-competition* testing." The rules did not allow the agency to single out an individual; it had to choose randomly from an identified group. "That [singling out Abdirahman] was not correct," Strand explained. "And John immediately jumped on that. How could they select an athlete from a group of only one person."

Abdirahman was a native of Somalia who had become an American citizen. He graduated from high school in Tucson, Arizona, and then ran successfully for the University of Arizona. He would eventually become the first and only American male athlete to run in five Olympics. He made the 2020 Olympic team by running a 2:10:03 marathon at age 43. (That's not to discount the fact that former WSU athlete Bernard Lagat also ran in five Olympics, two for his native Kenya and three for the US, narrowly missing a medal at 5,000 meters in 2016 at the age of 40.)

"A day or two later," Strand went on, "there is a confrontation with the head of the Australian Anti-drug Agency [a medical doctor]. The doctor comes up to John and says, 'Can we go somewhere to discuss this?' John says, 'No. We'll discuss it right here.' The doctor starts questioning John, and John states the obvious. *One person is not a group.* It got a little heated for a moment. I told him that I had never known John to be wrong on a point of the rules. He is meticulous, and he knows this stuff inside and out.

"They next tried to do an out-of-competition test in Brisbane," Strand said. "We were training at one of the Catholic high schools there. We had two track meets and raised a huge amount of money [for the school]. It was very well attended." (The money raised provided scholarships for youngsters from across southern Asia to attend the school.)

"The drug people show up during the meet," Strand continued. "But you can't do out-of-competition testing in the middle of a track meet."

Chaplin insisted that an out-of-competition test could not be done during a track & field meet, which is by definition (and obviously) not *out-of-competition*. "He was not being obnoxious. He was just being correct, protecting our athletes," Strand added, and then explained that the World Anti-Doping Agency did intervene, and just as you'd expect, Chaplin's interpretation of the rules concerning who could and who could not be tested and when they could be tested was proven correct.

"John Chaplin is going to do the right thing," Strand said. "For the right reason."

Even if that involves removing an American athlete from the team. Strand cited the C.J. Hunter situation as an example to demonstrate that Chaplin's attitude toward drug use by American athletes was based on his clear-eyed understanding of the rules and not on protecting American athletes in every instance.

"We knew C.J. Hunter had several positive tests," Strand said. "But that was not disclosed by USATF, the IAAF, or USOC. How do we get around that? John tells Hunter's agent, Charles Wells, 'You're going to have C.J. come down with an illness or an injury and resign his position as a US Olympic team member.'" And, Strand explained, "If Hunter did not do so, Chaplin himself would make Hunter's positive test public."

At this point in Strand's story, Chaplin noted, "We had a dilemma, and two things were at stake: the rights of the athletes under USOC rules and the Anti-Doping Agency's ability to keep the sport clean." *See a detailed account of this issue in the appendix.*

"Under the USOC rules," Chaplin continued, "to remove an athlete from the games, the athlete had to provide a written statement that he or she was withdrawing. And if I'd gone to the USOC, they'd want a written statement from Hunter before they would grant a credential for an alternate. I talked it over with my head manager, Fred Newhouse, and he was adamant that he would not submit Hunter's name. I agreed.

"But we had a way around this dilemma. John Godina was the alternate, and he already has a credential for the discus throw." So, Newhouse entered Godina and not Hunter.

Of course, even today, more than twenty years later, performance-enhancing drug use is still an issue. Suspensions are common, especially for an athlete failing to make themselves available for random out-of-competition testing. International-level athletes are required to make their whereabouts known to their national anti-drug agency at all times.

"It [the PED situation] is still not resolved," Strand said. "It really is a war between people who are cheating [and people who are not]. The purpose is to have a level playing field. Cheating is worth hundreds of millions of dollars to a country or to an athlete. There's more money on the cheating side than on the honest side."

The worst aspect of drug use by athletes, Strand suggested, is that it's become difficult to know which stunning performance is legitimate and which is not. "Every time someone does something wonderful, you wonder if they're cheating," he said, a clear note of dismay in his voice. "Almost all marks prior to 1988 are suspect [after the Olympics in Seoul]." Those Olympic Games in Korea are remembered primarily for 100-meter gold medalist Ben Johnson being disqualified for a positive drug test after defeating American star Carl Lewis.

At that point, Strand added that athletes like "Harvey Glance and Edwin Moses demanded we do something about drugs."

To emphasize how absurd the situation can become, Strand pointed out that one group of athletes bound for the Sydney Olympics did not even get on the ground in Australia. "There was a Chinese plane that turned around in midair and headed back to China." Clearly, the Chinese team at the time was operating under a different ethos than John Chaplin and Dr. Dick Strand.

"The key," Strand concluded, "is that John just didn't care [what people thought]. He wanted to do the right thing and then let the chips fall where they may. He did not seek adoration or approval. He didn't care about any of that, but he trusted our little team of myself, Charlie Greene, Alan Kolling, Linda Lanker, Jim Grogan, Ed Gorman, Bob Podkaminer, and a few others. He didn't interfere and let us do our job. He picked good people to do the right things."

AFTERWORD

I think there is a fundamental problem with the assumptions that members of the public, especially members of the media, make about prominent people. Often, the assumption is that a well-known person's most noticeable public characteristic is what defines their entire character. And then, unfairly (in almost every case), judgments are made about that person, opinions are expressed, and assumptions become some fact that is a version of the truth, which, in most cases, has no grounding in reality and is based on an incomplete understanding of what is actually going on.

John Prescott Chaplin rose to the very top of the track & field world as a phenomenally successful college coach and a national and international innovator and influencer. That is a fact. But the assumptions made about how he got there are often the subject of an incomplete understanding of the actual impact he had on the athletes under his direction or on the development of the sport that he dedicated his entire adult life to. There is a tendency to focus on high-profile individuals and incidents: Henry Rono's unprecedented achievements in 1978 or Chaplin's internationally televised removal of Linford Christie from the track after being disqualified from the 100-meter final at the 1996 Olympics.

But too often lost in any discussion of John Chaplin's legacy is his behind-the-scenes support for women's track & field, going all the way back to his days at Wapato High School in the mid-1960s. Or his determination to expand the track & field program by promoting the addition of the steeplechase and the hammer throw for both men and women and by insisting the women's triple jump, pole vault, and heptathlon be shown on TV at the USATF national championship and the Olympic trials so as to attract international attention and recognition. Or his work to advance women's opportunities for men's team coaching and management in a sport that had been dominated administratively for more than 100 years by men with a limited view of the benefits of the sport for women.

Had Chaplin's activities been limited to coaching or to administration alone, his impact on the world of track & field would have been historic. That he has been such a seminal figure as both a coach and an administrator marks John Chaplin as one of the indispensable figures in the development of track & field both in the US and internationally.

I spoke with a couple of dozen former WSU athletes during the course of this project. And I was privileged to encounter figures that I admired, even idolized, during my formative years in the sport—coaches like Brooks Johnson, Rose Monday, and Linda Lanker. And a great athlete like Stephanie Hightower, who has become one of the preeminent movers and shakers in the world of international and national track & field.

And, of course, to have been able to talk to two of my boyhood idols, Mel Pender and Charlie Greene, was an incomparable honor (and thrill). My lengthy interview with Mr. Greene may have been the last he granted before his death in March 2022. His expressed wish was that he hoped he had said something to advance Chaplin's reputation. Well, he did. And someone needs to get ahold of Pender's book—*Expression of Hope: The Mel Pender Story*—and make a movie about this singular American hero's life.

I regret and apologize that I was not able to include everyone so generous with their time and recollections, and I am grateful to all. Even those not quoted in these pages had an impact on my still incomplete understanding of Coach Chaplin.

When it came down to it, though, I needed three or four of Chaplin's protégés to sum up his story. The possibilities are, of course, endless. I settled on three of the most successful and one of the most interesting of WSU's galaxy of track & field stars. I chose these athletes because, despite their success, they are not as well-known as Henry Rono, Gerry Lindgren, Peter Koech, Julius Korir, Gabriel Tiacoh, or *The Viking*, Tore Gustafsson. But each, like every other athlete I spoke with, paid homage to the positive impact that Coach Chaplin and WSU had on their current lives.

The first is Patrick Muturi, who came to WSU from a level of poverty he says American kids cannot even imagine. The second is Chris Whitlock, who recognized immediately that Pullman's distraction-free environment made it the perfect place to pursue his athletic and academic goals. Then there is New Zealander John Delamere, who would eventually become a high-ranking official in his country's government, and who should have revolutionized the long jump. And finally, there is Dominique Arnold, who came to WSU without a full scholarship and became one the greatest high hurdlers in the history of US track & field.

Patrick Muturi's arrival at WSU was a revelation to the young Kenyan. "The change [from his boyhood in Kenya] was significant," he said. "Being in a situation where you can take a shower is a miracle. Three meals a day is a miracle. Those things are not common in other places."

On more than one occasion, Chaplin suggested that for athletes from much of the world, the benefits of an American education were not limited to advancing a specific individuals' career because education could also change the trajectory of an entire extended family.

"Growing up," Muturi explained, "I had a very difficult life as a child. Nobody cares about your future. Thank God I had a longing to be better. I just didn't know how to do it."

The catalyst for harnessing Muturi's desire to do better was Coach Ngata, who was familiar with the success that athletes from that region of Kenya had at WSU. "He said, 'You're a pretty good student and a good runner," Muturi went on. "He said, 'Look what is going on in Pullman. Rono, Kapkory, Kibiri.' The list is long."

Coach Ngata had planted a seed, and when it took root on the WSU campus, Patrick Muturi blossomed. His athletic credentials are impressive enough: cross country All-American in 1993 (behind national champ teammate Josephat Kapkory) and a 10,000-meter All-American on the track in 1994. He also holds the WSU school record in the marathon at 2:12:56, the ninth-best time in the world in 1994. But it was Chaplin's and the WSU program's impact on Muturi (and his family) away from the track that Muturi insisted we focus on.

"It changed my life," he said. "I had the drive to get out of poverty." Muturi indicated his family's situation back home in Kenya was so dire that "I'd send twenty dollars home in an envelope, and that takes care of them for a month.

"In America, you have so many opportunities. You can survive very well on minimum wage. You are able to work and make a living, and that is critical. Athletes [from developing countries] have not had that opportunity. Here they can work hard and make it."

It is worth noting that Chaplin's appeal to international athletes and a significant element of his success in developing those athletes, especially developing countries, had to do with his understanding of this basic reality. Athletes like Patrick Muturi were seeking an opportunity to advance themselves and their families, an opportunity often not available in their home countries. And track & field was the vehicle by which they would pursue that opportunity.

Muturi left WSU after Chaplin retired. He entered several marathons and other road races with some help from Chaplin, winning the San Francisco Marathon and placing third in the Chicago Marathon. His performance in these races provided Muturi with the necessary resources to continue his education and help his family. He subsequently joined the US Army, which helped him become a US citizen and return to school.

"Coach Chaplin," Muturi said. "I look at him, and I see what he had done, digging me and my family out of poverty." Muturi is unashamedly grateful for the opportunity "to provide basic necessities of life for my family, and by helping my brothers and sisters to get a college education. Athletics paved the way for me to run and get an education. As an athlete, you are good for five or ten years. Then what are you going to lean back on, whether you stay here or go back to Kenya? Chaplin tells me 'You can't go wrong with a good education. It's going to be good not only for you but for your family and for generations to come.'"

And how did the emphasis that John Chaplin placed on education work out for Patrick Muturi? Today he has a Ph.D. in nursing research and is an assistant professor of nursing at Pacific Lutheran University.

Chaplin is justifiably and understandably proud of the opportunities that intercollegiate track & field and, particularly, WSU track & field have provided to athletes from developing countries and, as a result, those athletes' academic and professional success.

Here, I think it is necessary to point out one more remarkable jumper from the early days of Chaplin's tenure, an athlete from a much different part of the world. Chaplin insists that a young athlete from New Zealand would have revolutionized the long jump (had the rule-making powers that be stayed out of the way) in the same way Dick Fosbury revolutionized the high jump.

Always an innovator, Chaplin had recruited John Delamere to WSU from New Zealand. He was the northern division long jump champion in 1971 with a best of 25-6¾ and the northern division triple jump champion in 1973 with a best of 52-6½. He was a four-year letterman who once held the school record for the triple jump. He had a perfect SAT score of 1600 and a photographic memory. He was the top Maori scholar his senior year in high school, and his father was a Maori elder. His mother was English.

"But as an athlete," Chaplin said, "he had one problem. His vision was such that he kept reaching for the toe board, so in the spring of 1974, I tell Coach Sloan, what if we just have him rotate into a summersault and land in the pit. That might fix the problem.

"So, Sloan tries it and says it might just work. We have John practice the somersault, but we don't use it in any meets until the Pac-8 conference meet in Los Angeles. How would you like to be that long jump official as Delamere flipped over into the pit right in front of him?"

Delamere tied the 1972 Olympic champion Randy Williams of USC for first but placed second based on Williams's better second jump.

"Of course," Chaplin said, "within a month or two, the IAAF banned this type of jumping just like they banned the 'Spanish javelin throw.'" Chaplin was referring to an innovative technique in the javelin in which the thrower spins before launching the implement, albeit uncertain about where it might end up, which could be a problem in a crowded stadium.

"If Dick Fosbury had not come out of nowhere and won the Olympic Games in 1968, the IAAF would probably have banned that technique also," he said. "The press went crazy and wanted Delamere to do it several more times, and I said, 'No way. It was for competition only.' But it was great press coverage for WSU."

WSU won four events at that Pac-8 championship meet—Gary Minor in the 220, John Ngeno in the three-mile and the six-mile, and Kip Ngeno in the high hurdles—but it was that second-place finish by a somersaulting Kiwi that garnered the lion's share of the press coverage.

"Not bad for recruiting in LA," Chaplin said.

Chaplin believes Delamere is as remarkable for where he came from as he is for his (since ignored) technical innovation in the long jump, a further example of the kind of disadvantaged situation many WSU athletes had to overcome. Chaplin relied on Delamere's own words to make his point. "I received this information from John Delamere in response to an e-mail I got from him about his father," Chaplin explained. "His background and upbringing are typical of many of the young men that came to WSU to compete for me." In the e-mail, Delamere explained that he was from a lost generation of indigenous youth born in the 1950s and 1960s.

"When I went to school in the 1950s and 1960s," Delamere expressed, "there was no Maori language, there was no Maori culture, there was no Maori kapa haka [dancing/singing/war dance, etc.] in our schools. There was nothing. And at home, our parents would not speak Te reo Maori [the indigenous Maori language] because our parents, like my father Eruera, were of that generation that had been beaten for speaking the Maori language.

"They had essentially been beaten into a cultural submission, and as a result, my parents made sure that my generation grew up as good little Pakeha [white Europeans].

"My father, Eruera Tuariki Delamere, was the son of Weihana Delamere and Tiaria Wikiriwhi and was born in 1928, a member of the Te Whanau an Apanui tribe in the remote Maori community of Maraenui. When he was seven, he started attending the local native school, which was when he started learning English.

"In 1945, he joined the New Zealand Army, and in the 1950s, he was a founding instructor of the New Zealand SAS [the equivalent of the US Navy SEALs]. He retired from the Army in 1965 and, for the rest of his working life, was an administrator for the New Zealand Road Services [the national inter-city bus company].

"His father, Weihana Delamere, was the chief of the Te Whanau, an Apanui tribe, which was why he was the principal speaker at the 1944 investiture for the Victoria Cross for his nephew Moana Ngarimu. Weihana's father was Te Kohi Delamere and was a founding member, in 1868, of the first Maori Christian religion, the Ringatu Church. Weihana's younger brother, Paora, was the supreme leader of the Ringatu for 42 years."

Note: Victoria Cross is the highest and most prestigious award in the system of British Military honors. It is awarded for valor in the presence of the enemy, much like the Congressional Medal of Honor in the US military.

"Te Kohi's father was known as 'By God' Sam Delamere. He was a whaler on an American whaling ship from Nantucket. He had four children with his Maori wife, Peti Te Ha. Today they have about 10,000 descendants.

"In February 1970, after I won the NZ Junior champs, I wrote to the coaches of the top 10 universities from the 1969 NCAA champs. They all wrote back offering me full scholarships. The only school that didn't write back at first was WSU.

"Instead, I got a telephone call from John Chaplin. And that was when, at least in New Zealand, it was a big deal to get a toll call from the next town—such as from Pullman to Colfax. It was that phone call that convinced me—along with the fact that I had never seen snow, and I wanted to see it, and Pullman had snow. Mind you, after my first three weeks of snow in November and December 1970, I had had enough snow."

Chaplin is typically and justifiably proud of all that Delamere accomplished in the years after he graduated from WSU. He married a young woman from Spokane, obtained resident alien status, and then got drafted into the US Army. During basic training, he took the test for admittance into Officer Candidate School, which he obviously passed (remember that perfect SAT score?). He rose to the rank of captain and was an assistant track & field coach at the US Military Academy under Mel Pender. While in the army, he earned a master's degree in business administration from Long Island University, then returned to New Zealand, became a successful businessman and politician, and served as New Zealand's minister of immigration from 1996 to 1999.

Chaplin noted the historical significance of John "Tuariki" Edward Delamere becoming the official in charge of immigration for his country. "He was a Maori from the *lost generation*," Chaplin said. "But it was Polynesian seafarers who discovered New Zealand originally, and they were the first peoples to colonize the islands. It is, therefore, ironic [that an individual of Maori heritage should become the minister of immigration] because Europeans and others were the real immigrants to New Zealand."

To add to the legacy, two of Delamere's grandnieces, Clarisse and Krystal Leger-Walker, were standouts on the WSU women's basketball team during the 2021-22 season. In fact, Charisse, just a sophomore at the time, was selected to the Pac-12 All-Conference team after averaging 21.1 points per game during the 2021-22 season.

Chris Whitlock was the first WSU athlete to run faster than 45 seconds in the 400. He came to Pullman from a small town in northern California and suspected that when he arrived, he would find a community much like the one he'd left.

"I was used to seeing prejudice," he said. "Coming from a small town in California [Whitlock attended Cardinal Newman High School], people weren't exactly friendly." But at WSU, he discovered a much different place than the one he'd left. "It was a friendly atmosphere. No racism. No prejudice. No one locked their doors."

Even Whitlock's roommate, Mark Langenherader, surprised him. "My roommate was a bull rider from Ritzville," Whitlock said.

I am not sure there is anything more typical of the rural environs of Eastern Washington than a bull rider from Ritzville, a tight-knit farm and ranch community smack in the middle of the eastern half of the state. "He had a brand-new truck, and he said, 'Chris, you can use my truck any time you want.'"

Whitlock recognizes that his status as one of the best athletes at WSU at the time may have had something to do with how he was received. "I felt appreciated," he said. "A lot of my friends were white, but I felt very comfortable in my own skin. I felt at home, that I was in the right place."

And, of course, John Chaplin had a role to play in the way Whitlock came to view his time in Pullman. "John Chaplin is trustworthy," he said, echoing a sentiment repeated by athletes from the very beginning of this project. "And he tells the truth."

There was nothing in Dominique Arnold's background to indicate that he would become one of the best 110-meter-high hurdlers in history with Chaplin's support and mentorship. He was an adequate hurdler, Chaplin remembered. The problem? He was…well…at least by world-class standards, slow.

"Dominique Arnold could not make WSU's 4x100-meter relay team," Chaplin said. "He was not fast enough. But he still ran 12.90. How could he do that?"

By this time, I'd begun to realize that Chaplin does not ask a question to which he does not already know the answer.

"Technique," Chaplin said. "You bring your knee up, and your foot comes down right under your body. I've only seen two hurdlers run off their lead leg like that. Skeets [Renaldo] Nehemiah and Dominique Arnold." For the record, so to speak, Nehemiah was the first athlete to run the 110-meter hurdles in less than thirteen seconds.

Chaplin recruited Arnold at the end of his WSU coaching career. "I was working for the provost office, and we would talk," Chaplin said. "I was not his coach. Mark McDonald was the coach. But I was a mentor. He came to me and asked questions. I talked to him about the fact that it was his technique that would have to be improved if his goal was to lower his time."

Arnold would eventually run even faster than Nehemiah's world record of 12.93, set in 1983. But ten years would pass between his 13.46 NCAA title in 1996 and his American record of 12.90 in 2006. And even though Chaplin was no longer the head coach by the time

Arnold reached his senior year, Arnold still credits Chaplin with the continued development that ultimately led to his American record.

"I came from gang-infested territory," Arnold said. "And seeing this white guy caring for me was different. We didn't grow up with white figures caring for you. But he showed me something different. I'd do anything for Chappy. He was everything I wanted in a father that I didn't have growing up."

Arnold pointed out that one aspect of Chaplin's character that he particularly appreciated is that he did not walk away from caring for his athletes after they stopped being useful to the WSU program.

"At the 2,000 Olympic Trials, I had the fastest time going into the finals. But I hit the fourth hurdle [and failed to make the team]. Chappy was there, patting me on the back, telling me it's okay, that I'll make it next time." It should be noted that at the time, Chaplin had not been Arnold's mentor for more than a decade.

"Chappy was my mental foundation," Arnold continued, explaining that prior to his senior year, circumstances had forced him to consider leaving WSU. He told Chaplin, "I trust you," adding, "Chappy talked me into staying. And I don't think I would have been NCAA champion if I had gone anywhere else."

I believe that last statement is more than likely true of most college athletes who succeed at the highest levels of the NCAA. The US has the best coaching and the broadest base of talent in the world, and it really isn't very close. But one of the pitfalls of the American system is that athletes must change coaches and programs at three critical points in their development: entering high school. Entering college. And entering the professional realm. A good match between the athlete, the coach, and the program is something of a crapshoot for most kids. When it doesn't work out and a kid does not continue to develop, it is not always a problem with the coach or the program. Maybe the entire situation was just not a great fit.

The amazing thing about John Chaplin's legacy is that the program *fit* so many different athletes from so many different backgrounds: Dominique Arnold from inner-city Los Angeles, Chris Whitlock from small-town Northern California, and Patrick Muturi from abject poverty in Kenya, along with John Delamere, "the smart kid from New Zealand," Chaplin said with a laugh. Plus, the likes of Robert Price, Chris McBride, Lee Gordon, Kris Durr, Tim Manson, and so many others from so many different parts of the world.

And Henry Rono.

Remarkable young men representing all five of the Olympic rings—North and South America, Europe, Asia, Africa, plus Oceania—all came together in a remote corner of a remote state and thrived under their coach's rough-edged nurturing. This is the truest and most accurate measure of John Chaplin's legacy.

POSTSCRIPT

W hat will coach Chaplin and I be doing in the future? Probably the same thing we've each been doing for the entirety of our adult lives. "Metaphorically," Coach John Prescott Chaplin said, "This is until the Great Trackman in the Sky calls us home because all the races have been run and all the finish lines have been crossed and our time in this world has run out and our stories have been recorded in the sands of time."

(ODDS AND ENDS, FACTS AND STATS)

Examples of confrontations and interactions with the Pac-8, 10, 12 Conference coaches and others (in John Chaplin's own words):

We can start with when Ray Nagel, the WSU Athletic Director at the time, let us go to Northern California during spring break for track meets against San Jose State and the University of California. It was my second year as head track & field coach. We lost to San Jose State 82-81 when Kip Ngeno stumbled in the 120-yard-high hurdles and got second. This was the first non-conference meet that WSU had ever lost. We went 7-3 that season, losing to Oregon State 93½ to 73½ in Corvallis on the way home from that spring break trip. Our other loss was to the University of Washington, 96 to 68. These were the only meets that OSU or the UW won against WSU during my tenure. It was my worst season, other than 1980 when we went 9-2.

Every other year, we were either undefeated or lost only one meet. After the San Jose State meet, Cal told us they were cancelling the meet for final exams. At the weekly press conference, they asked me what I thought about that. Again, without thinking my answer out, I said, "If they can't win, I guess the University of California does not want to play." The Conference Commissioner had a fit. When I got back to Pullman, Ray Nagel called me into his office and said, "The Conference wants me to reprimand you for your comments." He then said, "Put your hand out." I did. He gave me a little slap and said, "Watch your statements concerning other teams in the conference and conference polices in particular." A literal *slap on the wrist*.

In 1983 we finally win the conference title at Berkeley. What do I do? I tell Coach Sloan that he will have to accept the trophy because I am going to Modesto to recruit some junior college athletes at the Modesto Relays. Unknown to me, this is the first time the conference commissioner was going to award the trophy. So, when the team assembles for the presentation, the commissioner has no idea who coach Sloan is and thinks that he is talking to WSU's head coach. The conference office calls WSU's athletic director and tells him he is not pleased that I embarrassed the commissioner by not being there. Our AD calls me in and asks, "Why did you not stay for the presentation?" I say, "You pay me to win titles, not go to a silly presentation where my assistant coach can stand in for me". He says, "That might be true, but I have to listen to the commissioner about what he thinks about your behavior, and that is not good for our relationship with the conference." So, I say, "Okay. If he has thin skin, I will try not to cause you any more problems with the conference... if possible."

Another conversation with a conference commissioner had to do with cross country. In 1980, I sent an incomplete team to the Pac-10 Conference Championships at Palo Alto. The commissioner calls me up and demands to know why WSU sent an incomplete team. I tell him that WSU has a chance to become a conference power in track & field and win the conference track & field title, so I am shifting our focus on recruiting a more complete team. And since there are no designated scholarships for cross country, unless he wants to allow more scholarships for cross country, he no business telling WSU where to use its scholarships (or who to enter in the conference meet). And besides, say I have only one cross county fan, my mother, and she does not even like the sport.

Another time, the conference made a rule that only head coaches could attend conference sponsored meetings. This was fine, except that a school could have separate men's and woman's coaches or one person who coached both, so any vote could be split. So, prior to the conference meet, the assistant conference commissioner for track tells all the non-head coaches in the room that they have to leave. Twenty minutes goes by, nothing gets said, nothing gets accomplished, and finally she says to me, as the chair of rules and the guy running the meeting at the time, "What is the holdup?" and I say, "Lady, you kicked the meet manager out of the meeting." The assistant coach for the host school was the meet manager, and he obviously needed to be at the meeting. Needless to say, the conference was not happy with my comment, even though it was true.

Another time we get a message from the conference that they want us to have all our athletes sign a waiver for competition at the conference meeting in Seattle that year. I took it to our attorney general at WSU and say I don't want to do this. She says, "Of course. Don't do it." We are now in Seattle and the assistant conference commissioner for track & field stands up and ask the coaches if they will do this. It is an alphabet roll call, so WSU is last. One by one they each school say yes, but when it got to me, last on the list, I say NO!

She starts crying and says, "I was sent up here to get this done and you are a pied piper, and they are following you." I say, "Listen I just said that WSU was not signing this I did not tell anyone else what to do."

One of the other times when I got in trouble with the conference was at a scratch meeting at UCLA. Prior to having the meeting closed to the press, this when the annual meeting with the scratch meeting was held on the day before the competition and the press could see and hear what the coaches were saying about the team entries and the semi-annual general meeting where coaches discussed items of interest. I was the elected chair of the rules committee for the track & field coaches in the conference. The NCAA had just stated that there could be no more parttime track coaches. That meant that teams with a parttime assistant coach and a one full time assistant coach that would have to let one of them go. I stand up and ask, 'Who will UCLA have to drop?' "The coach with the drugs or the one with the money?" The Pac-10 Conference goes nuts and closes the meetings to the press. The next year the coach from Oregon, Bill Dillinger, stands up and says, "The answer to Coach Chaplin's question last year is that UCLA kept the coach with the drugs." Needless to say, that the conference about lost its mind with me and Bill. It was no secret that Dillinger and myself did not consider the conference commissioners we had during our tenure, as heavy weights." In short, the expertise of the people that we had to deal with at the conference office was not always of a high caliber or experience in track & field. But it is true that I was not always a team player with the Conference.

I had two of these type of phone calls with the NCAA on eligibility and neither went well. In fact, Walter Byers, the head of the NCAA at the time, once said on one these two calls. "You (the President) need to tell your coach that football counts and track does not." This was a conversation about some SMU players, who took money, and were running on the 4x400-meter relay team that cost WSU and another institution national titles. The second time, the faculty rep from another conference school asked our faculty rep if we had information on an athlete that the NCAA made eligible contrary to the transfer rules. WSU did know the rule and did not recruit him. So, me and the WSU president and our faculty rep and the admissions office (who had approved the foreign student transcripts for the NCAA) are all on a call with Byers. After we explain the rule to Byers he says, "You (speaking to the president of WSU) need to tell your coach that he needs to drop this matter and then the NCAA will be indebted to WSU."

Sometimes individuals would ask about my philosophy of running the International Competition Committee and the Men's Track & field Committee (USATF). It was simple. I got the best people that I could find and allowed them to do the job they were given. I never had a particular job, other than to supervise the whole operation. I believed that if I had a particular job, then when there is a crisis, I would have to leave that job to help with said crisis. And as I have said earlier, I am a lot of things but insecure is not one of them. As I said before, I had people who, in reality, ran the show. I just made sure all the parts were in synch. I had people like Charlie Green, Dr. Richard Strand, Linda Lanker, Allan Kolling, Ed Gorman, Bob Podkaminer, and many others, who, in reality, ran the show. I just made sure that all the parts were in sync.

As Chair of ICC and Men's Track & field, I made out the time schedule for TV and coordinated with TV and the host committees and then was in charge of managing the competition.

Another question I have been asked many times is how coaches and managers are selected for foreign trips. First, in those days, all coaches and managers had to be elected by the appropriate committee. The ICC was the committee of jurisdiction, but today it is either the men's or women's' track & field committees that select the coaches. Today, the managers are selected by the High-Performance Committee. It usually took about four hours each to manage the two subcommittees, one for men and one for women. In the fall of 1996, at the selection meeting of the ICC which consisted of 39 members, there were three candidates for the position of head coach, and I was selected. I was also selected three times by the Men's Track & field Committee.

Secondly, you have the Olympics Trials, which are put on by national federation (USATF). At the trials, we use a schedule that mirrors the time schedule of that particular Olympic Games. After the trials, the team becomes the property of the National Governing Body, the USOC in the case of the Olympics. Their rules on all matters of procedures and communications with the IAAF (WA), the IOC and the officials at the particular Olympic Games are the rules that the team is governed by. The Olympics are hosted by a city, not a nation. In the case of the 2000 Games, it was Sydney, where I was the head coach for the men's track & field team. The U.S. is the only nation that has two separate track & field teams at the Games - a women's team and a men's team with completely different coaching and managerial staffs. The two teams pretty much went their own way. Karen Dennis a Hall of Fame Coach at Las Vegas at the time, was the women's head coach for the U.S., but I arranged to get both the men's and women a great place on the Gold Coast from Ron Clark the great Australian world record holder, and a new hotel in Brisbane for the month prior going into the Olympic Village. I also got us a training camp with the Australian team. With the help of UCS for equipment and the USOC who shipped everything to the training site, we had a good training center. We left it all to the local college (really a high school), which hosted our camp as partial payment for the use of their facilities. I even set up a track meet with all the other nations who were training the area and donated the gate receipts to the school for their overseas scholarship program.

Speaking of the USOC, in 2000 I had to go to them to get an additional coach and basically informed them of who I wanted on the medical team. That was Dr. Ricard Strand for drug testing, Dr. Dean Clark as our chiropractor, and Cheryl Parker as head trainer. Cheryl who later became a physician's assistant.

What went down later was fascinating. Herman Fraizer, a teammate of my manager Fred Newhouse, was third in the 1976 Olympic Games 400M race and won a gold medal in the 4x400- meter relay. Anyway, the USOC had Herman, who was a vice president of the USOC come to Sydney to handle basketball, boxing, and all things *Chaplin*. Herman and I laugh about that today since we are still close friends. Use your imagination to figure out why?

With all this in mind let's move forward.

I had two situations prior to going to Australia: The press who wanted to know who would be on the relay teams, who was in charge of deciding the makeup of the team, and the position of the runners; And Doctors who were not in accord with the walkers taking and using a special type of altitude tent and. on medical drug testing with one particular athlete.

"In both cases I explain to the different groups the I use the "Mr. Lincoln Rule". President Lincoln had a six-member cabinet, and he was the seventh when they discussed policy. The Doctors voted by a show of hands that they did not think the walkers should take the tents to the Games. When the press wanted and an explanation of who would make the final calls on relay personnel, I applied "the Mr. Lincoln Rule". When Mr. Lincoln called for a vote regardless of the outcome, Mr. Lincoln won. In other words, I had the final say.

Dealing with the USOC or USATF at the Olympic Games is like "Whistling Dixie in the Dark". Other than Mike Conley, my liaison with both groups, who did a fabulous job, I had little contact with them. The only major issue came about when I received a call from a friend at the IAAF telling me that C. J. Hunter, the husband of Marion Jones, the eventual Champion in the 100 and 200 meters, at the time, and a shot putter on our team had had several positive drug tests from meets in Europe. I called my head manager Fred Newhouse, who was an Olympic gold medalist on the 4x400 and the silver medalist in the open 400 meters at the 1976 Games and explained the situation to him. We both agreed that under no circumstances should we enter E.J. in the shot put and if Hunter pressed his right to compete, we would just not enter him.

But under USOC rules, if you want to replace someone, for all practical purposes, the athlete would have had to agree in writing to give up his or her spot on the team. And if I'd gone to the USOC, they'd want a written statement from Hunter before they would grant a credential for an alternate. I talked it over with Fred Newhouse, and he was adamant that he would not submit Hunter's name. I agreed. But we had a way around this dilemma. John Godina was the alternate, and he already has a credential for the discus throw.

So, I did three things:

First, I called Hunter's Agent, Charlie Wells, and explained that he would withdraw E.J. one way or the other because he had positive tests, from Europe, or I would call a press conference and tell the world that he has tested positive for illegal drugs, period. Backing up, I should explain that teams in all individual events are made up of a maximum of three qualified athletes and one alternate athlete".

Second, I called the alternate athlete, John Godina, and asked him if he would like to compete in the shot put. He said "yes." Now remember, an athlete has to remove himself or herself from the team in writing. You have to be credentialed at the Olympic Games, and the USOC is the organization is in charge of submitting credentials for athletes and Staff. Ha! But our alternate athlete already had a credential for the discus throw.

And third under the rules, 48 prior hours to the start of competition, each nation must enter up to three competitors. Since the alternate, Godina, had a credential, Newhouse entered John Godina and not C.J. Hunter as our third entry. The shot put is always the first final on the first day of the Games with the preliminary in the morning and he final that night. All is well, right? That's what we thought.

And finally, all hell broke out the next morning when the world press awoke to find that C.J. Hunter had tested positive. So, I go to the press conference and on the stage is a lectern and a chair for me. A young lady is standing there with a paper in her hand and talking about *athletes' privacy, rights, etc.* I walk over and take the paper out of her hand and say, 'Please sit down. I will handle this.' I sit on the edge of the stage and say, 'questions.' A woman from France is yelling at me 'How did Hunter get a credential?' I say first of all, 'C.J. Hunter did not compete for the U.S. yesterday, so that is a moot question. And second of all, I do not give out credentials that is the USOC's job, so go talk to them. This is above my pay grade.' I sat there for almost two hours and answered questions, and that was the end of the matter.

The only other incident came up when an athlete came with a new pair of high jump shoes, and when he went to out to compete in them, they were the wrong size. He was the defending Olympic Champion, and he had to borrow a pair from another athlete and did not make the podium. He came to me and said, "What do I tell the press?" I told him "Don't make up any story about why it happened.

Just tell them the truth, that you made a mistake and should have check shoes and let it go at that." That's what he did, and the matter went away.

My job at the Games as the Head Coach was to be the leader for all the members of the team not just the medal winners. So, I mostly stayed in the Village until the assistant coach for the last group competing that day was in the call room, and then I went over to the Stadium.

One of the coaches that read an early version of this book said you need to explain how you handled us at a meet when we came screaming to you with a protest or a question on procedure etc.

So here goes.

When a coach, the athlete's manager, or anyone else the athlete has sent, came into protest, I would first give them my speech: "Coach let's understand the ground rules. I am a cynical, sarcastic S.O.B. Now that we both know what I am, you don't have to waste my mine and your time by you telling me that. Then I would say what is your problem and let's see if we can fix it. Then if things were got to the place where the coach is feeling sorry for him or herself and start talking about fairness, etc. I'd say Coach "if you want love, get a Puppy. The puppy will love you when you wife or husband or whoever may not." Then I would say, "I am here to make sure that the rules are followed, and my decision will be based on the facts, not on emotions." If this individual does get or does not like the answer or ruling, I'd suggest the coach or agent or whoever "go out and tell your wife or husband or your assistant coaches that I am a S.O.B but do it quietly so as to not get on YouTube."

I hope the reader finds these little tidbits informative or, at least, amusing.

More... "Hanky/Panky" ...

There are two items left that are rarely spoke about... the 800-pound gorillas in the room.... The honesty of the NCAA, the national governing body, for its handling of the influx of monies paid under the table in Division I sports and the issue of student-athlete eligibility to participate, especially for a foreign student.

In the first half of the Twentieth Century, such matters were handled by the colleges and universities themselves. The Ivy League, the ICAAAA, the NCAA in 1906, and the Pacific Coast Conference all set many of their own rules for eligibility. But after WWII, when millions of returning soldiers came home to attend school on the G.I. Bill, institutions of higher education expanded their athletic programs away from strictly regional competition to an emphasis on national-level competition. And so, a consistent set of rules that could be applied nationwide needed to be established. But, even at the beginning, the NCAA seems, in certain cases, to have ignored them.

Foreign Athletes at the time were a relatively small percentage of athletes in the NCAA, and there were no special rules that applied to them. But it was still left up to each institution to decide who to admit. With all this in mind, college athletes for men exploded in the sixties, then exploded again for women in the seventies after the advent of Title IX. As a result, money poured into these institutions, and of course, things got out of hand. An age requirement was added to the NCAA Division I eligibility rules. Division I (athletes one would lose a year of eligibility for every year after age 20, with exceptions granted for Military service and for religious missions, etc. Also, transfer rules were imposed to keep schools from poaching each other's athletes. Minimal standards had been set for high school test scores and grade point averages. But then, an influx of foreign athletes entered the system, and how to handle their eligibility became a problem. How do you prove an international athlete's age, for example? Or how do you evaluate kids from different educational systems' academic records? 'O' level exams – from 1951 to 1986 and the GCSEs since 1986. In West Africa, standardized tests were administered in the high schools, but scores could be purchased in certain countries.

For example, in Kenya, if you are in the tenth grade and decide to go to a *teachers' college* for two years (to qualify to teach elementary students), you are not considered a transfer student when you come to the U.S. to run in college. But if you enter the teacher's college after the twelfth grade, you *are* considered a transfer student and would have to sit out one year before you were eligible to compete in the NCAA. I know this is the case because I was involved with eligibility, and our faculty rep said he got a call from a conference member who wanted to know if I know anything about a particular athlete. I said, "yes, we tried to get him, but he would have been considered a transfer and would have had to sit out a year." When WSU asked the NCAA about why the athlete was allowed to compete at another university, we were told that the matter was closed, and that the NCAA would appreciate it if the faculty rep would "tell your coach to drop the matter."

And how to handle the age question? In many third-world countries where there had been colonial rule prior to the 1960s, there was no local government that recorded or kept track of birthdates for most of their population. If birthdates were recorded at all, it was on a baptism certificate from a religious institution. Many children did not enter elementary school until the age of seven or even eight. So even if you count back from high school, the age on a kid's passport may not be true.

Returning to the dirty money problem, an issue that would expose the NCAA in its dealing with SMU. SMU was given the "death penalty" for illegally paying football players for their performances. To make matters worse, the NCAA, behind closed doors, made a Faustian bargain when it stated the names of the players who were paid would not be released. Well, the Dallas Morning News found the players and published the names anyway. But the problem was that several of the football players were members of SMU's 4x400-meter relay. The ten points SMU earned by winning that relay cost WSU the NCAA team title. When WSU appealed, the NCAA's answer was, 'Coach, in the bigger picture, football counts, and track does not. How is that for an honest and responsible system?

**Henry Rono's 1978 Season. "The Greatest Cougar Ever"
1978 *Track & field News* MALE ATHLETE OF THE YEAR
WORLD RECORDS: 5,000m, 3,000M steeplechase,
10,000M, and 3,000M**

- April 8 ASU and California vs WSU at Berkeley, CA **13:08.4** (WR) 5,000 meters
- April 15 Oregon vs WSU Dual at Eugene, OR **8:14.8** (CR) Steeplechase
- April 22 CSU, UM and BSU vs WSU Duals at Pasco, WA **4:00.9** (MR) Mile
- April 29 Washington vs WSU Dual at Pullman, WA **8:24.4** (MR) Steeplechase
- May 7 Sunkist Invitational at Los Angeles, CA **7:43.0** (CR) 3,000 meters
- May 13 Northwest Relays at Seattle, WA **8:05.4** (WR) Steeplechase
- May 19 Pacific-8 Championships at Corvallis, OR **27:46.6** (MR) 10,000 meters

- May 20 Pacific-8 Championships at Corvallis, OR **13:20.2** (MR) 5,000 meters
- May 24 Crystal Palace at London GB **7:43.9** 3,000 meters
- June 1 NCAA championships at Eugene, OR **8:18.6** (MR) Steeplechase
- June 1 NCAA championships at Eugene, OR **13:21.8** (MR) 5,000 meters
- June 3 NCAA championships at Eugene, OR **8:12.4** (MR) Steeplechase
- June 11 Vienna at Austria **27:22.5** (WR) 10,000 meters
- June 17 Kenya Championships at Mombasa, Kenya **8:16.2** (MR) Steeplechase
- June 17 Kenya Championships at Mombasa, Kenya **13:31.4** 5,000 meters
- June 24 IAAF Meet at Cologne, WG **7:41.5** (CR) 3,000 meters.
- June 25 IAAF Meet at London, GB **13:20.8** (MR) 5,000 meters.
- June 27 IAAF Meet at Oslo, Norway **7:32.1** (WR) 3,000 meters.

Also included in Rono's 1978 Season...

The San Blas Half Marathon has been held in February annually since 1963. The race, besides having an individual champion, is also scored as a two-person team event. In 1978, Chaplin split his team: Henry Rono (first in 1:04.46) and Joe Cheruiyot (twelfth in 1:07.55.1) represented WSU, and Samson Kimombwa (sixth in 1:06.13.4) and Joshua Kimeto (eighth in at 1:08.1) represented Kenya. WSU beat Kenya 13-14. In 1978 Chaplin tells Jim Bush at the NCAA Nationals in Eugene, he was right about those African Athletes, and that WSU had beaten the Kenyans 13-14 in a team scored event in Coamo,

Puerto Rico. Chaplin pointed out that the irony of the result went over Bush's head. "He missed the whole point," Chaplin said.

***

An Overview of WSU Distance Training philosophy, Methods, and Tactics:

(What follows are the notes that Coach Chaplin has distributed when speaking at coaching clinics around the world)

Six Principles:

(1) A *hard day* of workouts must be followed by at least followed by one *easy day* in a four-day training sequence (Monday through Thursday).

(2) Every time **you put an athlete on the track** for interval or repetition work **the chance of injury is increased**. This is true for mature college athletes, so it makes sense to **limit hard track work even more for teenage athletes**.

(3) **Since** teenage runners compete at **3,000/3200** meters, **tailor their training** to those distances. We design training sessions for club and collegiate athletes to meet the demands of a 5,000-meter race since that is the most common distance run at that level.

(4) Focus on **quality** running as opposed to **quantity** (high mileage).

(5) When possible, adopt a racing strategy that uses runners working together, a primary runner and at least one secondary runner. "I have used a system of primary and secondary runners as the core strategy (to help with for scoring) at the Pacific 10 Conference

Championships and NCAA meets for thirty years. In high school this would include the league, district, or state championships."

(6) Practice and utilize racing tactics that exploit the **weaknesses of your opponents,** limiting their tactical choices during the race. Force you opponent to do what he/she does not like to do. If they do not like to change pace, **surge, that is dramatically increase the pace at critical points** in the race. Also, **negative splits** are not only the most efficient way to run a long race on the track, but they are also a good way to disrupt an opponent's race plan, as long as he/she is willing to allow your runner to lead from the gun. Note: These tactics are most effective at the longer track distances and may be of limited utility in a shorter high school race unless the athlete has practiced and mastered these techniques.

<u>There are three main race tactics a good distance runner should practice:</u>

Taking the lead from the gun, using a steady and superior race-pace that the competition cannot stay with.

Surging during the race. Increasing the pace for a predetermined distance (usually 800 for women or races of 3000M-1,000 meters for races of 5000M & 10,000M for men) and then returning to the original race pace.

Sprinting. WSU did not use the strategy of waiting until the end of the race and then simply trying to out-sprint the competition with a better kick. "This method is all too often used by American runners who use it from 1500 meters to 10,000 meters," Chaplin said. "The problem with too many American distance runners is that they use this tactic too much of the time. We here in the United States still train, for the most part, and race as if the distances we were competing are 1,500 meters or the mile instead of 5,000 and 10,000 meters.

<u>Tactical and Training Considerations</u>:

Never let less-talented runners stay in the race until the final sprint. "If you do you will increase your chances of losing. This is his or her big chance, and they will probably make the most of it.

If the athlete you are running against has real talent, you cannot shake him/her by running a steady pace, no matter how fast you run. This is because you cannot put enough stress on a good athlete to put them deep enough into oxygen debt. It takes a surge of at least 1,000 meters, often repeated several times, to break good runners in races of 5,000 and 10,000 meters. In high school and with college women a surge of 600 to 800 meters is sufficient, for a 3200-meters race). The reason for a shorter distance for these groups is because men have more strength than women not more talent.

Practice time spent on the track should be focused on the weakest part of each individual runner's race.

During light (sub-maximal) exercise, oxygen stored in the muscles can be recovered by the respiration and circulatory systems.

During moderate exercise (a slight increase short of maximum effort, anaerobic processes contribute to the energy output at the beginning of the workout and lasts until the aerobic oxidation can take over and completely cover the energy demand. Lactic acid can be produced, but as the work proceeds at the moderate level, the blood lactate concentration falls again to the resting level, and the work can continue for long periods of time.

During heavier workloads, the lactic acid production along with the rise in blood lactate concentration are elevated and remain elevated throughout the work period (or race), but heavy workload can be endured by well-motivated, well-trained, and well-conditioned individuals.

During severe exercise, there is an increasing oxygen deficit with elevated lactate content in the blood, which must be cleared before the next hard training session or race.

Examples of WSU successfully employing team tactics:

1976 NCAA 5,000 Meters: Joshua Kimeto first, John Ngeno second, Samson Kimombwa third.

1977 NCAA 5,000 Meters: Joshua Kimeto first, Samson Kimombwa second

1984 NCAA 5,000 meters: Julius Korir first, Peter Koech second.

1973 Pac-8 10,000 Meters: John Ngeno first, Dan Murphy second, Phil Burkwist third.

1978 Pac-8 10,000 Meters: Henry Rono first, Joel Cheruiyot second, Samson Kimombwa fourth.

1978 Pac-8 5,000 Meters: Henry Rono first Joel Cheruiyot second Josh Kimeto third, Samson Kimombwa fifth.

1983 Pac-10 Steeplechase: Julius Korir first, Richard Tuwei second, Steve James third.

1983 Pac-10 5,000 Meters: Richard Tuwei first, Peter Koech second, Julius Korir (third).

1994 Pac-10 5,000 and 10,000 Meters: Josephat Kapkory first, Patrick Muturi (second).

(Chaplin noted, "These results were made possible by running negative splits and surging at key points in the race in order to exploit the weaknesses of other runners in the race and by the using primary/secondary runner strategy in which the secondary runners create a situation during the race to give the primary runner the best chance to win.")

<u>Training considerations:</u> WSU did sprint drills between 180 meters and 300 meters after their twice weekly long runs. Chaplin explained: "For example, don't just run 15x400 when you're not tired. This type of repetitive intervals does not replicate what happens in a race."

BASIC PRINCIPLES

(1) Surging: At all levels of competition, the ability to cope with the surging (change of pace) is the main tactical problem most distance runners face today. Surging is more physical than mental, and the inability to surge is the result of the lack of proper training methods being used in the United States.

(2) Negative splits: Since 1965 All Cougar distance runners who broke world, American, collegiate, or conference records ran the second half of their race faster than the first half.

TRAINING METHODS AND SURGING TACTICS

"Here I must take a minute to explain a little about training philosophy, even though this is a review of the strategy and tactics mentioned earlier. I train runners on and off the track with three main objectives."

Training is specific to the most common racing distance, for example, 3,000 meters or 3,200 meters for high school athletes. 5000M for college athletes.

Time spent on the track should be focused on the weakest aspect of the athlete's racing arsenal.

Never do anything in a practice situation that does not have some practical application in a race.

FARTLEK AND INTERVAL CONCEPTS

Fartlek is a Swedish word meaning "speed play" and was originally explained as a system of training that alternates between strenuous segments and easy segments over varied terrain within a single training session.

Fartlek workouts are a **physically demanding hard-easy training system** that deploys an ever-increasing interval and pace during workouts on the road or on trails intended to push the athlete's aerobic threshold. These workouts, which increase heart rates and fatigue factors, are accomplished without any increase in the amount of mileage run per week. Note: The same strategy is use for the Anaerobic track workouts.

WSU distance athletes put in an average of 60-80 miles per week during the nine-month college year (from September to May). **Forty-to-sixty miles per week is sufficient for the average high school runner** (Unless they are nationally, ranked and even then, caution is called for, and individual circumstances should determine if more mileage is needed.

Important Note: I believe that from an athletic development standpoint, **long slow distance running has no more validity than running slow in an interval workout on the track**. If an athlete is running seven-minute or eight minute-mile pace in practice, it should come as no surprise that he will have a hard time running five-minute mile pace in a race.

Therefore, a program should divide fartlek training away from the track into two types: varied and steady. The difference is the length of the repetitions run during the fartlek workout. With varied fartlek, the distance of each repetition and with each recovery segment is different. Steady fartlek on the other hand means the length of each repetition and recovery segment remains the same throughout the workout.

For example, a steady fartlek workout might consist of a series of 800 to one-mile runs followed by a specified recovery time or distance. But a varied fartlek session might consist of a variety of distances for both the harder runs and for the recovery segments. It is important to keep in mind that the recovery segments provide an <u>adequate</u> and prescribed amount of easy running between each repetition.

When it comes to interval training, I do not subscribe to the general theory that each repetition should be no longer than 90 seconds for training to be maximized. I do feel that if the pulse remains above 140 ninety seconds after completion of any repetition, more rest is required.

Our system of training in conjunction with surging drills will develop a more complete runner. Compared to many distance programs, which use a fartlek system in combination with a ninety-second interval system on the track, we produced a better product.

ANAEROBIC and AEROBIC TRAINING

One needs to do both Aerobic and Anaerobic workouts to gain maximum racing efficiency. The distinction between anaerobic and aerobic training is the most critical element of modern distance running training.

Anaerobic Training is training at a faster pace than can be maintained at a steady pace for an extended period. This type of training requires more oxygen than can be supplied during the run. An oxygen debt is incurred, causing lactic acid to build up in the muscle tissue and in the blood stream, inevitably ending in exhaustion. Individual pulse rates can be as high as 180 to 190 beats per minute.

In contrast, **aerobic training is running at a pace that can be maintained indefinitely**. This is possible so long as an ample supply of oxygen sufficient to oxidize the carbohydrate sources of energy is available, allowing **no accumulation of lactic acid**. Note: This balanced condition is commonly called being in a "steady state". This state allows young adult athletes to run with a pulse rate in the range of 130 to 169.

Here a discussion of running tactics with anaerobic threshold is needed. One needs to know what his or her point of VO2 max is, beyond which lactic acid begin to build up rapidly in the athlete's blood causing "oxygen debt" (the point at which the athlete crosses the line from aerobic to anaerobic running). The coach needs to monitor the athlete's workouts by checking their pulse rates when the athletes are pushing their aerobic and anaerobic thresholds in workouts.

This translates into a program whose goal is to increase the steady state of the individual athlete by increasing the lowest pace that will produce maximal oxygen uptake without driving the runner into oxygen debt.

In simple terms, what we try to do is lower the race pace that is aerobic (say to 68-70 seconds per 400 meters) on one end and increase the anaerobic threshold (say to 62-65 seconds per 400 meters on the other end).

In practice we progressively increase the pace of our workouts both on and off the track but without increasing the mileage they run per week. If the runner has problems with the new workload as we increase the race pace (per 400 meters) or lower the recovery time between repetitions, we cut back on the workload (volume and/or intensity) until the runner is able to handle the new load.

This allows the athlete to run a progressively faster race pace while still maintaining a relatively low level of stress for longer periods of time, increasing the maximum oxygen uptake and oxygen debt thresholds.

The acquired technique of increasing the runner's oxygen debt threshold allows surging to become the primary race tactic. Being able to surge was the main goal of WSU's distance program.

ANEROBIC PROCESSES

The energy required during light work may be almost exclusively produced by aerobic processes (as mentioned in our subsequent discussion of distance training). During more severe work, anaerobic processes are brought into play (after four or five minutes of harder running).

Oxygen Debt - Lactic Acid Production: To some extent, lactic acid is eliminated during light exercise with the result that a portion of the aerobic energy deficit rate during the early sage of exercise will accelerate. The rate of lactic acid produced during heavy exercise exceeds tolerable levels because muscle PH drops (becomes more acidic). The outcome of this is that some of the lactic acid in used, some is stored in the blood, and some remains in the muscle. There is always oxygen debt after exercise. A gap exists between the oxygen debt at the beginning of work and the oxygen debt during heavy work.

Maximal Aerobic Power - Remember, maximal aerobic power is defined as the highest oxygen uptake the individual can maintain during physical work, breathing air at sea level. Understanding this concept is the basis for the training we used. Therefore, we are constantly pushing both aerobic and the anaerobic thresholds of our runners. The oxygen consumption curve rises toward the maximal consumption point until it levels off and maximum oxygen uptake has occurred. The lactic acid curve increases rapidly as the level of exercise intensity increases. But at higher altitudes, oxygen uptake goes down with the same workload, and lactic acid in the blood will increase sooner with the same workload.

***

WSU Track & Field/Cross Country Team Accomplishments

- 1977 NCAA National Indoor Champions.
- Pacific-8 Cross Country Champions 1971, 1972, 1974, 1975.
- Pacific-10 Outdoor Champions 1983, 1984, 1985. 1991.
- 202-15-0 Dual Meet Record (93.1 percent).
- All-Americans Certificates: Cross Country 29, Indoor T&F 75, and Outdoor T&F 114.
- Six *Track and Field News* National Dual Meet Titles 1981, 1983, 1984, 1985, 1991, 1992.
- 17 individuals with 37 NCAA Gold Medals
- WSU has won National Collegiate, Individual & Relay, Event Titles in 23 of the 29
- events currently contested at Cross Country. Indoor & Outdoor Track & field: Cross
- Country. Indoor: 60M HH, 60M, Distance Medley Relay, 35# weight & Distance
- Medley Relay, Outdoor: 100M, 200M. 400M, 1500M, Mile, 2-mile/3000M, 3-mile/
- 5,000M, 6-mile/10,000M, 110M HH, 400M IH,3000M Steeplechase, Long Jump
- Triple Jump, Pole Vault, Discus throw, Shot Put, Javelin Throw, & Hammer Throw
- Non-winning positions: 800M & High Jump 2nd, 4x400M Relay, 4x110M Relay &
- Decathlon 4th. No points in the Indoor Heptathlon.
- NCAA Cross Country Competition: Nine Top-10 Team Places: fourth in 1969, *second in 1971,* fourth in 1972, third in 1973, fourth in 1974, *second in 1975,* third in 1976, ninth

in 1977, seventh in 1984. Note: Chaplin's 1975 Cross Country Team lost the national title to UTEP by 4 points, 92 to 88.

- 300.5 total Points in NCAA Indoor Competition: Eleven top-10 Team Places: fifth in 1975, fourth in 1976, *first in 1977,* fourth in 1978, eighth in 1981, fifth in 1982, seventh in 1983, second in 1984, fifth in 1986, sixth in 1987, third in 1991.
- 652.5 total points in NCAA outdoor track & field competition: Twelve Top-10 Team Places: tenth in 1974, ninth in 1975, fourth in 1976 and 1977, ninth in 1978, tenth in 1979, third in 1982, fifth in 1983, and *second in 1984, 1985, 1986, and 1991.*
- Chaplin's teams won 19 NCAA top-four trophies. Note: John P. Chaplin's 1986 Outdoor NCAA track & field team lost to SMU by one point.

More stats and facts from the WSU Track & field History Books

- Washington State University graduates were major players on the international stage from 800 meters to the marathon. In 1909 Jack Nelson From tied world record for the 100- and 220-yard dashes, at a time when strings were used to mar the lanes in the 100-yard dash. In 2021 Eldon Jenne a 1920 U.S. Olympian won NCAA Pole Vault and in 1925 John Devine was the NCAA 2-mile Champion. *All these athletes were coached by Doc Bohler.*
- In 1939 Dixie Garner set a world record by running 9:11.1 and defeating two-mile world record holder Miklos Szabo from Hungary in 1939. WSU set a World Record for the Mile Relay. Loren Bence won the 1939 NCAA 440 Yard Title and in 1949 Lee Orr won the 1940 NCAA 440-yard Title. *All these athletes were coached by Karl Schliemann.*

- Bill Parnell won the gold medal at one mile in 4:11.0 at the 1950 Empire Games and a Bronze Medal at 800 meters, in 1:53.4. Don Bertoia won the gold medal at 800 meters, in 1:48.46 and the bronze medal in the 1,500 at 3:55.19 in the Pan-American Games. Gerry Lindgren beat the Russians at 10,000-meters as a high school athlete in the USA vs. The Soviet Union Dual Meet in 1965 and set a six-mile world record in a tie with Billy Miles, the 1964 Olympic 10,000 meters champion, in 27:11.6 in 1965.Art Sandison, a 1:46.1 800-meter runner won a silver Medal in the 800 at 1:50.67 in the Pan American Games in 1971. *All these athletes were coached by Jack Mooberry.*

- John Ngeno at 7:38.6 for 3,000 meters, 13:20.6 for 5,000 meters, and 28:04.6 for 10,000 meters in 1976. Also in 1976, Ngeno beat Lassi Viren at 5,000 meters in the 1972 and 1976 Olympic 5,000 and 10,000 champion in the pre-Olympic Meet in Canada. Joshua Kimeto at 13:26.8 for 5,000 and 28:00.6 for 10,000 who also competed in the Commonwealth Games. Samson Kimombwa set a 10,000-meter world record in 1977 of 27:30.47 and ran 13:20.6 for 5,000 meters Henry Rono set world records for 3,000 meters at 7:32.1, 5,000 meters, twice, at 13:08.4 and 13 06.2, for the 3,000 meters steeplechase at 8:05.4 and who broke Kimombwa's 10,000 meters record at 27:22.47. In 1978 Rono won the Commonwealth Games 3,000 meters Steeplechase at 8:26.3 in the heats and ran 8:26.54 in the final. He also won the 5,000 final at 13:23.0. Julius Korir – Olympic Steeplechase champion was the Olympic Champion in the steeple in 1984 at 8:11.5 and also won the 1982 Commonwealth Games steeplechase at 8:23.94. Korir also ran 7:48.70 for 3,000 meters, and 27:40.1 for the 10,000, both in 1986.Richard Tuwei

NCAA Champion at 8:18.22 for the 3,000 meters Steeplechase in 1983, 3:38.77 for the 1,500 in 1982 and at 7:45.28 for 3,000 and 13:30.60 for the 5,000 in 1983.

- Peter Koech at 3:35.67 for 1,500 meters, and 7:39.09 for 3,000 in 1982, plus an 8:17.05 two- mile the same year. Koech was the second fastest man in the world at 5,000 meters, at 13:09.50 in 1982. Koech won a silver medal in the Seoul Olympics in 1988 and then broke Henry Rono's steeplechase record with a time of 8:05.35 seven years later. Samuel Kibiri a NCAA 1500M Champion who ran 1,500 meters, in 3:38.38 and the steeplechase in 8:28.63 in 1991.Josephat Kapkory a versatile runner with personal bests of 3:39.87 for the 1,500, 7:50.91 for a NCAA Indoor Meet Record for the 3,000, 13:27.0 for the 5,000, and 8:20.67 for steeplechase, all run in 1994.

- Patrick Muturi was eighth in the World at the marathon with a 2:12:50, placing third at Chicago and first at San Francisco in 1994. *All these athletes were coached by John Chaplin.*

- Bernard Lagat anchored WSU to an indoor world best for the distance medley relay at 9:32.56. Then, at the World Championships in 2007, Lagat became the only man to win the 1,500 meters (3:34.77) and the 5,000 meters (at 13:45.87). Lagat won world indoor titles at 3,000 meters, for Kenya in 2004 at 7:56.34, and in 2010 for the U.S. at 7:37.97 and 2012 in 7:41.44. His lifetime marks were 3:26.34 for 1,500 meters, 7:29.00 for 3,000 meters and 12:53.60 for 5,000 meters. He ranked first in the U.S. in the 1,500, 3,000, and 5,000 several times. In 2013 Lagat ranked third in the World at 1,500 meters, and he was sixth in the 5,000 at the Rio de Janeiro Olympic Games in 2016 13:06.78 at age 41. Also, in 2016, Bernard Lagat posted a 27:49.0 10,000-meter time for a master's world record the first time he ever ran the event. At age 42, Lagat set 100,000-meter record on the road at 28:13. *Lagat was Coached by James Li*

Additional WSU Athletes of Note

- Six WSU javelin throwers were All-Americans and/or conference champions. Laslo Babits is the WSU record holder with the old javelin at 282-5 (86.08 meters), and Jan Johansson, Gerald Lyons, and Mark Babich all threw beyond 80 meters with the old javelin. Stephan Wikstrom at 257-2 (78.3) in the school record holder with the new javelin All competed during Chaplin's tenure, along with seven of the school's top ten throwers in the hammer: Tore Gustafsson held the collegiate, and he and a Stefan Jonsson were both NCAA Hammer Throw Champions.

- Five of WSU's top ten triple jumpers with Ian Campbell at 57'5" (17.56) a two-time NCAA indoor Champion and Joseph Taiwo at 56 4 ¾ (17.17) (Taiwo was the "Athlete of the Century" for the triple jump by the Pac-12 Conference) Chaplin recalls: "I was in Senegal for the African Championships when Lee Evans the head Coach for Nigeria and the 1968 Olympic 400-meter champion, brought up to me the skinny little kid Joseph Tawio and said, "he is a good student and has jumped over 50 feet will you scholarship him"? And I say, "Okay. That was the first of a long line of recruiting dealings with Lee" and Ray Kimble a football player at WSU that jumped a lifetime best 56'11 ½ (17.36) the third all-time American mark, set an over 40 triple jump record of 54' 4 ½, had a 57'11 ½ (17.56) wind added mark in 1987, a National USATF Champion and was fourth twice in the U.S. Olympic trials topping the list.

Closer to home: Athletes from the State of Washington

- Hammer Throwers (who learned the event after coming to WSU) like All-Americans Jim Jesernig and John Billingsley and walk-ons like Kyle Unland, Dwight Middles, and Ed VandeVoorde.

- Bill Ayears long jumped 26-5 ¾ and won the 1996 re-enactment of the 1896 Olympic Games in Athens, on his birthday.

- A veritable army of javelin throwers, all who threw at least 75 meters, (246 feet) like Carl O'Donnell the 1968 NCAA Champion, Foss Miller, Gene Lorenzen, Tom Deihl, Randy Mendenhall, and Mark Babich (who competed for Team U.S.A. in the world championships) and played Basketball for WSU. All were either All-Americans or conference champions.

- Brian Zinsser was a walk-on who cleared 17-0¾ in the pole vault.

- Bruce Anderson had been an NCAA Division II champion in the shot before transferring to WSU.

- Norm Kietges came to Pullman from tiny (fewer than 100 students) St. John High School in the wheat country along the Washington-Idaho border, but still managed to run 46.9 for 400 meters, and 1:49.4 for 800 meters.

- Sprinters like Dave Rorem who ran 9.5 for 100 yards. Tim Giesa from Gonzaga Prep in Spokane ran 9.5 for 100 yards and 46.5 in the quarter mile. Jim Carkner, a wrestler who Chaplin recruited onto the track team, ran 440 yards in 46.95.

- Other sprinters like Forey Walter from tiny Odessa, Washington, ran 9.5 for 100 yards and was one of the best sprinters in Washington High School history. Larry Scherer was an AAU All-American at 20.8 for 220 yards and had a best of 9.5 for 100, 20.8 for 220 yards, and 47.0 for 400 meters. Park Eng ran 5.1 for 50 yards indoors (a world best at the time). Steve Hoover, a cheerleader, ran 20.7 for 220 yards, set a WSU school Record, beat USC at the 4 x110 relays in a dual meet in Pullman, and scored in the NCAA 4x110-yard relay. And Lee Gordon from Mercer Island placed second at 100 meters, in 10.29 at the 1984 NCAA meet.

- Brent Harkin was a seven-foot-high jumper in high school who improved to 7' 7' (2.31) and set the still standing school record and then jumped 7' 8 ½ in 1991 after college, at the time the fourth-best jump ever by an American.

- Phil Burkwist, perhaps the most colorful athlete in Spokane's long tradition of distance running excellence, came to WSU from Spokane Community College and Lewis and Clark High School and was, in Chaplin's words "not fond of training", but he still became a cross country All American in 1972 and set an NCAA meet record of 13:54 for three miles (a preliminary round) at the 1971 ships in Seattle.

- Tom Robinson, another walk-on, who Chaplin introduced to the marathon in college and set the colligate record for that distance in 1971.

- In 1965, WSU led by a Washington prep athlete Bill Bleakney, who walked-on from the golf team, ran 14.0 in the high hurdles to beat Paul Kerry the NCAA 120-yard-high hurdle champion from USC as WSU downed USC 82-65 in a dual meet. This was the first dual meet loss for USC in the conference since before WWII. The all-time dual meet record between WSU and USC is currently tied.

Chaplin: *"WSU was more than just a distance dog and pony show."*

WSU is the only institution in the history of the Pac-12 to win an individual title in every event contested at the outdoor championships and the Cougars have done it twice.

E.J. Gou and Tony Li both came to WSU from China. Li broke the NCAA record for the 55-meter hurdles, and Gou was an All-American at 3,000 meters indoors and 5,000 and 10,000 meters, outdoors. Kenyan Samuel Kibiri was the NCAA 1,500-meter champion and runner-up in the steeplechase; NCAA long jump Champion George Ogbeide and NCAA 55-meter indoor champion Augustine Olobia were both from Nigeria; Swedes Stephen Jonsson who was twice NCAA hammer champ and Tore Gustafsson NCAA thirty-five-pound weight and Hammer Champion.

Chaplin provides another list of names and describes their accomplishments and contribution to WSU track & field. He insists that these athletes not get lost in any discussion of what it took for WSU to get to the top of the collegiate track & field world: Athletes like Hilary Mawindi, the Mountain Pacific Sports Federation indoor triple jump champion. Francis Dodoo, just 5-foot-5, a triple jumper from Ghana. Americans of West African heritage like Demetrius Murray, runner-up in the triple jump at the outdoor NCAA Outdoor Championships with a mark of 54'0 (16.46) and a Pac-10 outdoor triple jump champion, Chris Whitlock, a 44.80 400M runner. Gabriel Tiacoh an Olympic silver medalist in the 400; In 1984, Tiacoh ran 44.54. He led the world in the 400 at 44.32 in and again at 44.30 in 1986).

The 1977 WSU Team won the NCAA Indoor Title: Rono won the two-mile and was third in the mile. Campbell won the triple jump.

Also scoring were new 10,000-meter world record holder Samson Kimombwa in the three-mile and Joshua Kimeto in the two-mile. All-Americans Paul Buxton in the thirty-five-pound weight throw and Brian Wordon in the Pole Vault completed the WSU scoring. Plus, Jim Brewster from Puyallup, Washington was an All-American at 800 meters.

And back in the day...

- In 1909, Jack Nelson tied the world record at 9.6 for 100 yards. His actual recorded time was 9.5, but in those days, times were always rounded up and recorded in fifths of a second. Nelson won the 100 and 220-yard dashes at the National College Championships (the forerunner of the NCAA) that same year.

- In 1927, Wes Foster, one of the first great black track stars, set a national freshman record in the 220 at 20.8. Foster also placed third in the 1928 NCAA 100-yard dash. He went to Wenatchee High School, and after he won the State Meet 100-yard dash his junior year, and then went to the Washington State College Prep School for his senior year in 1927.

- Jack Mooberry had been playing baseball at Wenatchee, and then replaced Foster on the Wenatchee High School track tram and won the 1927 state title in the 100 his senior year. Mooberry followed Foster to WSU in 1928.

- Paul Swift tied the world 100-yard record with a 9.5 at the Kansas relays in 1931 and twice more in 1932.

- Lee Orr, as a 19-year-old freshman placed sixth in the 200-meter final at the 1936 Olympics and actually set the Olympic record of 21.2 in the heats. Of course, Jesse Owens broke that record in the final.

- And finally, there was Bob Gary who won six Pacific Coast Conference titles and placed second in the 100 and third in the 220 at the 1954 NCAA meet.

The LONG CRIMSON LINE"

For more 100 years (beginning in 1909), tradition has been the key. *The Long Crimson Line*, a special group of over 50 athletes, from 1500M to the Marathon, have led Washington State University to its present position as a major power in NCAA men's track & field. Distance running has been at the core of Cougar track & field success and young men from around the world continue to carry on this tradition.

WSU has scored more points in NCAA competition in the 3,000 meters, two-mile, 3,000-meter Steeplechase, 3-mile, 5,000 meters, Six-mile, and the 10,000 meters than any other collegiate institution in NCAA history by the time that Chaplin left WSU in 1994.

No university had more individuals from 3,000 meters to Cross-Country during Chaplin's tenure. No Collegiate institution has had an Olympic champion, an IAAF world champion, or a world record at any of the Olympic distance events except WSU. Cougar athletes set world Records in the 3,000 meters, 5,000 meters (twice), six miles, 10,000 meters (twice), 3,000-meter steeplechase (twice), and distance medley relay. Three times Cougars have held the top two world marks consecutively for Olympic events: the steeplechase, 5,000 meters, and 10,000 meters. 10,000-meter world records – Samson Kimombwa 27:30.47 in 1977 and Henry Rono 27:22.5 in 1978. 5,000-meter world records - Henry Rono 13:06.1 in 1981 and Peter Koech 13:09.50 in

1982. Steeplechase world records - Henry Rono 8:05.4 in 1978 and Peter Koech 8:05.37 in 1991. *Note: Gerry Lindgren held the six-mile world record and Bernard Lagat was the IAAF world champion at both 1,500 meters and 5,000 meters.*

Listed below are WSU athletes who have carried the tradition of the *"Long Crimson Line"* from 1909 to the present, by winning a conference title, NCAA title, receiving All-American honors, or by scoring at the NCAA national meet in events from 1,500 meters to 10,000 meters. Cougars have at some point been ranked first in world at 1,500 meters, 3,000 meters, the steeplechase, 5,000 meters and 10,000 meters.

Distance Events Listed in the *Long Crimson Line*

1,500 meters

Ken Wills (1932), Clem Eischen (1948), Richard Paeth (1948), Peter Koech`` (1985), Samuel Kibiri (NCAA champion in 1991), Josephat Kapkory` (1992), Bernard Lagat`` (1997, 1998, and 1999), Paulk Ryan (3:36.48) and Zack Stallings (3:39.32) were added to the list in 2021.

Other notables: Clem Eischen was on the U.S. Olympic Team in 1948. Bill Parnell was on the Canadian Olympic Team in 1948 and 1952. Don Bertoia won gold medal at 800 meters and a bronze medal 1,500 meters in 1962 Pan-American Games for Canada. Bernard Lagat won a silver medal at 1,500 meters in the 2001 and 2003 world championships and a bronze medal in the 2000 Olympics and a silver medal 2004 Olympics at 1,500 meters, running for Kenya. Lagat al so the collegiate record for 1,500 meters four times: 3:34.48, 3:33.32, 3:30.61, and 3:30.56. He only athlete in Pac-10 history to win three 1,500 meters titles and to win the 800 and 1,500 in the same year. In 2001, Lagat ran 1,500 meters in 3:26.34 to become second the fastest man with the third fastest time ever run at 1,500 meters. He set World Cup record and won the gold medal at 3:31.20 in 2002, set the American indoor 1,500-meter record at 3:33.34 in 2005 and the outdoor record of 3:29.30 in 2005. Lagat won the 2006 USATF title, the IAAF outdoor 1,500 Title in 2007, the first global championship for an American athlete in 99 years. Lagat was third at the 2009 IAAF Outdoor Championships, and ranked first in U.S. in 2005, 2006, 2007 and 2008.

One Mile

Conference Champions and All-Americans: C. J. Cooil (1909), Floyd Ratchford (1918-19), Ken Willis (1933), Roy Carriker (1934), Dixie Garner (1938-39), Noel Williams (1942), Roy Nuckolls (1945), Clem Eischen (1946 and 1948), Richard Paeth (1948), Bill Parnell (1951), Rick Riley (1970), Dean Clark (1973), Henry Rono (NCAA indoor champion in 1977 and 1978), Richard Tuwei (NCAA indoor champion in 1982 and 83), Henry Rono (NCAA champion and All-American in 1977 and 1978), Richard Tuwei (NCAA runner-up in both the mile and the 1,000 in 1983; was the first WSU athlete to break 4:00 - 3:59.66 - at an NCAA championship meet), Samuel Kibiri (NCAA indoor champion in 1991), Bernard Lagat (NCAA (door champion in 1997, 1999).

Other Notables: George Stimac - seventh in the NCAA mile in 1950. Rick Riley was the first athlete in conference history to run a sub-four-minute mile when he won the conference title in 3:59.2. Ten Cougars have run faster 4:00.0 (4:00.14 automatic) or better: 3:55.65i

- Bernard Lagat, 1999, 3:55.74 - Colton Johnsen, 2022, 3:57.00 - Zach Stallings, 2022, 3:57.51 – Paul Ryan, 2021, 3:57.84 - Samuel Kibiri, 1991, 3:57.51 - Paul Ryan, 2021, 3:58.1 - Peter Koech, 1983, 3:59.2 - Rick Riley, 1970, 3:59.2i - Henry Rono, 1977, 3:59.66i - Richard Tuwei, 1983, 3:59.87i - Jacinto Navarrete, 1987. Lagat ran 3:47.28 in 2001. Lagat in 1997 and Eric Kamau in 1998 each won Mountain Pacific Sports Federation indoor titles. Lagat set the American indoor mile record of 3:49.23 in 2005 and ranked first in the U.S. in 2005, 2006, and 2007. In 2009 he won his seventh Wanamaker Mile at Madison Square Garden to tie Irish great Eamon Coughlin's record. He also ran 3:52.87 in in the Wanamaker mile in 2005 to break Coughlin's 24-yard old meet record and the Madison Square Garden record of 3:52.99 by Noureddine Morceli set in 1992. Bill Parnell won the gold medal for Canada at 1950 Commonwealth Games.

3,000 meters

Indoor Conference Champions and All-Americans: Peter Koech (1984 and 1985), Jacinto Navarrete (1987), Josephat Kapkory (NCAA champion 1992 and 1994), Bernard Lagat (NCAA champion in 1998, All-American 1999). Dan Wolf (2004).

Other Notables: Gerry Lindgren - national freshman record of 7:58.0 and in indoor American and collegiate record of in 7:53.9. Joshua Kimeto - collegiate outdoor record of 7:37.5 and indoor collegiate record of 7:53.9. John Ngeno - two collegiate indoor records, 7:52.6 and 7:49.3. Henry Rono - collegiate indoor records of 7:47.4 and 7:39.2 and world and collegiate record of 7:32.1. Peter Koech - national freshman record of 7:39.09. Bernard Lagat in 1998 and 1999 and Dan Wolf in 2002 won the MPSF Indoor 3,000-meter titles. Bernard Lagat

- IAAF World Indoor 3,000 meters title at 7:34.96 in 2004 and 2012. Lagat set indoor American record at 7:32.43 in 2007 and outdoor American record of 7:29.00 in 2010. The top 15 best marks for WSU runners at 3,000 are all under 7:59.99. Lagat's world Rankings: first indoor in 2004 and fifth [in] 2005; U.S. rankings: first 2005, 2006, 2007, 2008, 2009, 2010, 2011, 2012 and 2013, and Colton Johnson was added to *The Long Crimson Line* when he ran 7:45.80 indoors in 29022.

Two Miles

All-Americans and conference champions: C. J. Cooil (1909), Clem Phillips (1918), Charles Smith (1915, 1916, 1919, 1920), John Devine (NCAA Champion in 1925), Dixie Garner (1938-39, 1940), Al Corsetto (1931), Clyde Wooton (1937 and 1939), Noel Williams (1941), Robert Selfridge (1948), Richard Paeth (1949), Al Fisher (1952-53). Chris Westman (1 1966), Gerry Lindgren (1967, 1967 and 1968), Joshua Kimeto (1975, 1976, 1977), Henry Rono (1977 NCAA Champion, 1978 All-American), Peter Koech (1982, 1983).

Other notables: Dixie Garner - American record and collegiate record at 9:07.9 outdoors and world, American and collegiate record of 9:11.1 for two-miles indoors in 1939 against world record holder Miklos Szabo from Hungary. Gerry Lindgren - national freshman record at 8:36.0 and American and collegiate records of 8:31.6 indoors. Henry Rono - collegiate record indoor at 8:15.9 and collegiate record outdoors at 8:14.7. Bernard Lagat - American record at 8:10.07. Note: Marks at English distances (other than the mile) and which are referred to as *world records* in the media are not officially recognized for record purposes by World Athletics (formerly the IAAF) and should be referred to as *world bests*.

Three Miles

All-Americans and conference champions: Chris Westman (1964, 1965, 1966), Gerry Lindgren (NCAA Champion in 1966, 1967, 1968), John Ngeno (NCAA Champion in 1973, All-American 1974 4th, 1975 1st) and (1974, 1975, 1976 all indoors), Samson Kimombwa (1976, 1977), Joel Cheruiyot (1978).

Other notables: Gerry Lindgren - collegiate record and national freshman record at 13:04.0 and American record and collegiate record at 12:53.0. John Ngeno - collegiate records at 13:08.2 indoors. Joshua Kimeto collegiate record at 12:58.2 indoor. Henry Rono - world best and collegiate record at 12:39.0 on the way to collegiate record 5,000 indoors at 12:56.1.

5,000 meters

NCAA Champions and All-Americans: Al Fisher (1932), Gerry Lindgren (NCAA Champion 1968), John Ngeno (NCAA champion 1976), Joshua Kimeto (NCAA champion 1976 and 1977, All-American 1978), Samson Kimombwa` (1976, 1977, 1979), Henry Rono` (1978, 1979), Peter Koech (1982 and 1984, 1985), Richard Tuwei (1983), Julius Korir` (1983, 1984 and 1986), E. J. Guo` (1990). E.J. Guo` (1990, 1991), Josephat Kapkory` (1992, 1994), Bernard Lagat (NCAA champion 1999).

Other notables: Gerry Lindgren - collegiate record and national freshman record at 13:45.4 and American record and collegiate record at 13:38.0 and 13:33.8 John Ngeno - collegiate record at 13:20.6 and indoor collegiate record at 13:34.6. Henry Rono - world record and collegiate record at 13:08.4 and 13:06.1 (ranked No. 1 in the world by *Track & Field News* in 1978). Peter Koech - national freshman record at 13:09.59 to become the second fastest individual in history at 5,000 meters. John Ngeno and Joshua Kimeto were on the 1976 Kenyan Olympic team (which ended up boycotting the Games). John Valiant – eighth place in the NCAA 5,000 in 1964. Bernard Lagat posted the second-best American mark at all-time at 12:59.29 in 2005, won the 2006 and 2010 USATF titles, and won the IAAF outdoor title in 2007. Lagat was also the first man to win the 1,500 and the 5,000 at the IAAF World Outdoor Championships. He was ranked tenth in the world in 2005 and fourth in 2007. He was also second at the 2009 IAAF Outdoor Championships and set the collegiate record at 12:54.12 in 2010. Lagat ranked first in U.S. in 2005, 2006, 2007, 2008, 2009, 2010, and 2011. In 2004, Danny Wolf was an indoor All-American at 7:58.00. And finally, Colton Johnson ran 13:39.75 indoors in 2022.

Six Miles

NCAA Champions and All-Americans: Chris Westman (1965-1966), (NCAA Champion in 1966 and 1967), Larry Almberg (1967), Rick Riley (1969-1970), John Ngeno (NCAA champion in 1974 and 1975).

Other notables: Gerry Lindgren - world and American record and national freshman record at 27:11.6. **John Ngeno** - collegiate record at 27:06.8 26:57.4.

10,000 meters

NCAA Champions and All-Americans: John Valiant (1964), Gerry Lindgren (NCAA champion 1968), John Ngeno (NCAA Champion

1976), Samson Kimombwa (NCAA champion 1977, All-American 1978, 1980), Joel Cheruiyot` (1978), Henry Rono` (1987), Peter Koech (1982, 1983, 1984, 1985), Jacinto Navarrete (1987), E.J. Guo (1991), Josephat Kapkory (1994), Patrick Muturi`` (1994).

Other notables: Gerry Lindgren - national freshman record at 29:00.8 and collegiate record at 28:40.2. John Ngeno - collegiate record at 28:04.6. Samson Kimombwa - world and collegiate record at 27:30.47. Henry Rono - national freshman record at 27:37.1, world and collegiate record at 27:22.5, and ranked first in the world by *Track&Field News*. John Ngeno was on the 1976 Kenyan Olympic Team (which subsequentially boycotted the Games; However, Ngeno had beaten Lasse Viren, who would go on to win the 5,000 and 10,000 at the 1976 Games, over 10,000 meters in a pre-Olympic event). Gerry Lindgren was on the 1964 U.S. Olympic Team while still in high school.

3,000-meter steeplechase

NCAA Champions and All-Americans: John Valiant` (1964). Rod Dahl (1968). Larry Almberg (1969). Dean Clark (1973). Henry Rono (All-American 1977, NCAA Champion 1978-1979). Richard Tuwei (NCAA Champion 1982, All-American 1983, 1985), Julius Korir (All-American 1983-1984, NCAA champion 1986). Peter Koech (NCAA Champion 1985), Marty Stroschein (1989). Nathan Morris (1986). Samuel Kibiri (1991). Robert Price (1991). John Hill (1991). Josephat Kapkory` (1994).

Other Notables: Henry Rono - world and collegiate records at 8:05.4, ranked first in the world by *Track&Field New,* and on the 1976 Kenyan Olympic Team (which subsequently boycotted the Games). Richard

Tuwei - national freshman record at 8:23.48. Julius Korir - national freshman record at 8:20.02 and 1984 Olympic Champion at 8:11.80 and ranked first in the world by *Track and Field News*, while running for Kenya. Peter was second in the 1988 Olympic Games at 8:06.79 for Kenya and broke Rono's world record at 8:05.37 and was ranked first in the world in 1991.

Cross Country

NCAA Champion and All-Americans: Gary Benson, (1965). Chris Westman (1965-66). Gerry Lindgren (NCAA Champion 1966, 1967, 1969). Rick Riley (1969). Mark Hayfield (1970). Don Smith (1970). Phil Burkwist (1971). Dan Murphy (1971, 1972, 1973). John Ngeno (1972-1973-1974-1975). Joshua Kimeto (1975-76). Kurt Beckman (1975). Henry Rono (NCAA Champion 1976, 1977, 1979). Samson Kimombwa (1976). Joel Cheruiyot (1977, 1979), Richard Tuwei (1981). Peter Koech (1984). Jacinto Navarrette (1987). Samuel Kibiri (1990). E. J. Guo` (1990). Josephat Kapkory (1991, 1992, NCAA Champion 1993), Patrick Muturi (1993). Bernard Lagat (1997-1998). Eric Kamau (1998).

Other Notables: Henry Rono (1976 and 1978-1979), Joel Cheruiyot (1977), Richard Tuwei (1981), and Josephat Kapkory (1991-1992-1993) were all NCAA Western Regional individual champions. John Ngeno in 1975 won the USA National Cross Country Title.

NCAA Distance Medley Relay (1200-400-800-1600)

NCAA Champions and All-Americans: Eric Kamau, Guillermo Macias. Rasto Kiplangat, Bernard Lagat (All-Americans in 1997, NCAA Champions in 1998).

Other notables: The team of Eric Kamau 2:55.5 (1200), Guillermo Macias 47.6 (400), Rasto Kiplangat` 1:47.7 (800), and Bernard Lagat 3:58.7 (1600) set the indoor world best and collegiate record mark of 9:29.54i at the NCAA Indoor Championships in 1998. Will Trift, J. K. Haines, Ian Johnson, and John Welsh in 2001 and Jim Neffway, Dan Brink, John Welsh, and Dan Wolf in 2002 won Indoor MPSF titles. Bernard Lagat (3:53.8) with Chris Lukezic (2:51.7), Jammer Carter (45.6) and Khadevis Robinson (1:44.5) broke the previous world record and set the American record in the DMR but placed second to Kenya 9:15.56 to 9:15.63 in 2006 at the Penn Relays.

More Facts and Stats

Josephat Kapkory is the only Pac-10 athlete to win conference titles at 1,500, 5,000, 10,000, the steeplechase, and Cross Country, and he was twice the NCAA indoor 3,000 champion. Kapkory is the only Pac-10 athlete to win conference titles at 5,000, 10,000, and the steeplechase in the same year. E. J. Guo is the only WSU athlete to earn All-American honors at 3,000 meters indoors 5,000 meters indoors and outdoors, 10,000 meters, and Cross Country. He won Pac-10 5,000 and 10,000 titles. Tom Robinson set a collegiate record in the marathon at 2:22:00 in 1971. In 1964 John Valiant competed at the NCAA meet in the 5,000, 10,000, and steeplechase. He placed eighth at 5,000 meters and fourth at 10,000 meters and fourth in the steeplechase. In 1976 John Ngeno set a collegiate record in the half marathon at 1:04.58, and in 1978. Henry Rono broke with record with a at 1:04:46.1. Rono is still the only athlete in history to hold the world record for 5,000 meters, 10,000 meters and the steeplechase. Bill Scott ran a 2:11:55 marathon in 1979 for the best time ever by a Cougar. He was ranked ninth in the World. Pat Muturi ran 2:12.56 for a national freshman record in

1994.Julius Korir won an Olympic Gold Medal in the steeplechase in 1984 and is the only collegiate athlete to ever win an Olympic title in the 5,000, 10,000, or steeple. In 1998 Bernard Lagat became the only athlete in Pacific-10 history to win the 800 meters and 1,500 meters in the same year. Lagat ranked first in the world at 2000 meters in 2005 after setting the collegiate record at 4:55.49 in 1999. Peter Koech ((in 1982) ANDE Joshua Kimeto (in 1978) had both previously held the collegiate 2,000 record, and Joel Cheruiyot has held the national freshman record.

John Chaplin's Washington State University Middle and Long-Distance Hall of Fame

(*An asterisk* indicates a member of the WSU Athletic Hall of Fame*)

(1) **Henry Rono*** - Set four world records in 90 days in 1978: 3,000 meters, 3,000 meters steeplechase, 5,000 meters, 10,000 meters. Ranked No. 1 in the world in all four. Set another 5,000-meter world record in 1981. The only individual to hold world records in every Olympic distance event.

(2) **Gerry Lindgren*** - Set a world record, American record, and collegiate record in the six-mile run. Set American and collegiate records at 3,000 meters, two-miles indoors and outdoors, and at three-miles. Also set the American and collegiate records at 5,000 meters. Won 11 NCAA titles from 1966 to 1969.

(3) **Barnard Lagat*** - Collegiate record, Olympic silver (2004) bronze (2000) medalist at 1,500 meters. Second fastest 1,500 meters mark in history at 3:26.34. Ranked No.1 in the world at 1,500 meters in 2004. IAAF Gold medalist indoors at 3000 meters, World Cup

Gold at 1,500 meters. Set American record at 1,500 meters outdoors at 3:29.30 and one mile at 3:49.89. American record indoors in 2005. Won Gold medals at 1500 and 5,000 meters at 2007 IAAF World Championships, the first to do so. World ranked No. 1 in the 1,500 and 5,000 in 2007. Set American record for 5,000 meters at 12:54.12 and 3,000 meters at 7:29.00 in 2010. He also ran 27:49.35 and was ranked fifth in the U.S. In 2017 at age 42, set U.S. master record for 10,000 meters on the road at 28:13.

(4) **Peter Koech*** - Olympic silver medalist in the steeplechase in 1988 and broke Rono's world record in in the steeple in 1991. Ranked No.1 in the world that year.

(5) **Julius Korir*** - National freshman record in the steeplechase and the and the 1984 Olympic steeplechase gold medalist. Ranked No.1 in the world. Only collegiate distance athlete to win an Olympic Gold Medal.

(6) **John Ngeno*** - 5,000 and 10,000 collegiate records. Seven-time NCAA Champion, and a National AAU Cross Country Champion.

(7) **Samson Kimombwa*** - In 1977, ran 27:30.47 set world and collegiate records at 10,000 meters. Won NCAA title in the 10,000 and was and NCAA 10,000 meters. An All-American at three miles indoors and 5,000 meters outdoors.

(8) **Relay team of Eric Kamau, Guillermo Macias, Rasto Kiplangat, and Bernard Lagat*** - Indoor world best and collegiate record at 9:29.54 in the distance medley relay (12,00, 400, 800, 1,600) in 1998 and ranked No.1 in the World.

(9) **Josephat Kapkory** - A two- time NCAA indoor 3,000 Champion, and an NCAA cross-country champion. NCAA 300-meter meet record holder. The only athlete to win Pac-10 1,500, steeplechase, 5,000, and 10,000, and cross-country titles.

(10) **Tie) Joshua Kimeto** - Two-time NCAA 5,000 champion. Collegiate records at 2,000 and 3,000 meters, both indoors and outdoors. Three-time two-mile All-American indoors. Cross-country All-American. **& Richard Tuwei** - Set a national freshman record and won an NCAA title in the steeplechase. Runner-up in the NCAA Indoor 1,000 meters and one mile in 1983. He ran 3:59.66 to become the first Cougar to break 4:00 indoors. Pac-10 Champion and All-American at 5,000 meters.

Honorable Mention
(Athletes are listed in chronological order)

John Divine* - The 1925 NCAA two-mile champion. **Dixie Garner*** - World, American, and collegiate record in the indoor two-mile in 1939. **Clem Eischen*** - A member of the 1948 U.S. Olympic Team in the 1,500. **Don Bertoia*** - 1963 Pan-American 800-meter gold and 1,500-meter bronze. **John Valiant** - First WSU athlete to run under 9:00 in the steeplechase. He ran 8:57.1 in 1964 at the NCAA Championships where he was fourth at the Steeple, fourth at 10,000 meters, and eighth at 5,000 meters. **Art Sandison*** - Current WSU school record at 800 meters at 1:45.5, and the silver medalist in the Pan-American Games. **Rick Riley** - The First WSU athlete to break 4:00 in the mile, winning the conference title at 3:59.2. **Tom Robinson** - 1971 collegiate record in the Marathon. **Samuel Kibiri** - NCAA 1,500 champion and second in the steeplechase in 1991. **Patrick Muturi** - National Freshman record of 2:12:58.0 for the marathon in 1994.

***

WSU's All-Time Dual Meet Team
(Three athletes per event, with no duplications,
and two additional for relays)

**An asterisk (*) indicates a mark adjusted to Meters from yards.
All marks are life-time bests.**

- **100 Meters** - Augustin Olobia 10.09 (NCAA Indoor 55M Champion), Lee Gordon 10.29 (NCAA Runner-up), Paul Swift 9.5 yards (world and American record holder).
- **200 Meters** - Bob Gary 20.7* (NCAA runner-up), Anson Henry 20.52 (Pacific-10 Champion), Jack Nelson 9.5/21.2 (world and American record holder at 100 and 220 yards).
- **400 Meters** - Gabriel Tiacoh 44.30 (collegiate record and Olympic silver medalist), Lee Orr 46.5* (NCAA Champion), Chris Whitlock 44.80 (Pacific-10 400 Meters Champion).
- **800 Meters** - Art Sandison 1:45.5* (NCAA runner-up at 880 yards), Sotirios Moutsanas 1:46.34 (NCAA Indoor runner-up at 1000 Meters), Don Bertoia 1:48.3 (Pan American Games Champion).
- **1,500 Meters and one mile** - Bernard Lagat 3:26.34 (American records at 1,500 Meters and 1 Mile, world champion), Sam Kibiri 3:38.38 (NCAA Champion), Richard Tuwei 3:38.78 (NCAA runner-up at one mile).
- **Steeplechase** - Henry Rono 8:05.4 (Word record holder in four events), Julius Korir 8:11.80 (1984 Olympic Champion), Peter Koech 8:05.37 (World record, NCAA Champion).

- **5,000 Meters** - Joshua Kimeto 13:26.8 (NCAA Champion 5,000 Meters), Gerry Lindgren 13:21.0* (American record at 5,000 Meters and three-miles, world record at six-miles), Samson Kimombwa 13:21.6 (world record at 10,000 Meters & NCAA Champion).

- **110-meter-high hurdles** - Tony Li 13.23 (NCAA indoor 55M HH Champion), Dominic Arnold 12.90 (American record, NCAA Champ), Arend Watkins 13.23 (U.S. ranked sixth & eighth, Pac-10 Champion).

- **400-meter hurdles** - Boyd Gittins 49.1 (Tied world and American /records, 1968 Olympic Team), Loren Benke 51.8 (American record, NCAA Champion), Jeshua Anderson 47.93 (USATF and world junior champion, NCAA Champion).

- **Long Jump** - George Ogbeide 27-½ (NCAA Champion), Bill Ayers 26-0 (First in the Athens Olympic centennial reenactment in 1996), Matt Mason 26-6 ¼ (All-American & MPSF Champion).

- **Shot Put** - Dimitrios Koutsoukis 67-6 ¾ (NCAA Indoor runner-up), Bruce Anderson 62-7 ½ (NCAA Division II champion), Tim Gehring 63-5 ½ (All-American).

- **Pole Vault** - Christos Pallakis 18-6 ½ (NCAA Runner-up), Patrik Johanssen 18-½ (All-American), Tom Byers 18-½ (All-American).

- **Discus**- John van Reenen 224-6 (World record, three-time NCAA champion), Ian Waltz 226-1 (Pacific-10 and USATF Champion), Matt Lamb 204-7 (All-American).

- **High Jump** - Brent Harken 7-8 ¾ (Pacific-10 champion), Doug Nordquist 7-8 ½ (second NCAA, USATF champion), Greg Jones 7-6 ½ (NCAA runner-up).

- **Javelin Throw** - Carl O'Donnell 258-11 (NCAA Champion), Laslo Babits 282-5 (Old javelin, Pan American champion), Jan Johansson 273-8 (Pacific-10 champion).

- **Triple Jump** - Ian Campbell 57-5 (NCAA indoor champion), Joseph Taiwo 56-4 ¾ (Pac-10 champion, Pac-12 100 Year Team), Ray Kimble 56-11 ½ (All-American, USATF champion).

- **Hammer** - Tore Gustafsson 262-11 (Collegiate record, NCAA champion & NCAA indoor 35-pound weight champion), Stefan Jonsson 244-5 (NCAA Champion), Paul Buxton 230-7 (National Freshman Rr4cord, All-American).

- **400-meter relay (Hypotheitical) Sub-38.00 team - Norbert Payton** (100 Meters finalist at the 1976 Olympic Trials, 9.9 [10.14]), **Lee Gordon** (NCAA 100-Meters runner-up, 10.29) **Augustin Olobia** (NCAA 55-meter champion, NCAA 100-meter runner-up 10.09), **Anson Henry** (Third in NCAA 60 Meters, 10.17 for 100 meter, Pacific-10 100-meter champion), **Gary Minor** (Pacific-8 200-meter champion,100 Meters in 10.0 [10.24]), **Anthony Buchanan** (Pacific-10 100-meter champion, 100 Meters in 10.21).

- **1600 Meters Relay – (Hypothetical) Sub-3:00 minutes team - Chris Whitlock** (Pacific-10 400-meter champion, 44.80), **Lee Orr** (NCAA 440-yard champion, world record one-mile relay, 46.5*), **Loren Benke** (NCAA 440-yard champion, world record one-mile relay, 46.6*), **Gabriel Tiacoh** (Silver medal at the 1984 Olympic Games, NCAA champion at 400 Meters, 44.30). **Chris Durr** (Pacific-10 1600-meter relay champion, 45.84), **Michael Joubert** (NCAA 400-meter All American, 45.62).

WSU Athletes All-Time Best Performances
Marks made while not competing
for WSU are listed in *italics*.

- 60 Meters - 06.53i: Emmanuel Wells, Albuquerque 2019
- 100 meter - *10.12: Anson Henry,* Doha, Qatar 2006
- 200 Meters - 20.52: Anson Henry, Pullman, WA 2002
- 3,000 Meters - 31.98: Gabriel Tiacoh, Strasbourg, France 1985
- 400 Meters - 44.30: Gabriel Tiacoh, Indianapolis 1986
- 600 Meters - 1:15.1i*: Jeff Ramsey, Moscow, ID 1980
- 800 Meters - 1:45.5n*: Art Sandison, Knoxville, TN 1969
- 1000 Meters - 2:15.9 - *Bernard Lagat,* Monaco 1999
- 1,500 Meters - *3:26.34n - Bernard Lagat,* Brussels Belgium 2001
- One mile - *3:47.28n - Bernard Lagat,* Rome, Italy 2001.
- 2000 Meters: 4:54.74i - *Bernard Lagat,* New York, 2014.
- 3000 Meters: *7:29.00 - Bernard Lagat,* Rieti, Italy 2010.
- 5000 Meters: *12:53.60 - Bernard Lagat,* Monaco 2011.
- 10,000 Meters: 27:22.47 - Henry Rono, Vienna, Austria 1978.
- 21 kilometers: 1:02.33 - *Bernard Lagat, New York* 2013.
- Marathon: *2:11:55.0 - Bill Scott,* Fukuoka, Japan 1979.
- 60-meter-High Hurdles: *7.51i - Dominique Arnold,* New York and Boston 2006.
- 110-meter High Hurdles: *12.9 - Dominique Arnold,* Lausanne, Switzerland 2006.
- 400-meter Intermediate Hurdles: 47.93 - Jeshua Anderson, Eugene, 2011.
- Steeplechase: *8:05.35 - Peter Koech,* Stockholm, Sweden 1989.
- 400-Meter Relay: 39.24 - George Ogbeide, Tony Li, Benari Burroughs, Augustin Olobia, Eugene 1991.

- Shuttle Hurdle Relay: 57.44* - Neil Knutson, Gary Minor, Steve Cochran, Kip Ngeno, Lewiston 1976.

- 800-Meters Relay: 1:23.9 - Mike Allen, Tim Giesa, Kip Ngeno, Gary Minor, Spokane 1975.

- 1600-Meter Relay: 3:05.58 - Lee Gordon, Dennis Livingston, Calvin Harris, Gabriel Tiacoh, Tucson 1985.

- Sprint Medley (200, 200, 400, 800): 3:15.75 - George Ogbeide, Augustin Olobia (200-200-400-800), Michael Joubert, Samuel Kibiri, Philadelphia 1991

- 3200-Meter Relay: 7:18.0n* - Dave Fox, Dennis Margadan, Bob Martin, Art Sandison, Modesto, 1969.

- 4x1500 Relay: 15:09.9 - Peter Koech, Jacinto Navarrete, Julius Korir, Richard Tuwei, Walla Walla, 1984.

- 4x1-Mile Relay: 16:28.0 - Peter Koech, Jacinto Navarrete, Julius Korir, Richard Tuwei, Walla Walla, WA 1984.

- Distance Medley Relay (1200-400-800-1600): 9:29.54i - Eric Kamau, Guillermo Macias, Rasto Kiplangat, Bernard Lagat (World best, collegiate record, NCAA champion), Indianapolis, 1998.

- Discus Throw - *226-1* (68.91m): *Ian Waltz*, Salinas, 2006.

- Hammer Throw - *262-1* (80.14m): *Tore Gustafsson*, Lappeenranta, Finland 1989.

- Old javelin - 282-5 Laslo Babits 1983.

- Javelin Throw - *260-9* (79.48m): *Jan Johansson*, Karlstad, Sweden 1989.

- Shot Put - *68-½* (20.74m): *Dimitrios Koutsoukis*, Drama, Greece 1989.

- 35-Pound Weight Throw: *75-9i* (23.08m) - *Tore Gustafsson*, Provo, 1988.

- High Jump - *7-8 ¾* (2.36m): *Doug Nordquist*, Moscow, Russia 1990.
- Long Jump - 27-½ (8.24m): George Ogbeide, Cottbus, Germany 1991.
- Pole Vault - 18-6 ½i (5.65m): Christos Pallakis, Barcelona, Spain 1995.
- Triple Jump* - 57-5 (17.50m): Ian Campbell Moscow, Russia 1980.

Notes

- In 2015, Athletes Australia credited Ian Campbell with a mark of 17.50m (57' 5") from his contested triple jump at the 1980 Olympic Games in Moscow. Athletics Australia has also asked the International Olympic Committee to review the triple jump results from 1980 and award Ian Campbell the Gold Medal.
- Prior to 2015 Athletes Australia's ruling Joseph Taiwo had a mark of 17.19 (56-4 ¾) at Lagos, Nigeria in 1984 the WSU and Pac-12 outdoor Triple Jump Records.
- Norbert Payton ran a 9.9 for 100 Meters hand timed at the 1972 U.S. Olympic Trials. Anson Henry had a wind aided time of 10.04w while still running for WSU. Augustine Olobia ran 55 Meters in 6.14 at Indianapolis in 1991.Gary Minor's 10.15 100 Meters (SAT) at Spokane in 1976 is still the best WSU mark all time. SAT marks were legal for record purposes in.
- Bernard Lagat's 1,500-Meters time is the second fastest ever run. Lagat held American indoor records at 1,500 Meters, one mile, 3000 Meters, two miles, and 5000 Meters. Lagat did not become eligible to set American records after 2014, so his American records may be a bit slower than of his personal best times, which he ran while representing his native Kenya.

- Henry Rono Held the (world and collegiate records for the 3000, 5000, 10,000, and steeplechase simultaneously, all set in 1978 while he was still in college. He is the only man in history to hold the world record in these four events.

- Dominique Arnold's 110-meter-hurdle mark was the second fastest time in history at the time. Tony Li's collegiate and NCAA meet record of 7.08 for the 55-meter hurdles was set at Indianapolis, Indiana in 1991.

- In 2006 at the Penn Relays, Chris Lukezic (2:51.7), James Carter (45.6), Khadevis Robinson (1:44.5), and Bernard Lagat (3:53.8) broke world best in the distance medley relay but placed second to Kenya 9:15.56 to 9:15.63.

- In 1986, the javelin was changed by moving the grip forward to prevent athletes from throwing more than 300 feet (see the reference to Laslo Babits above).

- A couple more notable performances by American athletes: In 1982, Casey Lewis from Boise, Idaho won the national junior pole vault title and the Pan-American junior gold medal in the pole vault; and in 2009, Joe Abbot won the national junior 800-meter championship at 1:46.84 and won a bronze medal in the Pan-American juniors. And in 1921, the First NCAA outdoor pole vault champion was 1920 U.S. Olympian Eldon Jenne. And finally in 1965, the first NCAA indoor Champion was Canadian Bob Yard.

WSU All-Time NCAA Scoring

Distance runners scored 727 of 1,58.80 points scored by WSU in the NCAA championships. Note: *Italic names are for races run in yards.* CAPITALIZED NAMES are NCAA Champions

Indoor Scoring listed are actual points earn. The NCAA has used several scoring systems -- 1965-1979 (6-4-3-2-1). 1980-1993 (10-8-6-4-2-1). 1994-present (10-8-6-5-4-3-2-1). 2020 canceled due to Covid.

Points per event: (1) 3000M/2-mile - 106 pts. **(2)** Triple Jump - 44 pts. **(3)**35# Weigh - 41 pts. **(4) tie** Shot Put - 35 pts. & Mile Run - 35 pts. **(6)** 5000M/3-mile - 28 pts. **(7)** 60M/55M HH - 25 pts. **(8)** Pole Vault - 24 ½ pts. **(9)** 60M/55M - 21 pts. **(10)** Distance Medley Relay - 18 pts. **(11)** 1000 yards 17 pts. **(12)** High Jump -16 pts. **(13)** 1600M Relay - 6 pts. **(14)** 600 yards - 4 pts. **(15)** Long Jump - 3 pts. **(16)** 800M - 2 pts.

Outdoor Scoring listed is actual points earn. The NCAA has used several scoring systems -- 1921-1922 (5-3-2-1-½), 1923 (5-4-3-2-1-½), 1924 *, 1925-1926 (6-4-3-2-1- ½), 1927-1981 (10-8-6-4-2-1), 1982-1984 (15-12-10-9-8-7-6-5-4-3-2-1), 1985-present (10-8-6-5-4-3-2-1). **Note:** * No Championship Meets held in 1924 and 2020 canceled due to Covid.

Points per event: (1) 5,000M/3-mile/2-mile - 217 pts. (2) 10,000M/6-mile - 152 pts. (3) 3000M Steeplechase -119 pts. (4) tie Hammer Throw - 77 pts. & Javelin Throw (Old & New) - 77 pts. (6) 400M/440 IH Yards - 75 pts. (7) Triple Jump - 68 pts. (8) Discus Throw - 57 pts. (9) 400M/440 yard - 56 pts. (10) High Jump - 51 ½ pts. (11) Shot Put - 44 pts. (12) 200M/220 yard - 40 pts. (13) tie 800M/800 yard - 37 pts. 100M/100 yard - 37 pts. & (15) 1500M/Mile - 35 pts. (16) Decathlon - 33 pts. (17) Pole Vault - 26.30 pts. (18) 110M/120 yard HH - 24 pts. (19) Long Jump - 16 pts. and (20) 400M Relay - 5 pts. Note: Only Current Outdoor Championship Event in the NCAA that WSU has never scored in is the 1600M Relay.

Indoor 3000 Meters (2-Mile Run) (1966-1999 – 34 yrs. 19 scoring places) *Chris Westman* ^ 1966-3 pts. (3rd); *GERRY*

LINDGREN 1966-6 pts. (1st), *GERRY LINDGREN* 1967-6 pts. (1st) *and GERRY LINDGREN* 1968-4 pts. (2nd); *Joshua Kimeto* 1975-4 pts. (2nd), *Joshua Kimeto*1976-3 pts. (3rd) and *Joshua Kimeto*1977-3 pts. (3rd); HENRY RONO 1977-6 pts. (1st) and *Henry Rono*1978-8 pts. (2nd); *Peter Koech* 1982-6 pts. (3rd),*Peter Koech,* 1983-1 pt. (6th),PETER KOECH, 1984-10 pts. (1st) and Peter Koech 1985-1 pt. (6th); Jacinto Navarrete 1987-6 pts. (3rd)' E.J. Guo 1989-1 pt. (6th); JOESPHAT KAPKORY 1992-10 pts. (1st) and JOSEPHAT KAPKORY 1994-10 pts. (1st); Bernard Lagat 1998-8 pts. (2nd) and BERNARD LAGAT 1999-10 pts. (1st.)

None scoring All-American: Dan Wolf 2004. **2nd Team All-American Honors:** Colton Johnson in 2021 & 2022.**Notes:** *GERRY LINDGREN* set a 2-mile NCAA (MR) @ 8:41.3 in 1966 and a 2-mile NCAA (MR) @ 8:34.7 in 1967.*HENRY RONO* set a 2-mile NCAA (MR) @ 8:24.83 in 1977. JOESPHAT KAPKORY set 3000M NCAA (MR) @ 7:50.90 in 1994.

Total Points: 106 -- Highest Finish 1st (7-times) -- 10 All-Americans Top Individual in scoring: JOSEPHAT KAPKORY 20 pts.

Outdoor 2-Mile Run *(1925-1949 – 25 yrs. 6 scoring places)* JOHN DIVINE 1925-6 pts. (1st); *Dixie Garner* 1938-1 pts. (6th), *Dixie Garner* 1939-2 pts. (5th) and *Dixie Garner* 1940-8 pts. (2nd); *Noel Williams* 1941-2 pts. (5th); *Richard Paeth* 1949-2 pts. (5th).

Total Points: 21 -- Highest Finish 1st -- 2 All-Americans Top Individual in scoring: Dixie Garner 11 pts.

Indoor 5000 Meters (3-mile run) **(1974-1990 – 17 yrs. 7 scoring places)** *JOHN NGENO*`1974-6 pts. (1st), *JOHN NGENO* 1975-6 pts. (1st) and *JOHN NGENO* 1976-6 pts. (1st); *Samson Kimombwa*1976-3 pt.

(3rd) *and Samson Kimombwa*1977-4 pt. (2nd); *Joel Cheruiyot*1978-2 pts. (5th); E.J. Guo 1990-1 pt. (6th). **2nd Team All-American Honors:** Colton Johnson in 2021. **Note:** *JOHN NGENO* set a 3-mile NCAA (MR) @ 13:20.8 1974 & a 3-mile NCAA (MR) @ 13:14.4 in 1975.

Total Points: 28 -- Highest Finish 1st (3 times) -- 4 All-Americans
Top Individual in scoring: JOHN NGENO 18 pts.

Outdoor 5000 Meters (3-mile run)*(1952-1999 – 48 yrs. 26 scoring places)*Al Fisher 1952-4 pts. (4th); *Chris Westman 1965-6 pts. (3rd) and Chris Westman^ 1966-6 pts. (3rd);* GERRY LINDGREN 1966-10 pts. (1st), GERRY LINDGREN 1967-10 pts. (1st) and GERRY LINDGREN 1968-10 pts. (1st); *John Ngeno*1973-4 pts. (4th), *John Ngeno* 1974-4 pts. (4th), *JOHN NGENO* 1975-10 pts. (1st) and John Ngeno 1976-8 pts. (2nd); JOSHUA KIMETO 1976-10 pts. (1st), JOSHUA KIMETO 1977-10 pts. (1st) and Joshua Kimeto 1978-4 pts. (4th); Samson Kimombwa 1976-6 pts. (3rd), Samson Kimombwa 1977-8 pts. (2nd), Samson Kimombwa 1978-6 pts. (3rd), Peter Koech 1982-12 pts. (2nd), Peter Koech 1984-12 pts. (2nd) and Peter Koech 1985-8 pts. (2nd); Richard Tuwei 1983-4 pts. (8th); Julius Korir 1983-8 pts. (5th), JULIUS KORIR 1984-15 pts. (1st), Julius Korir 1986-2 pts. (7th); E. J. Guo 1991-1 pt. (8th); Josephat Kapkory 1992-8 pts. (2nd), BERNARD LAGAT 1999-10 pts. (1st). **Other Finalists:** John Valiant 8th in 1964, Phil Burkwist 8th in 1972, Joel Cheruiyot 8th in 1978. Josephat Kapkory in 1994. **Non-Scoring All-Americans:** Henry Rono in 1978. **Notes:** GERRY LINDGREN set a NCAA (MR) in 1966 at yards with a 13:33.7 and in 1968 a 13:29.9 yards NCAA (MR) on the way to a 13:51.2 5000M NCAA (MR). Rick Riley was an AAU All-American at 3rd in the 3-mile in 1970. Henry Rono set a NCAA (MR) of 13:21.79 in 1978 prelims. His foot was injured he did not run the Final. Awarded All-American Honors for his unprecedented record breaking 3000M Steeple/5000M double in the heats. GERRY LINDGREN never lost a NCAA 3-mile/5000M final. Won all three times he competed. **Note:** Peter Koech posted three 5000M seconds in his WSU Career.

Total Points: 196 -- Highest Finish 1st (8 times) -- 12 All-Americans Top Individuals in scoring: Peter Koech 32 pts.

Outdoor 10,000 Meters (6-mile run) *(1964-1994 – 31 yrs. 23 Scoring places)* John Valiant 1964-4 pts. (4th), *Chris Westman* 1965-8 pts. (2nd) and *Chris Westman* 1966-2 pts. (5th); *GERRY LINDGREN* 1966-10 pts. (1st, *GERRY LINDGREN* 1967-10 pts. (1st), GERRY LINDGREN 1968-10 pts. (1st); *Larry Almberg* 1967-1 pt. (6th); *Rick Riley* 1969-8 pts. (2nd) and *Rick Riley* 1970-1 pt. (6th); *JOHN NGENO* 1974-10 pts. (1st), *JOHN NGEN* 1975-10 pts. (1st) and JOHN NGENO 1976-10 pts. (1st); SAMSON KIMOMBWA 1977-10 pts. (1st), Samson Kimombwa 1978-4 pts. (4th) and Samson Kimombwa 1980-8 pts. (2nd); Joel Cheruiyot 1979-4 pts. (4th); Peter Koech 1982-10 pts. (3rd), Peter Koech 1983-5 pts. (8th) and Peter Koech 1984-7 pts. (6th); E. J. Guo 1991-4 pts. (5th); E.J. Guo 1992-2 pts. (7th); Josephat Kapkory 1994-8 pts. (2nd); Pat Muturi 1994-6 pts. (3rd). **Other Finalists:** Rick Riley ^ 8th in 1968, *Dan Murphy* 8th in 1973, Samson Kimombwa in 1976, Henry Rono in 1978. **Notes:** JOHN NGENO set a NCAA (MR) @ 28:22.7 in 1976. Samson Kimombwa injured and dropped out in 1976. Samson Kimombwa set a NCAA (MR) @ 28:10.66 in 1977. Henry Rono qualified and entered in 1978 but due to a foot injury from the 3000M Steeplechase did not run. Both GERRY LINDGREN & JOHN NGENO were never defeated at 6-miles and/or 10,000M. They both won all three (3) times they ran the 6-mile and/or 10,000M in outdoor NCAA Championship competition.

Total Points: 152 -- Highest Finish 1st (7 times) -- 12 All-Americans
Top Individuals in scoring: GERRY LINDGREN & JOHN NGENO
30 pts.

3000M Steeplechase (Barriers 36") *(1964-1991 -- 38 yrs. 15 scoring places)*John Valiant 1964-4 pts. (4th); Dean Clark 1973-6 pts. (3rd); Henry Rono 1977-8 pts. (2nd), HENRY RONO 1978-10 pts. (1st) and HENRY RONO 1979-10 pts. (1st); RICHARD TUWEI 1982-15 pts. (1st), Richard Tuwei 1983-10 pts. (3rd) and Richard Tuwei 1985-2 pts. (7th); Julius Korir 1983-12 pts. (2nd), Julius Korir 1984-12 pts. (2nd) and JULIUS KORIR 1986-10 pts. (1st); PETER KOECH 1985-10 pts. (1st); Nathan Morris 1986-1 pt. (8th), Samuel Kibiri 1991-8 pts. (2nd); Robert Price 1991-1 pt. (8th). **Non scoring All-American:** John Hill 1991. **Other Finalists:** Rod Dahl 1968; Larry Almberg 1969; Graham Hutchinson in 1972; Rob Evans 1980; Steve James in 1983; Marty Stroschein 1989 & 1990. **Honorable Mention:** Andrew Gonzales in 2015. **Note:** Henry Rono set a NCAA (MR) in the Heats @ 8:18.63 in 1978 and the current NCAA (MR) in the Final @ 8:12.39 in 1978. **Note:** JULIUS KORIR was the 3000M Steeplechase 1982 Commonwealth Games and 1984 Olympic Champion.

Total Points: 119 -- Highest Finish 1st (5 times) -- 10-All Americans
Top Individual in scoring: JUILUS KORIR 34 pts.